A0688763

THE DEPARTMENT OF PUBLIC PROSECUTION AND JUDICIAL POLICE IN CAMEROON

CHIMONTOH Z. AKOMANDOH

The Department of Public Prosecution and Judicial Police in Cameroon

Chimontoh Zonipoh Akomandoh

First Published in 2020

Miraclaire Publishing
Kansas City, MO 64133, USA
www.miraclairepublishing.com / info@miraclairepublishing.com

In association with
Ken Scholars Publishing, USA

ISBN-13: 978-0-9978977-6-0
© 2020 Miraclaire Publishing

All rights reserved
No part of this book may be reproduced, stored in a retrieval system, or transmitted, in any form or by any means, electronic, mechanical, photocopying, recording or otherwise, without the prior permission of the copyright owner.

Printed in the United States of America

Miraclaire Publishing makes every effort to ensure the accuracy of all the information ("Content") in its publications. However, Miraclaire and its agents and licensors make no representations or warranties whatsoever as to the accuracy, completeness, or suitability for any purpose of the Content and disclaim all such representations and warranties, whether expressed or implied to the maximum extent permitted by law. Any views expressed in this publication are the views of the author and are not necessarily the views of Miraclaire.

DEDICATION

To my father,

Chimontoh Richard Ngopang
of blessed memory

PREFACE

One of the most acclaimed merits of Law N°2005/007 of 27 July 2005 instituting the Criminal Procedure Code of the Republic of Cameroon is the resurrection of the Examining Magistrate (member of the bench) to conduct preliminary inquiry in the place of the State Counsel. This ground-breaking innovation led to a popular opinion according to which the Legal Department will henceforth be relegated to the background as far as the conduct of criminal proceedings are concerned.

The Department of Public Prosecution and Judicial Police in Cameroon, while tracing the historical background of the Legal Department, carefully walks you through its institutional framework and governing principles, while highlighting its omnipresence at all phases of the procedure (police investigation, preliminary inquiry, hearing before the Courts as well as in the execution of Court Judgments). The said ubiquitous presence is accentuated by the lawmakers who in some instances render it not only necessary but mandatory as well. Curiously, the Department of Public Prosecution is presented as that principal party who is not responsible for malicious prosecution.

First of its kind on the subject in the queen's language, the author in a doctrinal but practical approach raises issues tainted with polemic, whose application is yet to be harmonised in Courts West and East of the Moungo. While preserving the position of the code and tapping from his rich experience in both systems, he substantiates his views in a typical Anglo-Saxon style with case law from Courts across the country and around the globe.

The author with much audacity traces a path in this domain worth pursuing. To my mind, this book is thus an essential reference point for the law and practice as far the Legal Department and Judicial Police structures are concerned, beneficial to both legal professionals of all spectrums as well as legal scholars.

Chief Justice Bechem Eyong Eneke
President Court of Appeal
Buea, South West Region

FOREWORD

In 2018, within the framework of a Professional Masters II program, I opted to conduct research on the topic: "Remand in Police Custody in The Criminal Procedure Code and the Respect of the Rights of Suspects". During the research, I made a startling observation. I noticed that civil law practitioners had written abundantly and extensively on the subject as well as on other aspects of practice and procedure as far as criminal law and the application of the Criminal Procedure Code (CPC) is concerned. Common Law practitioners on the contrary made little or no effort in this domain. In fact, I did not come across any scientific paper or book written by a practitioner of common law origin as far as the application of the CPC is concerned. More astounding were the incongruities I observed in the application of the CPC in courts East and West of the Moungo thanks to my very enriching experience in both systems. I resolved it was time we start telling our own story and sharing our experience just like our Civil Law colleagues.

The Department of Public Prosecution and Judicial Police in Cameroon is one among many other books that I embarked on writing as far as practice and procedure in criminal law in Cameroon is concerned. It traces the origin of the Legal Department, presents its organisation and governing principles, while critically and pragmatically analysing its enfolding role at all phases of criminal proceeding

At the initial phase, the Legal Department is not only an initiator, but that overseer, who oversees the instigation and conduct of investigations by judicial police officers, correcting every irregularity observed and sanctioning any misconduct as well. In the Course of preliminary inquiry, it has been considered as the alpha and omega. In fact, all proceedings are initiated or commenced with its express authorisation and can only be concluded as well after its opinion has been expressed. At the trial phase, unlike all other parties in criminal proceedings, the law explicitly styles it "the principal party", which must be represented at such trials under pain of rendering the entire proceedings and the decision null and void. Inquiringly, the Legal

Department is that principal party who is not responsible for damages to the prosecuted party in case of no case ruling or acquittal. To crown it up all, not only is the Legal Department actively involved in the execution of decisions, but the law has made it the supervisor of all such execution.

This book destined to legal professionals, legal scholars as well as citizens does not in any way assert an exhaustive reflection on this subject which in my opinion is inexhaustible. It is a gateway for a deeper reflection on the subject. It is on this node that I sincerely wish to extend my gratitude to Mrs. Bih Che épouse Anye Nde Abegley who formed in me a sense of objectivity and integrity in this divine mission. I am equally indebted to Mr. Bechem Eyong Eneke, Chief Justice of the South West Court of Appeal who accepted to preface this book.

It is an uphill task for any civil servant to treat such a sensitive subject linked to his profession without from time to time unconsciously breaking the barrier of the obligation of reserve. With utmost humility, I plead for forgiveness of my hierarchy if at any point I transgressed this rule.

Chimontoh Zonipoh Akomandoh
Edea, 5th June 2020

CONTENTS

LIST OF LEGISLATIONS

International Covenant on civil and political rights 16th December 1966

Vienna Convention of the 18th April 1961.

Law N° 2008/001 of 14 April 2008 to amend and supplement some provisions of Law N° 96/6 of 18 January 1996 to amend the constitution of 2 June 1972.

Law N° 2006/015 of 29 December 2006 modified and supplemented by Law N° 2011/027 of 14 December 2011 on judicial organisation.

Law N° 96 – 06 of the 18 January 1996 modified by law N° 2008/001 of 14 February 2008 on the constitution of the Republic of Cameroon.

Law N° 82/14 of 26 November 1982 establishing the organisation and functioning of the Higher Judicial Council.

Law N° 82/14 of 26 November 1982 supplemented by Law N° 89/016 of 28 July 1989 on the organisation and functioning of the Higher Judicial Council.

Law N° 2017/014 of 12 July 2017 to amend and supplement some provisions of law N° 2006/16 of the 29 December to lay down the organization and functioning of the Supreme Court.

Law N° 90/060 of 19 December 1990 on the creation and organisation of the State Security Court.

Law N° 2017/012 of 12 July 2017 on the code of military justice.

Law N° 2014/028 of 23 December 2014 on the repression of acts of terrorism.

Law N° 2002/003 of the 19 February 2002 on the general tax code.

Law N° 94/01 of the 20 of January 1994 on the regime of forestry, fauna and fishery, completed by ordinance n° 99/001 of the 31 August 1999.

Law N° 96/12 of the 5 August 1996 on environmental management.

Decree N° 2012/389 of 18 September 2012 on the organisation of the ministry of Justice.

Decree N° 2012/223 of 15 Mai 2012 on the administrative organisation of the Special Criminal Court.

Decree N° 2013/202 of 28 June 2013 amending and supplementing Decree N° 80/299 of 26 July 1980 on the administrative organisations of courts.

Decree N° 2012/389 of 18 September 2012 organising the Ministry of Justice.

Decree N° 95/048 of 8 March 1995 on the Status of the Magistracy.

Décret N° 2012/552 DU 20 NOV.2012 portant délimitation territoriale de commissariats d'Arrondissement dans certains Commissariats Centraux de sécurité Publique

LIST OF CASES

Abdoulaye Mazou C/ Etat de Cameroun
Aff. MP et CNPS contre ELOUNDOU Pierre Jean Marie et autres. Inédit
Affaire MP et Olama Hubert c / Six policiers, TGI, jugement N° 122/crim.2007
Arret N° 27/P du 9 avril 2007, MP, Etondé Ekotto Nathanael et autres c. PAD (Port Autonome de Douala) et al. Inédit
Arrêt N° 016/2004 du 29 avril 2004 (affaire scierie d'AgnibilekrouWahabNouhab dite SDA, Wahab Nouhab Rachid C/ Hassan Hahly
Arrêt N°003/2002 du 10 Janvier 2002 (affaire Siem C/ Société Atou et Bicici)
Arret n°72/P du 16 juillet 2015, affaire Kingue Paul Eric c/ commune de Njombe-Penja
Arrêt n0 28/P du 27 Mai 2010, Aff. Hazim Marcel et Samir Camil El Chamas c/ MP et Etat du Cameroun (MINFI), inédit
CEDH ,30 aout 1990, Fox. Campbell et Hartley C/ Royaume Uni
CEDH, 6 février 2003, Zeynep Avic c. Turquie§ 46, et 3 juin 2004
Chambers V Mississippi, 410 U.S. 284, 294 (1973)
Chimel v. California (1996) 395 U.S 752, 764-63
Communication N° 143/95 and 150/96, Constitutional Right Project and Civil Liberties Organisation Vs. Nigeria
Communication N° 48/90, 50/9, 52/91, 89/93, Amnesty and ors Vs. Sudan
Crim, 24 juin 1987, Bull.crim n° 267
Crim. 20 juin 2000; Bull.n° 237
Crim. 14 Oct. 2003, Bull. n° 189
CS, arrêt n0 28/P du 27 Mai 2010, Aff. Hazim Marcel et Samir Camil El Chamas c/ MP et Etat du Cameroun (MINFI), inédit
Horton vs. California (1990) 496 U.S 128, 136
F.N Eko v. Sam Mofor, WACA/11/71, 1971, (unreported)
Jim Nwabodo v. John Nwobodo (2002) 2 A RR
Kirby V United States, 147, U.S. 47, 55 (1899)

Lorence A. M. &1or Vs. The People of Cameroon, (2016)1, CCLR part 18

Maizga v. Kvello Estate, 2009 SCC 51

Maryland V. Craig, 497, U.S. 836, 845 (1990)

Miranda v. Arizona, 384 U.S. 436 (1966)

MP et Ebale Fombo Emmanuel c. Bissack Emmanuel, n° 239/cor/ADD

Ohio V. Roberts, 448, U.S. 56, 65 (1980)

Ord. N° 698/PTGI/W/DLA du 29 aout 2007 du Pres. Du TGI du Wouri, Jacques Makaké C. Ministère Public

Ord. N° 001/ORD du 14 décembre 2007 du Prés. du TGI de la valée du Ntem, Zogo Ongolo Abraham C. Ministère Public

Ord. N° 003/ORD du 19 mars 2009 du Prés. du TGI de la valée du Ntem, Zo'o Engo Charles, Bekoung Mba Philibert, Mba Mba Fils et Zo'o Zo'o Charles Materne

Ordonnance N° 76/HC, TGI du Mfoundi, du 28/07/2011, aff. Nchuafane Daouda et Mballa Bénédicte c/ MP, (inédit)

Ordonnance N° 132/HC du 15/09/2011, aff. Fatouma épouse Abdouramane c/MP

Regina v Denton: CACD 22 Oct (1981)

Riley v. California, 573 U.S. 373 (2014)

Schneckloth v. Bustamonte (1973) 412 U.S.218,219

ShenZhanghua V. Republic [2006]

Sigilani v. Republic [2004] 2 KLR 480

State V. Gilroy, 199 NW 2d 63

Suit No. CANWR/MS/30C/2015: Bangha Grace & 1or Vs The People of Cameroon and 1or. SLR, 6(2017)

Suit No. CANWR/MS/39C/2014: Fuh Gideon Bakeh & 4 ors Vs The People of Cameroon & 3ors, SLR, (2016)

Suit No. BCA/MS/32C/2008: Isaiah Mbunkur V. The People of Cameroon & 1or

Suit No. CANWR/MS/70C/2014; Loh Emmanuel & 2ors Vs The people of Cameroon & 1or, SLR, 6, {2017}:

Suit n° CANWR/MS/60C /2012: Ndi Tangiri and 54 others Vs The People of Cameroon: SLR, 4, (2016)

Suit No. CANWR/ICC/2C/2014, Nyamsekwen Christopher Kunbuma Vs the People of Cameroon & 2ors SLR,6 {2017

Suit No. CANWR/MS/35C/2014: Nguelle Nguelle Felix & Sakiri Usmanu alias Sarkiri usman Balarabe, SLR, 4 (2016)

Suit N°. CANWR/MS/52C/2013: The People of Cameoon and Dr. Yoh Peter Tingem Vs Tume Evelyne Mainsah: SLR, 4, (2016)

Suit No. CASWR/04ICC/2015: The People of Cameroon Vs Gabriel Lyonga, SLR, 6 (2017)

Suit No. CFIB/40P/2009: The People &anor Vs Njina Kevin Ndango: CCLR, PART 14

Suit No. CANWR/ICC/6C/2012: The People of Cameroon Vs Tanoh Lawrence Ndangoh: SLR, 4 (2016)

The People V. Ray (1999) Cal. 4th 464, 472

The People vs. Carter (2005) 36 Cal.4th 1114, 1141

TPI d'Akonolinga, jug. Du 20 septembre 2007, MP et Ebale Fombo Emmanuel c. Bissack Emmanuel, N° 239/cor/ADD

United States V. Arnold (9th Cir. 2008) 523 F.3d 941, 945

Yen v. Avoyelles Parish Police Jury, 5 So. 3d 1002 (2009)

Yosefa v. Uganda [1969] E.A. 236

Young v. Valcourt (1982) 1WWR 575 (BCSC)

LIST OF ABREVIATIONS

ADD: Avant-Dire Droit
CANWR: Court of Appeal North West Region
CCLR: Cameroon Common Law report
CEDH: Cour européen de droit de l'homme (European court of human rights)
CFI: Court of First Instance
CIC: Code d'Instruction Criminelle
CPC: Criminal Procedure Code
CPO: Criminal Procedure Ordinance
EM: Examining Magistrate
HC: High Court
ICC: Inquiry control chambers
ICCPR: International covenant on civil and political right
ICTY: International Criminal Tribunal of ex- Yugoslavia
ICTR: International Criminal Tribunal for Rwanda
JPA: Judicial Police Agent
JPO: Judicial Police Officer
PG: Procureur Général
PUA: Presses Universitaires d'Afrique
OHADA: Organisation for the harmonisation of business law in Africa
SC: Supreme Court
SCC: Special Criminal Court
SLR: South West Law Report
TGI: Tribunal de Grande Instance
TPI: Tribunal de Première Instance

INTRODUCTION

The Department of Public Prosecutions better known as the Legal Department within the Cameroonian context or better still "*parquet*" or "*ministère public*" in Molière's tongue is one of the oldest judicial institutions in the legal arsenal of independent Cameroon but one of the least understood .The lack of mastery of this legal structure is illustrated by an author [1] through a conversation between two friends. In their dialogue, Gerard explains to his friend Paul that he has been convoked to the Legal Department as witness in a divorce proceeding. Paul panic stricken at the mention of Legal Department hopes that he will not be remanded in custody.[2] The deficit of mastery even among legal professionals is quite visible in the divergent practices observed East and West of the Moungo, which can partly be justified by the reminiscence of colonialism. One would have expected a synchronization of practice with the promulgation of Law n° 2005 of 27 July 2005 on the Criminal Procedure Code ,which according to an author[3] had as main objective among others, the harmonisation of norms commenced with the penal code since 1967 and in the domain of criminal procedure, as well with the unification of norms of the "*Code d'Instruction Criminelle*" and the Criminal Procedure Ordinance as practiced in the French and English parts of the country respectively.

The Legal Department as it exists in Cameroon is not an original creation of the Cameroonian lawmakers. It is the result of an evolution which is both historical and legal. A comprehensive understanding of the Legal Department can better be achieved by a scrutiny of the two major legal systems from which it originates their characteristics, as well as their origin and evolution.

---

[1] Ndjere (E.), *Le ministère public ou parquet*, édit. Apprendre, Tome I, PUCAC, 2009, p.13

[2] In essence Gerard is convoked as witness in a divorce proceeding before the High court and not at the Legal Department.

[3] Mahouvé (M.) and Kembo (H.T.), in *Les droits de l'homme au cœur de la procédure pénale Camerounaise: Entre volonté humaniste et tentative régressive*, Bruylant, p.20

According to Roger Merle and Andre Vitu[4] two great procedural systems succeeded each other throughout history in most European countries; the accusatory and the inquisitorial systems. The accusatory system is reputed as the oldest. It responds fundamentally to the idea according to which a proceeding is nothing more than a dispute solemnly adjudicated before an impartial and passive witness; a judge, whose rule is limited to handing down a verdict by declaring one of the parties' winner. It has three main characteristics notably:

- Complete equality between prosecution and the defense
- The judge plays a passive role
- The tendering of evidence is subjected to a strict formality

However, this system is criticised for encouraging impunity of many offences, as most persons avoid taking the disagreeable and perilous function of complainant. What accounts for this unfortunate situation is the fact that the rich and influential offenders can trade the silence of witnesses or paralyse eventual proceedings for fear of reprisal. That notwithstanding these authors hold that the real shortcoming of this system is the absence of preliminary investigation, which prevents cases from going to court already clarified and thus scrapping off useless elements thereby orientating hearing only to fundamental aspects. The authors hold that the inquisitorial system only surfaced lately when certain factors were consolidated to provoke the disappearance of the accusatory system till date in place. The introduction of the inquisitorial system was initially motivated by political transformation which led to the birth and later on the reinforcement of centralised and autocratic power. Sovereignty moved from the people to the Prince, who was henceforth invested with the mission of maintaining public order and the appointment of judge in charge of punishing offenders. Within this perspective, offences were seen more as an infringement on established public order than a damage caused to a civilian or his family. Punishment here was not limited to the reparation of the

[4] Merle (R.) et. Vitu (A.), *Traité de droit criminelle*, édition Cujas, 1997, p. 169-184

damage suffered by the victim, it assumed a public character, and public vengeance overrode private vengeance.

It is for this reason that the accusatory procedure was considered as not adapted to an efficient fight against criminality, due to the absence of a public authority to institute prosecution, the tardiness of the procedure instituted etc.

The inquisitorial system has the following aspects:

- The organisation of justice in this system manifest the decline of the role of victims and of third parties in prosecution, this role is played by « *parquet*» or "*ministère public*"; that is by a magistrate directly representing the central power,
- The Presiding Magistrate is attributed the power to be seised of a matter *suo moto* "toute juge est Procureur Général", flawing or destabilising the right to a fair trial to the disadvantage of the defence. Citizens do not participate in the trial of offenders, the right to judge is the exclusive role of professional judges, permanent and specialised officers of justice instituted by the state,
- The Presiding Magistrate plays an active role in the search of evidence, the proceedings are written, secret and non-contradictory, in the course of investigations as during the hearings. In some legislation, publicity is permitted but preliminary inquiry and investigations are carried out in camera.
- The considerable power given to Magistrates permits them to freely decide on matters before them
- To obtain confession regarded as the supreme evidence, torture is admitted based on the idea that God will rescue the innocent to overcome the pains and torments inflicted on them

The Cameroonian system as aforementioned as a heritage of colonisation is a mixed system with both elements of the accusatory and the inquisitorial procedure, just like the French system adopted by most European countries. On the other hand, modern day Great Britain has remained faithful to the accusatory system with little or no influence from the inquisitorial system. The accusatory principle from all angles is fundamental, prosecution is commenced by citizens and most often carried out by the police and wholly funded by the director of public prosecution which appeared in 1809. The Crown Prosecutor only intervene before the Magistrates Court and the Crown Court, prosecution is conducted by a lawyer more or less specialised, chosen by the complainant. Such is the system adopted by most West African countries colonised by Great Britain such as Ghana and Kenya.

Incarnated by the "*magistrate débout*" [5] the Legal Department has been defined diversely by different authors. According to Dashaco John[6], the Public Prosecutor's Department refers to all the legal officers on whom the society has conferred the authority to initiate and conduct criminal proceedings on its behalf in court. The French dictionary "*Le Lexigue des termes juridique*" defines it as an assembly of career magistrates who are charged before certain courts to submit for the application of the law as well as safeguarding the general interest of society. According to the First President of the Cameroonian Supreme Court as cited by Emmanuel Ndjere[7] "the Legal Department is comprised of a category of magistrates established within certain jurisdictions with the objective of representing the society. Stating further that this same category of magistrates charged with prosecution are not constrained sorely on the said task, apart from court sessions during which they submit in criminal as well as civil and commercial matters, their attributes are so varied such that getting a globally accepted definition is almost impossible...."

In the same line with Carlson Anyangwe, Emmanuel Ndjere making allusion to Jean Pradel in his work "*Procédure Pénale*", traces the origin of the Legal Department as instituted in the Cameroonian legislation to ancient France wherein its members referred to as standing magistrates stood below the dais

---

[5]So called because unlike the judge, the state prosecutor must while in court, stand up each time he wishes to speak. During a criminal trial the ministère public is sometimes referred to as l'acussation, that is, the prosecution.

[6]Dashaco (J.), "The public prosecutor's power to prosecute in Cameroon: A clash of two legal systems?", in *Annales de la faculté des sciences juridique et politique de l'université de Dschang*, Tome II 1998, p .103

[7] Ndjere (E.), op.cit., p .15.

reserved for magistrates of the bench otherwise referred to as seating magistrates and submitted the inverse position held by the said judges. He states further that the interest of the Legal Department is not limited to criminal matters only; in civil matters he provides written submissions at times as a principal party but most often as a parasite to the proceedings. His presence in civil matters can be justified by the fact that most often disputes of purely private nature can at times raise issues of public policy. Such is the case with nationality, adoption as well as divorce. In criminal proceedings he plays a central role, in fact he is referred to as a principal party[8]. Such is not the case however with most countries of Anglo-Saxon origin. In England for example the prosecution of cases wherein the sanction is death penalty and other statutory offences are the reserve of the Director of public prosecution. All other prosecution is instituted by the police through the crown prosecution service[9]. In Nigeria on the contrary, the police single handedly conducts investigations right up to charging the accused before a law court irrespective of the offence. As such the police literally constitute the DPP. As a result, their presence during hearing or trial is mandatory.

As regards the Legal Department in the Cameroonian context, which is basically of French extraction ensuing from colonialism as codified in the *Code d'Instruction Criminelle*, it has always been subject of criticism. Curiously enough after independence, in the ordinance of the 26th August 1972, the Legal Department for structural reasons and for an effective fight against criminality, was armed with enlarged powers, conferring to it not only the functions of prosecution but that of preliminary inquiry as well. By so doing, the Legal Department in the words of Anoukaha F.[10] was transformed into a god with two heads "Le Janus" - guard of the temple gate in the Greek mythology. The

---

[8]Section 128 CPC.

[9] Philip James, *Introduction to English Law*, E .L.B.S.,Butterworths,1989.p.174 et seq. Cited by Dashaco (J.), Ibid. p.104

[10] Anoukaha (F.), « Le Procureur de la République « Janus » de la magistrature Camerounaise », *Penant*, 1985, p.115 et suivants.

critics of this institution[11] hold that the Legal Department is a strongly controlled arm of government and as such the intrusion of the Legal Department in the domain of individual liberty constitutes a malicious shortcut, which unfortunately permits the interference of the Executive in the Judiciary contrary to the principle of separation of power. They equally hold that the management by the Legal Department of individual liberty is nauseating to the right to fair trial. This can be justified by the fact that one of the ingredients of a fair trial is equality before the law, but the Legal Department has been attributed the power to tamper with the liberty of a suspect who will be his adversary before a court of law or an Examining Magistrate.

In fact the Legal Department in the words of the CPC shall be a principal party in a criminal trial before the court and shall always be represented at such trials under pain of rendering the entire proceedings and the decision null and void[12]. It further provides that "subject to the powers of the Presiding Magistrate to maintain order in Court the Legal Department may intervene at any stage of the trial" and that "at the close of hearing, the Legal Department shall in every case, address the court or tender written submissions without being denied the right of hearing or stopped when addressing the court"[13] A situation which is not only illogical, but which raises *apriori* a problem of equality before the law.

At a time when legal practitioners[14] prone for an urgent repositioning of the Legal Department, placing it at the same footing with the civil party and the defence so as to guarantee the preservation of theoretical equilibrium between the three main parties in a criminal proceedings, at a time when the European Court of Human Rights[15] strongly condemn the role of judge and a party played by the Legal Department in the same procedure. Law N° 2005/007 of 27 July 2005 instituting the Criminal Procedure Code, made very little efforts to this regards in its

---

[11] ²Eteme Eteme, « Le Parquet et la privation de liberté : Mauvais ménage ? Réflexion sur le devenir d'une relation antinomique », *Miroir de droit*, N° 02 Avril-Mai-Juin 2011, p. 14- 21.

[12]Section 128(1), CPC.

[13]Section 129(2 and 3), CPC.

[14] Ibid.

[15]Affaire Medvedev, cited by Me Eteme Eteme,Ibid.

efforts to put in conformity the said code with the exigencies of a fair trial as it resulted from international legal instruments of the protection of human rights, the most outstanding of which include ; the International Covenant on Civil and Political Rights of the 26th of December 1966[16] ,the African Charter on Human and Peoples' Rights of the 27th June 1981 [17] ,the Convention against ,cruel ,inhuman or degrading treatment or torture of the 10th December 1984[18] ,the United Nations Conventions on the Rights of the Child of the 20th November 1989[19] ,texts that were integrated in the constitutional block of the Cameroonian constitution of 1996, the ambiguous and problematic powers of the Legal Department has been maintained.

According to an author [20], the philosophy underlying prosecution is that anti-social conduct must be punished. Since anti-social behaviour threatens the very fabric of society, the suppression of such conduct is a matter of public interest for society. Consequently, the right to exert punishment or to refrain from doing so is the sole prerogative of the society or the state. But since society or the state can only act through natural persons, it has delegated its powers to prosecute offenders to certain qualified persons in the community styled "Public prosecutors" or State prosecutors" for their job is to prosecute all breaches of the criminal law on behalf of the public at large

Whatever the case the Legal Department within the context of the CPC plays a primordial role in criminal proceedings as a whole, fundamental among which we can cite the exercise of prosecution, the supervision of investigations carried out by Judicial Police Officers, more especially measures of remand in police custody, active participation in preliminary inquiry proceedings, trials and in the execution of judgments. The CPC equally spells out the organisation of this institution, implicitly bringing out its guiding principles.

---

[16]Cameroon adhered to this pact on the 27[th]June 1984.

[17] Cameroon ratified the charter on the 21st October 1986.

[18] Cameroon ratified the convention on the 19th December 1986.

[19] Cameroon ratified the convention on the 11 January 1993.

[20]Fwang (S.), "Can the state prosecutor discontinue a private prosecution by entering a nolle prosequi ?, F.NEKO V. Sam Mofor (1971) Appeal N° WCCA/11/71, unreported _ Judgment per O'Brien Quinn, J.". in *Juridis péridique* N° 31, July-August-September 97,p. 39-44.

PART I

THE INSTITUTIONAL FRAMEWORK AND THE GUIDING PRINCIPLES OF THE LEGAL DEPARTMENT

The organisation and functioning of the Legal Department is well thought-out. Its structure is perfected by some cardinal guiding principles worth examining. The peculiarity of the organisation of this department lies in the fact that it constitutes an arm of the executive within the judicial arsenal hierarchically submitted under the direct tutelage of the Ministry of Justice. This intrusion, in a supposed functionally distinct arm of government, has been partially justified[21] by the fact that this ministry and its minister, who happens to be the vice president of the Higher Judicial Council[22]is in charge of the follow up and the putting in place of the criminal policy of the state. It should be noted that the aforementioned organ is presided over by the President of the Republic[23] who happens to be the Head of State[24] and guarantor of the independence of the judiciary.[25] According to Carlson Anyangwe [26] the constitutional provision which makes the executive guarantor of the independence of the judiciary does not assure the Cameroonian judiciary of control over matters of judicial administration. Rather the minister and not a Chief Justice exercise considerable control over such matters. As such it is clear that the judiciary like the Legal Department is administratively under the supervision of the Ministry of Justice. This is in staggering contrast to what obtains in common law countries where the legal system places the judiciary outside the civil service and gives the legal profession such a central place in the constitution. Ulrich Xavier Ovono Ondoua[27] while opining that the implication of the executive in the judiciary is problematic and compromises the independence of the judiciary, goes further to point out that the text that fixes the organisation

[21]Article 2, Decree N° 2012/389 of 18 September 2012 on the organisation of the Ministry of Justice.

[22]Article 2, Law N° 82/14 of 26 November 1982 establishing the organisation and functioning of the Higher Judicial Council.

[23] Article 1 Law N° 82/14 of 26 November 1982 establishing the organisation and functioning of the Higher Judicial Council.

[24] Article 5, Law N° 2008/001 of I4 April 2008 to amend and supplement some provisions of Law N° 96/6 of 18 January 1996.

[25] Article 37(3) Law N° 2008/001 of I4 April 2008 to amend and supplement some provisions of Law N° 96/6 of 18 January 1996.

[26]Anyangwe (C.), *The Magistracy and the Bar in Cameroon*, CEPER 1989 p. 37,

[27] Ovono Ondoua (U.), *Sous le bandeau de thémis, les larmes, panser et repenser la justice camerounaise*, Harmattan 2019, p.88

and functioning of the Higher Judicial Council[28] and practice at the Bar are laws[29], whereas the Status of the Magistracy is a decree.[30] According to him this is quite unusual taking into cognizance the fact that the Judiciary, just like the Executive and Legislature, is a constitutionally guaranteed power. He opts for a Judiciary void of the implication of the executive and the legislative and headed by the First President of the Supreme Court.

That notwithstanding, far from this constitutional debate on the separation of power, it has been established that the Legal Department is the principal party in a criminal trial before the court under pain of nullity of both the proceedings and decisions. The Legal Department as noted can intervene at any stage of the trial without being denied the right or stopped and even when such interventions are based only on civil claims[31].

Generally, the Code provides that any judicial act done by any magistrate of the Legal Department is considered to have been done in the name of the entire Legal Department.

A better comprehension of the Legal Department can be achieved by looking at its organisation as well as its characteristics.

---

[28] Law N° 82/14 of 26 November 1982 establishing the organisation and functioning of the Higher Judicial Council.

[29] Law N° 90/059 of 19 December 1990 to organise practice at the Bar

[30] Decree N° 95/048 of 8 March 1995 modified on several occasions

[31] Section 129 CPC

CHAPTER I
THE ORGANISATION OF THE DEPARTMENT OF PUBLIC PROSECUTION

The court system of Cameroon falls under two major categories: Courts of ordinary jurisdiction and courts with special jurisdiction. Ordinary law courts in our context can be seen as courts with an all-embracing jurisdiction to hear and determine actions of every kind whether civil or criminal. While providing that justice shall be rendered on the entire territory of the Republic of Cameroon in the name of the Cameroonian people[32], the law on judicial organisation emphasize on the fact that judicial power shall be exercised by the Supreme Court, Appeal Courts and Courts with original jurisdiction [33](Customary Courts, Magistrates Court or Court of First Instance and High Court). Globally speaking and as per the provisions of Article 3 of the afore-cited text, judicial organisation is comprised of the Supreme Court, the Courts of Appeal, the Special Criminal Court, Lower Administrative Courts, Lower Audit Courts, Military Tribunals, High Courts, Courts of First Instance and customary Courts. The said classification which seems to be incomplete leaves every keen observer with the question as to whether the Court of State Security created and organised by Law N° 90/060 of the 19 December 1990 has been scraped off the legal arsenal. This law while failing to make a distinction with regards to the ordinary or special nature of the courts listed equally fails as well to give an exhaustive list of all the courts irrespective of their nature. Ordinary law courts in our context refers to the courts provided for in the provisions of article 2 of the law on judicial organisation namely the Supreme Court, Appeal Courts and Courts with original jurisdiction (Customary Courts, Magistrates Court or Court of First Instance and High Court). It should be noted however that our interest is focused on

[32] Article 1, Law N° 2006/015 of 29 December 2006 modified and supplemented by Law N° 2011/027 of 14 December 2011 on judicial organisation.

[33] Article 2 Law N° 2006/015 of 29 December 2006 modified and supplemented by Law N° 2011/027 of 14 December 2011 on judicial organisation.

the Department of Public Prosecution of the said institutions and not its entirety.

The CPC provides for a hierarchical organisation of the Legal Department whereas functionally its administrative set-up is put in place by Decree n° 80/299 of 26 July 1980, modified by Decree n° 81/264 of 8 July 1981 and other isolated texts as regards certain jurisdictions such as the case of the Special Criminal Court.[34]

I. JUDICIAL ORGANISATION OF THE DEPARTMENT OF PUBLIC PROSECUTION

Judicially, the Legal Department as per the CPC is organised at three levels, at the level of the Supreme Court, the Courts of Appeal and at the level of Courts with original jurisdiction. It is common to find a dual organisation as well most especially from authors of Anglo-Saxon extraction. Their dual organisation limits it to the Legal Department at the level of courts with appellate jurisdiction as well as the Legal Department at the level of Courts with original jurisdiction.

A. Organisation of the Department Public Prosecution of Courts with Appellate Jurisdiction

The term "appellate jurisdiction" refers to the authority of a Court to hear appeals of cases decided by lower Courts. Courts that have such power to reverse or modify the lower Courts decision. No cases originate from these Courts.

The CPC has formally identified the Supreme Court and Courts of Appeal as Courts with appellate jurisdiction. However, we are interested in the organisation of the Legal Department of the said Courts.

1. At the Level of the Supreme Court

The Legal Department of the Supreme Court[35] is made up of the Procureur General at the said court and all the magistrates of the said Legal Department. Curiously, the law on judicial

[34] Decree N° 2012/223 of 15 Mai 2012 on the administrative organisation of the Special Criminal Court

[35] Section 127 (3), CPC.

organisation[36] consecrated on Judicial Organisation while making mention of this structure fails to precise its organisation. This loophole is however filled up by a special text on the organisation and functioning of the Supreme Court[37]. It provides that the Legal Department at the Supreme Court is composed of a Procureur General, a First Advocate General and Advocate Generals[38].

As regards his duties, he is a party to all appeals lodged by parties and may of his own motion raise grounds for the annulment of the decisions appealed against. He is the principal party in all appeals brought by him before the Supreme Court[39]. Its jurisdiction is national unlike that of the Court of Appeal.

2. At the Level of the Courts of Appeal

The organisation of the Legal Department at the Courts of Appeal is not vastly different from that of the Supreme Court. The CPC provides that it is composed of the Procureur General and all the magistrates of the said Court. The law on Judicial Organisation[40] throwing more light on this, precise that it is made up of the Procureur General, one or more Advocate Generals, (his senior assistant), then the junior assistant known in French as (Substituts du Procureur Général). At the bottom of the prosecutorial corps are legal assistants (attachés). Its jurisdiction is the Court of Appeal.

The functions of the Procureur General at the Court of Appeal are varied and more extensive than those of his colleague at the Supreme Court. He does not only ensure the application of criminal law throughout the jurisdiction of the Court, but as well, charged with the supervision of the activities of judicial police

---

[36]Law N° 2006/015 of 29 December 2006 modified and supplemented by Law N° 2011/027 of 14 December 2011 on judicial organisation.

[37] Law N° 2006/016 of 29 December 2006 as modified and supplemented by Law N° 2017/014 of 12 July 2017.

[38] Article 4 Law N° 2006/016 of 29 December 2006 as modified and supplemented by Law N° 2017/014 of 12 July 2017.

[39]Section 132(2), CPC.

[40] Article 20(1)b° 2006/016 of 29 December 2006 as modified and supplemented by Law N° 2017/014 of 12 July 2017.

officers and agents within his jurisdiction, submitting half yearly reports to the minister of justice on their activities and conduct[41]

Practically the application of criminal law within the jurisdiction of the Court of Appeal is made possible through directives of a general or specific nature given by the Procureur General to the various State Counsels within his jurisdiction as well as regular cell controls. Phillipe Keubou[42] in line with the provisions of the law is of the opinion that the Procureur General can carry out cell controls. Practically however, it is quite unusual to see a Procureur General personally carrying out cell controls. This is usually done by State counsels on instruction or by an Advocate General commissioned by the later. In the same line, the law provides that he may direct JPO or agents to obtain any information he deems useful for the proper administration of justice. An effective control of the Procureur General can only be ensured by the actual implementation of the provisions of section 134(2) of the CPC which empowers him to supervise and evaluate JPO and agents. Without an enforcement of the said prerogatives through a text of application, the above-mentioned provision will be of no essence, since JPO and their agents continue to be answerable to their direct hierarchy. It is rather an unfortunate situation since in some cases the Procureur General is obliged to pass through the Regional security heads to enforce some instructions.

B. At the Level of Courts with Original Jurisdiction

Courts with original jurisdiction hear and determine matters for the first time[43]. The courts in question include the customary courts, Courts of First Instance and High Courts. At the level of the Court of First Instance and High Courts the Legal Departments are comprised of the State Counsels of the said Legal Departments and all the magistrates of same. Its jurisdiction is the Court of First instance and High Courts respectively depending on the organisation of such courts. It should be noted however that the State Counsel's Chambers is a

---

[41] Section 134(2), CPC.

[42] Keubou (Ph.), *Précis de procédure pénale Camerounaise*, PUA, p.40.

[43] Ewang (S.), "The organisation of the judiciary in Cameroon : An appraisal", in *Annales de la Faculté des sciences Juridiques et politique*, Tome 10, 2006, p.24.

one-man office made up of the State Counsel alone and, in some cases, he conducts prosecutions both before the Courts of First Instance and the High Court. Such is the case with jurisdictions like Mezam, Ngoketunjia, Sanaga Maritime and Lebialem.

The jurisdiction of the Legal Department has been succinctly spelt out by the lawmakers in the provisions of the CPC[44]. This section of the law provides that the competent State Counsel can either be

- That of the place of commission of the offence; or
- That of the place of residence of the suspect; or
- That of the place of arrest.

It further resolves any conflict of jurisdiction by emphasizing that when more than one State Counsel are seized of the same matter, priority shall be given to the State Counsel in whose jurisdiction the offence was committed[45]. Matters are brought to the State Counsel either by way of a written or oral complaint, or a report by the competent authority, public servant of any person who has knowledge of an offence classified as felony or misdemeanour as well as a victim of an offence. It is not however excluded that the State Counsel be seized *suo moto*.[46]

As regards the attributes of the Legal Department incarnated by the State Counsel, it includes among others the direction and control of the operations of officers and agents of the judicial police[47]. Visiting of cells lodged within the police or gendarmerie units in order to verify the conditions of detention and the situation of suspects falls within his material jurisdiction. During such visits, he can of his own motion or by virtue of an order of habeas corpus order the immediate release of unlawfully remanded suspects[48]. Such persons must be immediately set free under pain of prosecution for unlawful detention against the JPO in charge of the investigating unit where the custody took place. Considering the very demanding task of prosecution of criminal offences shouldered by the Legal Department, the lawmakers have accompanied such responsibilities with corresponding

[44] Section 140(1), CPC.
[45] Section 140(2), CPC.
[46] Section 135, CPC.
[47] Section 137(1), CPC.
[48] Section 137(2), CPC.

measures. Such is the case with the possibility which is at the same time a right to directly request the use of the forces of law and order. He may as well request the assistance of persons who are likely to help in the discovery of the truth. The CPC equally attributes to him the powers of a judicial officer, even though it is to him that all case files are destined. The organisation of these common law courts is slightly different from Courts with special attributes or jurisdiction.

C. The Department of Public Prosecution of Courts with Special Jurisdiction

A court with special jurisdiction is one which deals either with specific matters formally provided for by statute or with a particular class of persons. Our statutes provide for five courts with special jurisdiction to wit, the Military Court, the State Security Court, the Court of Impeachment, the Special Criminal Court, and the Constitutional Council. The organisation and structures as well as mission of some of the courts account for the absence of the Public Prosecution Department. Such is the Case with the Constitutional Council. Our focus here is centred on Courts whose structure provides for the Legal Department.

1. The Department of Public Prosecution of the Military Court

The organisation of military justice in Cameroon is governed by Law N° 2017/012 July 2017 laying down the rules of military justice. This law while specifying that the military tribunal is a special tribunal[49], fixes the territorial attributions of the tribunal[50], its composition[51] and material jurisdiction in the provisions of Section 8.[52]

---

[49] Article 1, Law N° 2017/012 of 12 July 2017 laying down the rules of Military Justice.
[50] Article 3 and 4, Law N° 2017/012 of 12 July 2017 laying down the rules of Military Justice.
[51] Article 5 Law N° 2017/012 of 12 July 2017 laying down the rules of Military Justice.
[52] The military Tribunal shall be competent to hear:

a. Military offences and war crimes,
b. Crimes against humanity and war crimes,
c. Offences linked with acts of terrorism and to state security,
d. Offenses of piracy and illicit acts against security of maritime navigation and platforms,
e. Any offense committed by servicemen, with or without civil co-offenders or accomplices, in a military establishment or in the exercise of their duties,

The Public Prosecuting Department or the Legal Department of the Military Court as per the provisions of the law is made up of a Commissioner of Government (Commissiare du Gouvernement) one or many deputies of the commissioner of government one or more registrars. Commissioner of Government in this context plays a role similar to that of State Counsels of ordinary law Courts with the exception that the case files from investigating units in this case, are destined initially to the Commissioner of government and a copy is forwarded to the Minister in charge of military Justice[53]

2. The Department of Public Prosecution of the State Security Court

Created by Law N° 90/060 of 19 December 1990, the State Security Court with its seat in Yaoundé, has jurisdiction to try offenders, co-offenders as well as accessories for felonies and misdemeanours against the internal and external security of the State, as well as related offences. Minors, less than 14 years do not fall within the jurisdiction of this court.[54]

Classical threats to the internal and external security include terrorism, espionage, cyber threats, and proliferation of arms of mass destruction. Book II of the Cameroon Penal Code treats this category of offences as particular offences. Among threats to the external security of the state, features offences such as hostilities against the fatherland[55], espionage and treason[56]. It

---

f. Offences against the arms law of the 1st, 2nd, 3rd and 4th category such as specified in the in the law on the general regime of arms in Cameroon,
g. Offenses of all types committed with the use of firearms of the categories specified above,
h. Armed robbery,
i. Any offence involving a serviceman, or any person considered as such, committed in times of war or In a region under state of emergency or emergency measures,
j. Any offence committed by civilians in a military establishment causing damage to the military equipment or installations or prejudicial to the physical integrity of a serviceman,
k. All offences relating to the purchase, sale, production, distribution, wearing or keeping of military effects or insignia as defined by military regulations,
l. All offences related to those specified above.

[53] Article 11(2)

[54] Article 4 (1) and (2)

[55] Section 102, Penal Code « any citizen;

a) Taking part in hostilities against the republic;
b) Or assisting or offering to assist the said hostilities;
c) Shall be guilty of treason punishable with death.

[56]Section 103, Penal Code.

is worth noting that some of the militants of the Cameroon Renaissance Movement party (CRM) including their leaders are being court marshalled for the offence of hostility against the fatherland[57]. The following offences as per the provisions of the penal code constitutes threat to the internal security of the State; secession[58], civil war[59], propagation of false information[60], revolution[61], armed band[62], insurrection.[63]

That notwithstanding, globally speaking, the court is made up of a President, a magistrate of judicial order, six assessors with a deliberative voice made up of two military magistrates, two magistrates of judicial order and two personalities designed by presidential decree.

The Legal Department is manned by a Procureur General and many deputies. Intriguingly the law alludes to the registry while précising that it is composed of one or more registrars[64]. It should however be noted that the registry of this Court is that of the Court of Appeal of the Centre Region. The provisions of Article 5 states that criminal action before the Court is commenced by the PG personally or by delegation to JPO who proceed where necessary to the investigation of offences,

---

[57] On Saturday the 26th January 2019, the Cameroon Renaissance Movement in spite of the refusal by administrative authorities to grant an authorisation for a public demonstration, Maurice Kamto and his militants staged a purported peaceful march against what they termed electoral hold up in many towns across the country. Meanwhile some of the protesters were injured the Cameroonian embassies in France, Belgium and Germany were devastated by an angry population; many protesters in Cameroon were arrested and remanded in custody. On Monday, the 28th January 2019, the President of the CRM, Maurice Kamto, executives and allies of his party as well as several activists were arrested by the police in the residence of Albert Ndzogang at about 7:30pm and transferred to Yaoundé for investigation and prosecution.

[58] Section 111(1), Penal Code, « whoever undertakes in whatever manner to infringe the territorial integrity of the Republic shall be punished with imprisonment for life;

2) In time of war, or in a state of emergency or siege the penalty shall be death.

[59] Section 112, Penal Code, "whoever provokes civil war by arming the people or by inciting them to take up arms against each other shall be punished with death"

[60] Section 113, Penal Code "whoever sends out or propagates false information liable to injure public authorities or national unity shall be punished with imprisonment for from 3 (three) ,months to 3 (three) years and with a fine of from CFAF 100 000 (one hundred) to CFAF 2 000 000 (two million).

[61] Section 114 "Whoever by force attempt to alter the laws composing the constitution or to overthrow the political authorities set up by the said laws or to render them incapable of exercising their powers shall be punished with life imprisonment".

[62] Section 115, Penal Code.

[63] Section 116, Penal Code.

[64] Article 2(1) law N° 90/060 of 19 December 1990 on the creation and organisation of the State Security Court

collecting of evidence and prosecution just like the State Prosecutor[65].

Regulated by a special law[66], one would have expected acts of terrorism as laid down in article 2 of the said law, which in essence constitutes crimes against the internal and external security of the state to fall within the jurisdiction of this Court. In the absence of a universally accepted definition of terrorism, an author[67] has attempted a definition[68] of this phenomenon which has taken a frightening escalating proportion with the advent of globalization, catching the interest of the security council of the United Nations[69].

By dint of its appellation "Court of State Security", its composition (a President, a Magistrate of Judicial Order, six assessors with a deliberative voice made up of two military magistrates, two magistrates of judicial order and two personalities designed by presidential decree) as well as its material jurisdiction (trial of offenders, co-offenders as well as accessories for felonies and misdemeanours against the internal and external security of the State), it is crystal clear that terrorism constitutes an aspect of its material jurisdiction. Unfortunately, the repression of acts of terrorism has been placed under the exclusive jurisdiction of the Military Tribunal[70].

The conclusion every keen observer will arrive at after a critical perusal of Law N° 2008/015 of December 2008 organising military justice and laying down the rules of procedure applicable before the military Court and law N° 2017/017 of 12 July 2017 to lay down the code of military justice

---

[65] Article 5

[66] Law N° 2014/028 of 23 December 2014 on the repression of acts of terrorism.

[67] Assira (C.), "La loi du 4 Décembre 2014 sur la lutte contre le terrorisme: Le retour de du talion", *Miroir du droit*, p.8

[68] "An attack against life, physical integrity, or personal liberties with the guarantee of international protection including diplomatic agents ; kidnappings, hostage taking or arbitrary arrest ; the use of explosives, grenades, automatic fire arms, trapped mails in such a manner that the use of such items constitutes danger to persons; or an attempt to commit one of such offences or participation in the commission of same either as a co offender or as an accessory of a person who commits or attempts to commit such offences.

[69] Considering the global threat caused by this phenomenon, the United Nations Security Council by resolution 2178 of 24 September attempts a definition which according to Claude Assira is limping due to the fact that it treats terrorism as a phenomenon resulting from the violent extremism of foreign terrorist.

[70] Article 3, Law N° 2014/028 of 23 December 2014, on the repression of acts of terrorism.

is the usurpation of the jurisdiction of the State Security and an extraordinary extension of the jurisdiction of the military Court which has rendered the effective putting in place of this jurisdiction of no essence.[71]

3. The Department of Public Prosecution of the Special Criminal Court

In spite of the existence of the Courts of First Instance and High Court with jurisdiction respectively over misdemeanour and felonies including offenses against misappropriation as defined by the penal code[72], the Cameroonian policy makers by virtue of Law N° 2011/028 of 14 December 2011 supplemented by Law of 06 July 2012 created the Special Criminal Court, wherein its jurisdiction is well spelt out[73]. Its territorial jurisdiction is national, with its seat in Yaoundé. This was in a bit to enhance efficiency and rapidity in the trial of offences against misappropriation of public funds as well as eradicating inertia as well as poor functioning observed notably with the courts of original jurisdiction.

A keen observer of the activities of the Special Criminal Court[74] noticed and from statistics that just six months after the commencement of work at the Court i.e. on the 15 October 2012, six judgments were passed, listing the cases in question and the verdicts of the Court.

As regards its composition and more especially as concerns the Legal Department, the law provides that the Legal Department shall be headed by the Procureur General, one or

---

[71] The 2017 law laying down the Code of Military Justice has added to the original material competence of the military Court as laid down by the 2008 law, exclusive jurisdiction on crimes against humanity and war crimes and offences relating to acts of terrorism. The security of the State which was intended initially as the exclusive jurisdiction of the State Security Court has been devolved exclusively to the Military Court. This change coincides with the Head of States crusade against terrorism with Boko Haram and the secessionist of the North and South West Regions of Cameroon.

[72] Section 184 PC.

[73] Section 2 "The court shall be competent to hear and determine matters, where the loss amounts to at least FCFA 50, 000,000 relating to the misappropriation of public funds and other related offences provided for in the penal code and international conventions ratified by Cameroon", the law further states that where the loss is below FCFA 50,000,000 the Procureur General of the Special Criminal Court shall transfer the case file to the competent Procureur General.

[74] Claude (A.), "Le Tribunal Criminel Spécial à l'épreuve de la justice", *Miroir de droit* N° spécial avril-septembre 2012 P.50

more Advocate Generals, one or more Deputies "*Substituts Généraux*"[75]. In the same section it is provided that the bench is made up of the President, one or more Vice Presidents, one or more Judges "*conseillers*", one or more Examining Magistrates. The registry on the other hand is comprised of the Registrar in Chief, one or more section heads, one or more registrars and inquiry registrars.

Complaints and accusations relating to any offence over which the Special Criminal Court has jurisdiction are subject to investigation[76]. Such investigations are ordered by the Procureur General of the said court[77], who perform the functions of the State Counsel during preliminary investigations[78]and has control over a specialised corps of the Judicial Police Officers charged with the responsibility of investigations and carrying out rogatory commissions[79]. The time limit for the closure of investigations commenced by this special corps is fixed at 30 days renewable twice[80]. At the end, the file is submitted to the Procureur General, who with his prosecutorial prerogative can either chose to close the case file or request that preliminary inquiry be opened[81]. Summarily the Legal Department of the Special Criminal Court is charged with prosecution of offences spelt out in section 2 of the law establishing the Special Criminal Court.

4. The Department of Public Prosecution of the Court of Impeachment

The Court of Impeachment created by the provisions of the constitution[82] has been vested with jurisdiction in respect of acts

---

[75] Section 4, Law N° 2011/028 of 14 December 2011 supplemented by Law of 06 July 2012 creating the Special Criminal Court.

[76] Section 7(1), Law N° 2011/028 of 14 December 2011 supplemented by Law of 06 July 2012 creating the Special Criminal Court.

[77] Section 7(1), Law N° 2011/028 of 14 December 2011 supplemented by Law of 06 July 2012 creating the Special Criminal Court.

[78] Section 7(2), Law N° 2011/028 of 14 December 2011 supplemented by Law of 06 July 2012 creating the Special Criminal Court.

[79] Section 7(3), Law N° 2011/028 of 14 December 2011 supplemented by Law of 06 July 2012 creating the Special Criminal Court.

[80] Section 7(4), Law N° 2011/028 of 14 December 2011 supplemented by Law of 06 July 2012 creating the Special Criminal Court.

[81] Section 7(5),(6), Law N° 2011/028 of 14 December 2011 supplemented by Law of 06 July 2012 creating the Special Criminal Court.

[82] Article 53(1) Law N° 96 – 06 of the 18 January 1996 modified by law N° 2008/001 of 14 February 2008 on the constitution of the Republic of Cameroon.

committed in the exercise of their functions to try the President of the Republic for high treason and the Prime Minister, members of government and persons ranking as such and senior government officials to whom powers have been delegated pursuant to article 10 and 12 for conspiracy against the State security.

The Department of Public Prosecution of this institution is still to be put in place alongside other institutions as well as its composition and the procedure applicable by law[83]. This is not the case of the Constitutional Council wherein the Department of Public prosecution is inexistent for strategic reasons.

5. The Constitutional Council

The Constitutional Council most often occupy a place of pride when it comes to study of judicial organisation in Cameroon. By virtue of its classification among the other Courts that makes up our judicial organisation, most onlookers mistakenly think that its organisation is similar to that of all other courts notably at the level of the bench, the Legal Department and the registry.

It is worth noting however, that by virtue of its mission as defined in the provisions of article 46[84], 47[85] and 48[86]of the constitution and its composition as well as the mode of designation of its members[87], and seizure[88] this Court is a special Court of a peculiar nature. Unlike common law courts, its

---

[83] Article 53(2) Law N° 96 – 06 of the 18 January 1996 modified by law N° 2008/001 of 14 February 2008 on the constitution of the Republic of Cameroon.

[84] "The constitutional Council shall have jurisdiction in matters pertaining to the constitution. It shall rule on the constitutionality of laws. It shall be the organ regulating the functioning of institutions.

[85] "The constitutional Council shall give final rulings on:

- The constitutionality of laws, treaties and international agreements;
- The constitutionality of the standing orders of the National Assembly and the Senate prior to their implementation;
- Conflicts of power between state institutions, between the State and regions and between Regions

[86] The Constitutional Council shall ensure the regularity of presidential election, parliamentary elections, and referendum operations. It shall proclaim the results thereof;

[87] Article 51(2) Members of the constitutional Council shall be appointed by the president of the Republic. They shall be designated as follows;

- Three including the President of the Council by the President of the Republic;
- Three by the president of the National Assembly after consultation with the Bureau;
- Three by the president of the Senate after consultation with the Bureau;
- Two by the Higher Judicial Council;

[88] Article 47(2) Law N° 96 – 06 of the 18 January 1996 modified by law N° 2008/001 of 14 February 2008 on the constitution of the Republic of Cameroon.

litigants are state institutions, as such it will be funny for another state institution of a lower standing to play the role of prosecution for an institution whose mission is supra-national i.e. judge of constitutionality of Laws, treaties and international agreements. It should equally be noted that far from being sorely jurisdictional as aforementioned, it equally performs extra-judicial roles such as that of regularity and control of state institutions. As such, the mode of commencement as well as procedure depends on the matter at stake.

Apart from the judicial organisation of the Legal Department its administrative set up has partially been regulated as well and worth examining.

II. ADMINISTRATIVE ORGANISATION OF THE DEPARTMENT OF PUBLIC PROSECUTION

The administrative organisations of courts in the Republic of Cameroon is governed by the provisions of Decree N° 80/299 of 26 July 1980 as modified by decree N° 81/254 of 8 July 1981. This text does not make mention of the administrative organisation of the Supreme Court. According to an author[89]the texts needs complete modification for the following reasons; initially it does not take into consideration the constitutional evolution of our country brought in by Law N° 96-06 of 18 January 1996 as well as Law N° 2008/001 of 14 January 2008 raising the judiciary from a simple judicial authority into a judicial power. In fact, Part V of the said constitution provides not only that justice shall be administered in the territory of the Republic in the name of the people of Cameroon but that the judicial power shall be exercised by the Supreme Court, Courts of Appeal and Tribunals. It also precise that the judicial power shall be independent of executive and legislative powers[90]. It should however be noted that as per the provisions of the same article the independence of the judiciary seems to be limited to the magistrates of the bench sorely[91]. Secondly, with the

[89] Ndjere (E.), op.cit. p .326

[90] Article 37 Law N° 96 – 06 of the 18 January 1996 modified by law N° 2008/001 of 14 February 2008 on the constitution of the Republic of Cameroon.

[91] « Magistrates of the bench shall in the discharge of their duties, be governed only by the law and their conscience »

introduction of the Criminal Procedure Code by law N° 2005/007 of the 27 of July 2005 putting in place new practices regarding the role of the Legal Department in criminal procedure and more specifically as regards preliminary inquiry, one would have expected a modification of the text taking into consideration the said legal instruments.

However in the absence of an all enclosing text that particularly treats the administrative organisation of courts in Cameroon, the vacuum in some cases have been filled by a presidential decrees as it's the case with the judicial organisation of the Special Criminal Court[92], a court whose instrument of creation[93] and according to Agbor A .A.[94] addresses issues that are purely procedural in content: the jurisdiction and composition of the SCC, its conduct of proceedings, the initiation of an appeal and the right to bail without touching any substantial issue such as the creation and definition of any crime, nor spelling out of penalties to be imposed by the court if an accused were found guilty. Such is equally the case with the administrative organisation of Administrative Courts[95] as well as the Supreme Court which seems to be partially organised on the administrative plan by a law[96]. As it stands, the administrative organisation of the Courts of Appeal and courts with common law jurisdiction are governed by Decree N° 80/299 of 26 July 1980 as modified by decree N° 81/254 OF 8 July 1981 and are presented as analysed here below.

A. The Administrative Organisation of the Court of Appeal

As afore mentioned, the Legal Department of the Court of Appeal which functions under the direct control and supervision of the Procureur General administratively is composed of three services:

[92] Decree N° 2012/223 of 15 May 2012 on the Administrative Organisation of the SCC.

[93] Law N° 2011/28 of 14 December 2011 amended by law N° 2012/011 of 16 July 2012

[94]Agbor (A.A.), « Prosecuting the offences of Misappropriation of public funds : An insight into Cameroons Special Criminal Court » PER/PELJ 2017 (20) p.12

[95]Decree N° 2013/202 of 28 June 2013 amending and supplementing Decree N° 80/299 of 26 July 1980 on the administrative organisation of courts.

[96] Law N° 2017/014 of 12 July 2017 to amend and supplement some provisions of law N° 2006/16 of the 29 December to lay down the organization and functioning of the Supreme Court.

- The service of administrative and financial affairs
- The service of judicial affairs
- The service of the control of registry, Legal Departments and judicial professions

Placed under the control of a chief of service, at least with the rank of a registrar or of a civil servant of general administration, the service of administrative and financial affairs is made up of the following bureaux:

- ➢ The bureau of administrative affairs, charged with the treatment of issues related to the management of personnel, internship, reception, typing of documents as well as printing, translation and the function of stores accountant and the maintenance of vehicles and buildings.
- ➢ The bureau of financial affairs is charged with the elaboration and execution of budget, accounting as well as maintenance.

Placed under the control of a chief of service with the rank of registrar or a civil servant of general administration, the service of judicial affairs is structured as follow; the bureau of mails and documentation, the bureau of repressive matters, the bureau of non-repressive matters and transit, the bureau of the execution of sentences and judicial statistics.

- The bureau of mails and documentation is charged with the reception, registration, and dispatch of mails. It ensures the keeping of archives and proceeds with the opening of administrative case files,
- The bureau of repressive matters takes care of repressive matters,
- The bureau of non-repressive matters and transit is charged with the follow up of "cause communicable", the execution of written instructions on case files emanating from traditional law courts, the follow up of all matters on transit, transmitted to the Legal Department by other Legal Departments of the Court of Appeal as well as foreign services,
- The bureau of the execution of sentences and criminal statistics is charged with the keeping of non-conviction records in collaboration with the registrars of the Court of

Appeal. It is equally attributed the duty of assembling and putting in order documents of execution of the registry of the Court of Appeal in view of its signature by the Procureur General, as well as its transmission to the police posts ,gendarmerie, Legal Departments for execution. This bureau takes care of the updating of registers for the execution of sentences, the filing of administrative files, the expedition of judgments handed down as well as rulings, the collection of statistics from other Legal Departments within the jurisdiction of the Court of Appeal and the establishment of same to reflect the volume of work done at the Legal department of the Court of Appeal ;

Placed under the authority of the chief of service with at least the rank of principal registrar, the service of the control of the registry, the Legal Department and judiciary profession is comprised of two bureaux:

- The bureau of the control of the Legal Department and registry,
- The bureau of judicial professions.

While the former is charged with the control of activities of the registry and the Legal Department, verification of emoluments for the visa of the registrar in chief and auxiliaries of justice, the latter is charged with the activities of the cabinets of lawyers, notary public as well as bailiffs.

B. The Administrative Organisation of the Department of Public Prosecution of Courts with Original Jurisdiction

The Legal Department of courts with original jurisdictions which functions under the direct control and supervision of the State Counsel is made up of the service of judicial affairs, the service of financial and administrative affair.

The service of judicial affairs is placed under the authority of a registry worker with at least the rank of registrar, whereas the service of administrative and financial affairs is placed under the supervision or control of a civil servant of general administration or a registrar:

1) The Service of Judicial Affairs

It is comprised of three bureaux namely;

- The bureau of criminal matters and matters on transit,
- The bureau of the execution of sentences,
- The bureau of the control of ministerial officers or judicial professionals.

The bureau of criminal matters and matters on transit handles the register of complaints and simple offences, follows up the enrolling of criminal matters before the court as well as its pasting of the cause list at the registry. It oversees the execution of all instructions given by the court during court sessions, oversees the execution of services demanded or solicited by parties or third parties, holds the register of the service of summons.

The bureau of the execution of sentences handles the register of sentences, puts together execution documents and forwards same to the registry for signature by the State Counsel. It is endowed with the responsibility of transmitting to JPO and external Legal Departments such documents and oversees their effective execution. Follows up files for clemency and judicial rehabilitation as well as establish statistics of the activities of the Legal Department.

The bureau of the control of judicial professions ensures the control of public or ministerial officers through documents and on the spot verifications. The chief of bureau keeps the register of all bailiffs' acts and verifies same for visa as well as emoluments.

2) The service of Administrative and Financial Affairs

It is made up of two bureaux to wit: the bureau of mails and documentation and the bureau of general affair.

The mails bureau receives, registers, and treats incoming mails as well as the expedition of outgoing mails. It is charged with documentation and oversees the opening of administrative files.

The bureau of general affairs is charged with the management of credits and personnel of the Legal Department. On the material level it is responsible for the logistic organisation of ceremonies and meetings of the court, receives persons on mission, maintain buildings and vehicles as well as ensuring the functioning of the library and the conservation of archives and documentation. However, the Courts of Yaoundé, Douala and Nkongsamba for some special reasons seem to have benefitted from special considerations in its classification.

C. The Administrative Organisation of the Department of Public Prosecution of Nkongsamba, Douala and Yaoundé Courts

The administrative set up of the Legal Departments of the Courts benefitted from a special regime since 1980 and as such is different from that of similar jurisdictions.

Like the other Legal Departments, the Legal Departments of the said jurisdictions are under the control of the State Counsel and have two services each namely; the service of judicial affairs and the service of administrative and financial affairs .But unlike the other courts with original jurisdiction and as the Legal Department at the Court of Appeal, the service of judicial affairs of these Courts comprises five bureaux, namely, the bureau of mails and archives, the bureau of repressive matters, the bureau of non-repressive matters and transit, the bureau of the execution of sentences and the bureau of the control of ministerial or public officers with almost the same attributes but adapted to the said court. It should be noted that the service of judicial affairs of other Courts has just three bureaux, namely the bureau of repressive matters and matters on transit, the bureau of the execution of sentences and the bureau of the control of ministerial or public officers

If in the 80s the administrative organisation of Courts permitted such a distinction, perhaps due to the volume of work and judgments delivered, the essence of such discrimination today as spelt out by the aforementioned text is been put to question. The special considerations that worked in favour of this special treatment, needs to be revisited, considering the tremendous changes and innovations within the judicial arsenal of this nation. This cacophony as regards the administrative organisation of Courts with special jurisdiction has taken a different dimension. Out of the many jurisdictions created with special attributes, some are still to be put in place[97] meanwhile most of those whose creation has been materialised, the decree setting up its administrative structure is inexistent. Such is the case with the Military Tribunal whose instrument of creation[98] while précising its special attribute, provides for the administrative organisation of the said Court by a special text[99]which is still awaited. The scenario is not different in the Court of State Security which at moment exists only on paper.

D. The Administrative Organisation of Courts with Special Jurisdiction

As mentioned above not all the courts with special attributes are regulated administratively. In most cases, the decree regulating the administration of such Courts are still been awaited, meanwhile the actual text regulating the administration of common law courts though outdated is still to be modified to meet up with recent developments of legal instruments within the judiciary. However, in some cases this issue has been adequately taken care of. Such is the case with jurisdictions such as the Special Criminal Court.

E. The Administrative Organisation of the Special Criminal Court

Organised by Decree N° 2012/223 of 15 May 2012, the administration of the Special Criminal Court is placed under the responsibility of the Procureur General and the President of Court[100], with the responsibility of common services to both structures i.e. the Bench and the Legal Department placed under the supervision of the Procureur General[101]. These services include[102]the service of reception, the service of cleaning, the library and archive service, the linguistic service, the stationeries services (*reluire et de l'impression*), the accounting Service and the service of internship.

---

[97] Court of Impeachment.
[98]Law N° 2017/012 of 12 July 2017 on the code of military justice.
[99]Article 2 Law N° 2017/012 of 12 July 2017 on the code of military justice.
[100] Article 4(1) Decree N° 2012/223 of 15 Mai 2012.
[101] Article 4(2) Decree N° 2012/223 of 15 Mai 2012.
[102]Article 4(3) Decree N° 2012/223 of 15 Mai 2012.

The Registry of the Court functions under the direct responsibility of the Registrar-in-Chief, who must at least hold the grade of "*greffier principal*" and is comprised of two criminal sections notably: Criminal Section I and Criminal Section II.

As far as the Legal Department is concerned there are three services in this Department namely:

- The service of administrative and financial affairs
- The service of criminal matters
- The service of control of the registry, the Legal Department and judicial professions

The organization and attributes of these bureaux and the services under them are not different from those of the common law Courts. For fear of repetition we will not look at the organisation and role of the said bureau and services. It should however be noted that it is well spelled out in the text mentioned here above[103].

A comprehensive understanding of the organisation of the Legal Department can best be achieved not only by the study of its judicial and administrative setup, but equally by an analysis of the underlying principles of the said organisation as well.

[103]Article 6,7,8,9 and 10 Decree N° 2012/223 of 15 Mai 2012.

CHAPTER II
THE CHARACTERISTICS OR PRINCIPLES THAT GOVERN THE ORGANISATION OF THE DEPARTMENT OF PUBLIC PROSECUTION

The Legal Department is characterised or governed by the following cardinal principles:

- The principle of hierarchical subordination;
- The principle of homogeneity;
- The principle of independence and
- The principle of no challenge or recusal (*irrecusabilité*)

A better comprehension of these characteristics or principles governing the Legal Department warrants that the principles be regrouped under two major heads:

- Principles linked to the nature of the organization of the legal department and
- Principles linked to the role of prosecution of the Legal Department.

I. PRINCIPLES LINKED TO THE NATURE OF ITS ORGANISATION

The principles directly linked to the organisation of the Legal Department include the principle of hierarchical subordination and the principle of independence.

A. The Principle of Hierarchical Subordination

The fundamental trait of the organisation of the Legal Department is its hierarchical subordination. Unlike magistrates of the bench who in the exercise of their duties are bound sorely by the law and their conscience, the magistrates of the Legal Department are subordinate to the Minister of Justice.

According to Emmanuel Ndjere[104] the terms subordinate and hierarchy are complimentary, and the complementarities can be justified by the fact that one cannot be conceived without the other. Hierarchy, necessarily and will always implicate subordination and subordination cannot exist as well in the absence of an established hierarchy. Summarily, he sees

[104] Ndjere (E.), op.cit., p.44

hierarchy as a certain superposition of one thing on another making allusion to rank and power. Subordination in other words consists in a certain established order among persons organised such that one depends on the other, following the norms of an established discipline.

As such members of the Legal Department are subordinate to the Minister of Justice. They receive directives and orders from their immediate superiors to whom they owe respect and obedience. At the top of the hierarchy is the minister of Justice. He is not a member of the Legal Department and has no such status. But as head of the Government Department which deals with justice in general, the Minister of Justice is the overall boss of the Legal Department. As the embodiment of the executive in this area, he may issue orders to the Procureur Generals, the Procureur Generals at the Appeal Courts to the State Counsels and all legal officers. In fact, section 134 of the CPC[105] is quite instructive to this regard. Furthermore, the Status of the Magistracy[106] in clear terms states that the Magistrates of the Legal Department and assimilated structures are hierarchically subordinate to the Ministry of Justice.

Several reasons have been advanced to justify the existence of this principle which to an extent constitutes an interference of the executive in the judiciary. This assertion is more evident in the composition of the Higher Judicial Council wherein the President of the Republic is President and his Vice is the Minister of Justice[107], not even the President of the Supreme Court. Whatever the case, as a representative of the executive power within the judiciary, the Minister is charged with coordinating and harmonising the judiciary policies of his ministry such that it conforms to government option as regards the maintenance of public peace, public order as well as tranquillity, vital elements of economic growth. The Decree that organises the Ministry of Justice charges him with the duty of

---

[105] (1) The Procureur General at the Court of Appeal shall ensure that the criminal law is applied throughout the jurisdiction of the Court of Appeal; (2) He shall have authority over all the magistrates of the Legal Department within his jurisdiction.

[106] Article 3(2) Decree N° 95/048 of 8 March 1995 on the Status of the Magistracy.

[107] Article 1 and 2 Law N° 82/14 of 26 November 1982 supplemented by Law N° 89/016 of 28 July 1989 on the organisation and functioning of the Higher Judicial Council.

putting in place and follow up of state criminal policy[108]. The exigencies of development and economic growth can at one point require that government concentrates on the fight against certain ills which by nature can compromise government option such as corruption, misappropriation, violation of human rights etc. This mission can only be accomplished if the minister has the possibility of exercising authority by way of instructions which must be executed. The structure and nature of the Legal Department[109] renders it just like all other administrations.

Considering the importance of the principle, law makers and regulatory powers have spared no effort to set up adequate legal instruments to this regard. Such is the case with the provisions of section 127(2), (7)[110] as well as article 3(1) and (2) of the Statute of Magistracy which summarily provides that magistrates of the Legal Department are hierarchically placed under the Ministry of Justice. The said hierarchical subordination as evident in the organisation of the Legal Department, places the Procureur General of the Supreme Court, the Procureur General of the Supreme Court under the direct control of the Minister of Justice Keeper of the Great Seal. The other magistrates hierarchically depend on the Procureur General of the Courts of Appeal; meanwhile magistrates in courts with original jurisdiction take instructions from the State Counsels.

Simply articulated, the Minister who is found at the top of the pyramid can issue instructions to all the legal officers of the Legal Department and this is normally done through the Procureur General at the Courts of Appeal who are answerable to him. The Procureur General of the Supreme Court, who is next in line in hierarchy, may issue orders and instructions to any legal officer serving at the Legal Department of the Supreme Court.

---

[108] Article 2, Decree N° 2012/389 of 18 September 2012 organising the Ministry of Justice.

[109] An arm of the executive in the judiciary.

[110] (2) The Legal Department as provided for this section comprises the magistrates of the Legal Department of the Supreme Court, the Court of Appeal, the High Court and the Court of First Instance.

(7) The magistrates of the Legal Department the Supreme Court, the Court of Appeal, the High Court and the Court of First Instance shall under the control, direction and authority of the heads of the said Legal Departments, exercise the powers conferred by the law on the Procureur General of the Supreme Court, the Procureur General of the Court of Appeal and the State Counsel respectively.

Below the Procureur General is the Procureur General of the Courts of Appeal who give orders to all his Deputies and all legal officers serving in the High Courts and Courts of First Instance. At the bottom of the hierarchy is the State Counsel who heads the Prosecution Departments of the High Court and the Courts of First Instance. The non-respect of instructions that flow from this pyramidal arrangement is considered as a professional fault liable to sanction.

Far from simply regulating the principle of hierarchical subordination, its jurisdiction has been fixed by two circulars of the Minister of justice. The first circular details the notion of reporting «*render compte*» [111], while the second precise its domain of application as regards prosecution[112]. But it should be noted that the principle of hierarchical subordination practically refers to two essential notions; the obligation of reporting and the obligation of conforming to received instructions.

1. The obligation of reporting

The obligation to report can only function efficiently within a context wherein the domains are meticulously circumscribed. Within a vague context it will be practically difficult if not impossible to obtain the required or awaited outcome, which is that of coordinating and harmonising the criminal policy of the State. This is the object of the 1962 circular which spells out some of the matters for which reporting is absolute. Such is the case with;

- Matters concerning State security and the repression of seditious activities;
  Matters involving;
  Parliamentarians;
  Former parliamentarians;
  Mayors and traditional rulers;
  Senior Divisional Officers, Divisional Officers, in short Senior Civil Servants;
  Magistrates, auxiliaries of justice and Judicial Police Officers;

[111] Circular N° 11of 16 April 1962.

[112] Circular N° 9186 of 25 February 1967.

- Offences which though present the characteristics of common law offences are of an exceptionally serious nature. Such cases otherwise referred to as "affaire signalée" are appreciated subjectively by each State Counsel.

Other circulars within the same context instruct Procureur Generals to address reports on defendants remanded in custody for more than six months[113], on the evaluation of cost as regards car insurance[114], on drugs[115] and as regards the prosecution of foreigners[116]. Reports from courts with original jurisdiction are channelled to the Minister through the Procureur General. However, the possibility of direct transmission is not excluded, though limited to cases of extreme gravity.

According to an author[117], this circular unfortunately operates a discriminatory categorisation of litigants into two distinct categories: the governing class and the popular class contrary to the principle of equality before the law. This is so because a State Counsel who receives a complaint against any of the personalities aforementioned "personne signalée", is obliged to report to the PG and wait for instructions whether to open investigations or not. More disturbing is the fact that as long as he does not receive any instructions the complaint is laid in abeyance and the complainant has no remedy. The author equally notes that, on the contrary, when the complainant is a "personne signalée", investigations are conducted with the speed of light without need for instructions from the hierarchy. This double standard in the dispensation of justice and the impression of impunity gives the governing authorities the delusion that they are above the law.

That notwithstanding, the purpose of the existence of the principle of hierarchical subordination will be defeated, if instructions received are not complied with. The obligation of compliance is not absolute; it has its limitations as well.

---

[113] Circular N° 9062/DAJS of 8 April 1965.

[114] Circular N° 30/033 of 13 August 1971.

[115] Circular N° 9007 of 18 December 1975

[116] Circular N° 30/047 of 6 February 1974.

[117] Ovono Ondoua (U.), *Sous le bandeau de thémis, les larmes, panser et repenser la justice camerounaise*, Harmattan 2019, p.68

2. The obligation of conforming to instructions received

According to Carlson Anyangwe [118] as a general rule, the Cameroonian Prosecutor monopolises the institution of and conduct of prosecution. However, he does not monopolise the discretion whether to prosecute or not. He shares it with the Minister of Justice, with each of them intervening in a well-defined area. He states and rightly so, that whenever the Minister of Justice decides to prosecute in respect of a certain matter, the State Prosecutor must abide by the decision and institute criminal proceedings irrespective of his own views in the case. Conversely, where the Minister decides against prosecution, the State Prosecutor must drop the matter, his own view notwithstanding. In these cases, the Minister's view to order or not to order prosecution is absolute and is exercised whether there is compelling evidence to warrant prosecution or not. He needs no reason for his decision.

However, criminal proceedings regularly instituted by the Legal Department in violation of ministerial injunction is said to be valid as it is not affected by nullity. Even though the State Counsel who initiates such a proceeding is opened to disciplinary measures, the Court is said to have been properly seized of such matters. If they refuse to prosecute in defiance of orders from their superior to do so the later cannot step into their shoes and prosecute in their place.

The Status of the Magistracy expressly gives the Deputy State Prosecutor the liberty to drift from received instructions during his oral submission[119], such a drift however must have been preceded by prior notice given to his superior and in due time, explicitly notifying him of his intention of orally differing in his submission or pleadings. In Francophone Courts, pleadings hardly carry any substantial weight. This provision in other words admits that the State Counsel or his Deputy can differ in opinion with the received instructions during his oral submission, summarized in the French expression *la plume est serve mais la*

[118] Anyangwe (C.), op.cit. p.87.

[119] Article 3(3) Decree N° 95/048 of 8 March 1995 on the Status of the Magistracy.

parole est libre[120], literally translated in latin, *scripta manen, verba Volant.* This position has been finely articulated by Elie Faustin, cited by Emmanuel Ndjere[121] in the following word, *le pourvoir exécutitif peut imposer au parquet des actes mais il ne peut imposer une opinion; il peut prescrire une poursuite, un appel ou un pourvoir mais il ne peut enchainer cette opinion……*[122]. While emphasizing on the indispensable and grounded nature of this principle , Emmanuel Ndjere[123] advises that if in the course of hearing, in a particular matter where conforming to the received instruction becomes difficult due to new facts, a Deputy is always expected to submit for a suspension of court session in other to ask for fresh instructions. It should however be noted, that in written submissions the instructions of the Minister must be respected to the letter. There is no possibility of drifting.

Despite the subordinate nature of the Legal Department to the Ministry of Justice, its independence is however established when it comes to its relationship with the Court.

B. The Principle of Independence of the Legal Department

The members of the Legal Department are independent of the bench in the jurisdiction wherein they exercise their duties. The members of the bench cannot orally reprimand or give instructions to Legal officers of the Legal Department.

As Carlson Anyangwe[124] rightly puts it, a judge cannot take cognizance of an offence and by himself initiate criminal proceedings. He must wait until he has been seized of the matter by the Legal Department. Similarly, the court cannot enjoin the Legal Department to amend a charge with the intent of either adding a count or including an accused that was left out. By virtue of this principle, the Court is obliged to respond to the

---

[120] It can be translated to mean 'the written word remains but the spoken word passes'.
[121]Ndjere (E.), op.cit. p.51.
[122] Summarily translated to mean that the executive power can impose its acts on the Legal Department but cannot impose its opinion, he can instruct the institution of appeal but cannot execute its opinion
[123] Ibid.
[124]Anyangwe (C.), op.cit. p.81.

submissions or pleadings of the Legal Department. In fact, the law provides that the Legal Department shall at the close of hearing in every case address the court or tender written submissions without being denied the right of hearing or stopped when addressing the Court[125]. Such is equally the case even where his submissions are based only on civil claim[126]. Exceptionally in some cases the bench can proceed to initiate or take cognizance of an offence and proceed to try it[127]. The Court does not need a fiat from the Legal Department to take cognizance of such an offence. The law as well exceptionally gives the Judge the possibility of prematurely putting an end to prosecution commenced by the Legal Department and under conditions laid down in the provisions of section 62 of the CPC[128]. The principles that govern the Legal Department are not limited sorely to its organisation. In its functional dimension the Legal Department is equally governed by principles worth examining as well.

---

[125]Section 128(3) of the CPC.

[126]Section 129 of the CPC.

[127] Such is the case with contempt of court under section 152(1) as read with section 154(a) OF The Cameroonian Penal Code

[128](1) Criminal proceedings shall be discontinued in the following cases:
(a) the death of the suspect, the defendant or of the accused;
(b) prescription;
(c) amnesty;
(d) repeal of the law
(e) after a successful plea of conviction or acquittal;
(f) by agreement between the parties if the law expressly so provides;
(g) the withdrawal of a complaint where the lodging of such a complaint is a precondition for the commencement of prosecution;
(h) the withdrawal of a complaint or the civil claim by the civil party who lodged the complaint in respect of a simple offence or a misdemeanor
(2) the provisions of subsection (1) (h) above are applicable only where:
- the withdrawal is voluntary;
- the matter has not been heard on the merits;
- the offence committed does not disturb public order, good morals; in case of many civil claimants, all of them must withdraw their complaint or civil claim;
- the withdrawal is not as a result of violence, fraud or deceit.
(3) in the case referred to in sub section (2) above the court shall grant the application and award cost against the civil claimant.

II. PRINCIPLES LINKED TO THE ROLE OF PROSECUTION OF THE DEPARTMENT OF PUBLIC PROSECUTION

The principles linked to the role of prosecution of the Legal Department or its prosecutorial mission are dual in nature; the principle of homogeneity (*indivisibilité*) and the principle of non-challenge or recusal (*irrecusabilité*).

A. The Principle of Homogeneity *(indivisibilité)*

Carlson Anyangwe [129] while painting a vivid picture of this principle explains that each Department of Public Prosecution attached to a court is legally regarded as one homogenous, indivisible entity. Although it is made up of several members, it is referred to and regarded as though it were one person. He further explains that no member of the Legal Department acts in his own personal name. When he speaks in Court, when he prosecutes, it is the Legal Department speaking, it is the Legal Department prosecuting. The members of the Legal Department are as if it were anonymous entities with one nomenclature.

The Criminal Procedure Code has expressly made provision to this principle. It provides that any judicial act done by any magistrate of the Legal Department shall be presumed to be done in the name of the entire Legal Department[130].

A fundamental effect of this being that in the course of a trial, members of the Legal Department may replace each other in prosecuting a single case. A typical illustration can be seen where in the course of a trial commenced by the 1st Deputy, in subsequent Court sessions the seat of the Legal Department is occupied by the 2nd and 3rd deputies respectively without any risk of challenge.

B. The Principle of Non-Challenge or recusal *(irrecusabilité)*

Generally, the law[131] provides that magistrates of the bench or a judge may be challenged for diverse reasons[132], while giving the

---

[129] Anyangwe (C.), op. cit., pp.82.
[130] Section 127(1) of the CPC.
[131] Section 591 of the CPC

said magistrates the opportunity of abstaining from hearing such matters if they think they could be challenged[133]. The Magistrates of the Legal Department who happens to be the principal party in all criminal trials before the court and whose absence is liable to rendering the whole procedure null and void[134] are excluded from challenge[135]. In a more profound reflection Emmanuel Ndjere[136] questions if a Deputy State Counsel who had previously represented the Legal Department during preliminary inquiry can as well take part in the trial in the same capacity. He opine that there is no legal provisions to the effect that the Deputy should desist while admitting that in the past there existed a circular to this effect from the Minister in charge of justice, instructing that such Magistrates should abstain from representing the Legal Department in the course of the trial. As regards Examining Magistrates, the law explicitly prohibits them from proceeding to the hearing of a matter wherein they had conducted preliminary inquiry.

The Legal Department's role in criminal proceedings is not limited to initiating and carrying out prosecution sorely. The Legal Department as well supervises the conduct of preliminary investigations, the recording of statements, issue warrants. In its mission of preliminary investigation, the Legal Department has as privileged collaborators judicial police officer, whose role is worth analysing.

---

[132] (a) where he or his spouse is a relative, guardian or relative by marriage up to the degree of uncle, nephew, first cousins or the child of the first cousin of one of the parties;
(b) where he or his spouse is employer, employee, next of kin, donnee, creditor, debtor, companion of one of the parties, or director of an enterprise or company involved in the case;
(c) where he has previously taken part in the proceedings or if he has been an arbitrator or counsel or witness;
(d) where he or his spouse is party in a case which shall be tried by one of the parties;
(e) Where he or his spouse is involved in any incident tending to show friendship or hatred towards any of the parties and likely to cast doubt on his personality.

[133] Section 592 of the CPC.

[134] Section 128 of the CPC.

[135] Section 593 of the CPC.

[136] E. Ndjere, op. cit.,p.53.

PART II

JUDICIAL POLICE: AUXILIARIES OF THE DEPARTMENT OF PUBLIC PROSECUTIONS

The term judicial police has not been defined by any legal instrument. The Criminal Procedure Code just like the "*Code d'Intruction Criminelle*", simply describe the status and duties of the judicial police.

However, an author[137] has defined it as "*l'ensemble des fonctionnaires des nature variée charges de rechercher les crimes, les délits et les contraventions, d'en rassembler les preuves et de livrer les auteurs aux tribunaux charges de les punir*"[138]. This definition is not different from paragraph 1 of section 82 of the Criminal Procedure Code which spells out the duties of JPO.

Judicial police as authorities charged with investigation perform their duties under the supervision of the State Counsel. They are composed of judicial police officers, judicial police agents and all other civil servants or persons to whom judicial police duties are assigned by law. In every jurisdiction of the Court of Appeal the judicial police is under the control of the Procureur General[139], who at the end of each year is supposed to evaluate their work[140]. Phillipe Keubou[141] makes a distinction between judicial and administrative police carried out by the same officers. According to him, the role of administrative police is the prevention of the commission of offences. This, he says, is achieved by instructions given to citizens, by interventions that it carries out and at times by the simple presence of the judicial police. In the execution of duties of the administrative police, the officers or agents are answerable to administrative authorities. Judicial police only come in when, in spite of the preventive measures put in place, an offence is committed. Law makers have however clearly spelt out the status and duties of JPO.

---

[137]Keubou (Ph.), op. cit., p. 31.

[138]Translated in English, Judicial police will be defined as an assembly of civil servants of varied backgrounds with the duty of investigating offences, collecting evidence, identifying offenders and accomplices and bringing them before the courts for them to be punished.

[139]Section 78 of the CPC.

[140]The laudable nature of the evaluation powers of the Procureur General of Judicial police authorities has remained a vain wish more than ten years after the promulgation of Law N° 2005 of 27july 2005. Its implementation would have been a milestone towards curbing the excessive violation of human rights in the course of investigation.

[141] Ibid.

CHAPTER III
THE STRUCTURE, STATUS AND DUTIES OF THE JUDICIAL POLICE

As a privileged collaborator of the State Counsel, the law makers have succinctly spelt out those on whom the duties of judicial police officers can be attributed. At first sight one may be tempted to think that it is basically made up of uniform men of the gendarmerie or police units.

I. THE STRUCTURE OF THE JUDICIAL POLICE

According to Emmanuel Ndjere[142] structurally the services of the judicial police is organised at the level of the Legal Department [143], at the level of the Delegation of National Security[144]as laid down by decree N° 2002/003 of 4 January 2002

---

[142]Ndjere (E.), op. cit., pp. 68-75.

[143] Summarily translated, the State Counsel who is a judicial police officer, ensures the running and control of the Legal Department: To this regard, he is assisted by his Deputies. This magistrate therefore carries out or caused to be carried out all the acts that he deems necessary in the search and to the prosecution of offences against criminal law. He controls and oversees the activities of the judicial police within his jurisdiction notably remand in police custody. He can at any time and place act as a judicial police officer.

The Procureur General at the Appeal Court ensures that the criminal law is applied throughout the jurisdiction of the Court of Appeal; he has authority over the magistrates within his jurisdiction. He can instruct the magistrates of the Legal Department within his jurisdiction to investigate offences of which he has knowledge, to close a file or to institute proceedings. He equally has as attribute in his capacity of a judicial police officer supervising the activities of the judicial police officers and agents working within his jurisdiction, submitting half yearly reports to the Minister in charge of justice on their activities and conduct and may direct them to obtain any information which he deems useful for the proper administration of justice. The appreciation of their work as well as the transmission of such appreciation and marks is still to be effectively implemented.

[144] Summarily translated, at the level of Central Services, the General Delegation of National Security is made up of a directorate in charge of judicial police which have as duty coordinating the techniques of criminal research, the fight against national, international and transnational criminality, coordination the activities of the judicial police of the external services, carrying out economic and criminal investigations, coordinating the methods and techniques of identification, diffusing and ensuring the execution of the instructions of magistrates of the Legal Department, establishing and issuing national identity cards etc .It is made up of the following sub directorates;

- The sub directorate of criminal investigations;
- The sub directorate of economic and financial investigations;
- The sub directorate of scientific police and identification;
- The sub directorate in charge of drugs.

All this sub directorates are charged with carrying out investigations under the control of the competent Legal Department in compliance with the law. This law equally provides for;

- A directorate of public security;
- A directorate of frontier police,

At the level of the external services;

on the organisation of the General Delegation of National Security, according to which the judicial police is exercised at the level of the central and external services. He equally looks at the structure of judicial police at the level of the Gendarmerie[145]

II. THE STATUS OF JUDICIAL POLICE OFFICERS

According to the provisions of section 79 of the CPC the status of JPO are attributed to the following:

- Officers and non-commissioned officers of the gendarmerie;
- Gendarmes in charge even in an acting capacity of a gendarmerie brigade or gendarmerie post;
- Superintendent of Police;
- Gendarmes or inspectors of police who have passed the judicial police examination and taken oath;
- Public servants even if they are temporarily performing the functions of head of external service of the National security.

Among the directorates that make up this section, we can name;

- The provincial division of the judicial police
- The emi-immigration police stations;
- Special branch police stations with diverse and numerous judicial police duties.

[145]The service of the Gendarmerie is organized by decree N° 60/280 of the 31 December 1960.It is a military force under the control of administrative and judicial authorities, to ensure public security, the maintenance of order, the execution of laws; a preventive and repressive surveillance constitutes the essence of its mission throughout the national territory. Their role constitutes essentially the security of the rural population and communication channels.

The Gendarmerie forms an integral part of the military. It is made up of territorial and mobile units. In order to ensure the execution of the task given to it notably the respect of laws and regulations the entire gendarmerie though under the direct control of the Minister Delegate in charge of the armed force is equally subdued under the control of the Minister in charge of Justice as regards the exercise of the duties of the judicial police as well as under the Minister of Territorial Administration for the exercise of the duties of administrative police. As regards the organization of the Gendarmerie, at the Regional level we have the Gendarmerie Legion which is placed under the control of a superior officer of the Gendarmerie. At the Divisional level we have Companies and at the Sub-divisional levels Brigades and Gendarmerie Posts. The National Gendarmerie has special units such as;

- Brigade in charge of traffic at the regional levels and charged with the repression of traffic offences as provided for in the highway code
- The Brigade de Recherche, implanted within the Gendarmerie company;
- Airport Brigades
- Seaport Brigade which exercises its duties at the seaport;
- Maritime Brigade whose mission is deployed over the seas. The Legal Department works in strict collaboration with all this units.

Section 80 of the CPC further provides that public servants and other public employees who have been assigned judicial police duties by special instruments shall discharge those duties under the conditions and within the limits fixed by the said instrument. Such is the case with the public servants of forestry and wildlife charged with carrying out investigations and recording statements in cases of wildlife offences.

Non-judicial police officers otherwise referred to as police agents are not excluded from judicial police duties notably investigation. They assist their superior officers but have no authority to take decisions to remand in police custody.

From the aforementioned, it is crystal clear that the term judicial police as defined by the CPC cannot be understood literally as referring sorely to the police force but encloses gendarmes as well as public servants of other administration with jurisdiction to carry out investigation.

Whatever the case it is worth noting that the duties performed by judicial police officers irrespective of whether their status is similar.

III. THE CLASSICAL DUTIES OF THE JUDICIAL POLICE

Judicial police officers are responsible for:

- The investigating of offences, collecting of evidence, identifying offenders and accomplices and bringing them before the Legal Department;
- Executing rogatory commission of judicial authorities;
- Serving court processes;
- Executing warrants and court decisions[146]

Apart from the duties mentioned here above the law equally provides that they are vested with the powers of receiving complaints[147] and reports[148] against persons and carrying our investigations. It further precise that in cases of felonies and misdemeanours committed flagrante delicto their powers are

[146]Section 82 of the CPC.

[147] Complaints within this context refer to a report from the victim of an offence against a suspect addressed to law enforcement officers.

[148] Reports on the other hand refers to a complaint by a third party who is not victim to an offence of which he has knowledge addressed to judicial police officers

exercised under the conditions laid down in the provisions of Section 104 to 115. The said duties are accomplished with the assistance of the forces of law and order and under the supervision of the State Counsel from whom they receive instructions[149].

Judicial police officers within the scope of section 82(a) can be seized directly by the victim of an offence, by a report from a third party or may be instructed by the State Counsel to carry out investigations. Such are cases wherein the State Counsel is directly seized by the victim of an offence. In any of such cases he opens preliminary investigations, which enables him to collect evidence, identify offenders and accomplices and bring them before the Legal Department.

A. Preliminary Investigations

Considering the fact that an investigative process is not limited to criminal justice only, an investigation has globally been defined[150] as “the examination, study, searching, tracking and gathering of factual information that answers questions or solves problems”. According to these authors, it is more of an art than a science, précising that although the person engaged in the investigation is a gatherer of facts, he or she must develop hypotheses and draw conclusions based on available information. It is a comprehensive activity involving information collection, the application of logic and the exercise of sound reasoning, the end been the factual explanation of what transpired, if the incident or issue is history or what is occurring, if the issue is of present.

Applied to the criminal realm, a criminal investigation refers to the process of collecting information (or evidence) about a crime, in order to:

- Determine if a crime has been committed;
- Identify the perpetrators;
- Apprehend the perpetrators;

---

[149]Section 83 of the CPC.

[150]Charles A. Senezald and John K. Tsukayama, *The process of investigation: Concepts and strategies for investigators of the Private sector*, second edition, Butterworth-Heinemann,2001, p. 3

- Provide evidence to support a conviction in court.

The above is similar to the mission of judicial police officers as defined by the CPC.[151]

According to Charles A. Senewald and John K. Tsukayama [152] investigation within this context have as main objective seeking answers to basic questions- the what, who, where, when, how and why regarding a condition, incident, or action deemed organisationally unacceptable.

In line with the CPC an author has summarily defined preliminary investigation as a procedure conducted by a judicial police officer of his own initiative or on the instructions of the State Counsel with the aim of collecting evidence of the commission of an offence, thus permitting the state Counsel to decide whether to prosecute or not. He distinguishes preliminary inquiry from offences committed flagrante delicto[153].

B. The Power of judicial police officers in the course of investigation

Specialists in investigation have been attributed significant powers to enable them effectively carryout their functions. Out of the definition of this power, springs a conflict between the right of the society and that of individuals and more especially suspects. Criminal law must thus maintain an equilibrium between this dual interest of almost equal importance, sacredness and worthy of protection. The general interest of the society requires the prompt repression of offences as well as the interest of the suspect, which necessitate complete guarantee of his right of defence[154].

Among the prerogatives of the judicial police officer in the course of investigation features; questioning of any person whose statement is likely to lead to the discovery of the truth, conduct searches, remand in custody, and request the assistance of experts. In cases of offences committed flagrante delicto the powers are more extensive and can include the interception of

---

[151] Section 82(a) CPC

[152] Charles A. Senewald and John K.Tsukayama, op.cit., p.4.

[153] Keubou (Ph.), op. cit., p.34.

[154] Cesare Beccaria, *Traités des délits et peine*, trad. Par Mme Khaiat, Paris Cujas, 1966, p. 123.

recordings, transcription of correspondences and taking of photographs at private premises or recording statements of persons vicariously liable.

The law provides that in the course of investigations, judicial police officers may question any persons whose statement is likely to lead to the manifestation of the truth[155]. Such persons who are supposed to have been summoned must appear and answer questions, failure of which a writ of capias shall be issued against them at the instance of the State Counsel[156].

At the level of police investigation all the operations carried out are geared towards the manifestation of the truth. The JPO just like the Examining Magistrate is not out to nail the suspect, in fact it is not an inquisition, he searches for elements that are favourable or unfavourable to the suspect with the paramount objective being the discovery of the truth. It is to this regards that he precedes with the questioning of witnesses as well as suspects and where necessary makes use of confrontation.

Who is a witness?

A witness can summarily be defined as "the eyes and the ears of justice" as Bentham rightly puts it[157]. The term witness in its strict legal sense, means one who gives evidence in a case before a Court of law, but has also been defined as one who has knowledge of a fact or occurrence sufficient to testify with respect to it, while an eye witness has been defined as one who testifies to what he or she has seen. In 1972, Justice Rawlings wrote this in State V. Gilroy, 199 NW 2d 63, "***the term witness… ordinarily means one who gives evidence under oath or affirmation, in person or by affidavit or deposition, in any proceeding in any court of justice, or before any officer thereof or before any tribunal or officer created by law, or in any proceeding in regard to any matter or thing in or respecting an oath or affirmation is required or may be required or***

---

[155] Section 92(1) (a) CPC.

[156] Section 92(1) (b) CPC.

[157] Jérémie Bentham, « Traité des preuves », I, N° 93, cited by Mbunja (Y.), in, *Les revenants : Le Juge d'instruction*, op. cit., p.123.

authorised by law". The CPC within the context of the procedure of trial, provides that to be admissible, oral evidence must be direct i.e. if it refers to facts which could be heard, by the person who heard, if it refers to facts which could be seen, by the person who saw, if it refer to facts which could be perceived by any sense, by the person who perceived and finally if it refers to an opinion by the person who hold the opinion[158].

Without the evidence of witnesses and their contribution to the law and justice system as reporters of events, the justice system would not be sustainable. Witnesses reconstruct events and tell the court or JPO what happened. The importance of witnesses can be summarised in the Latin maxim "***testis oculatus unus plus valet quam auriti decem***" meaning one eyewitness is worth more than ten ear witnesses[159].

1. Recording of Statements from witnesses

In the course of police investigation victims of offences are privileged witnesses due to the fact that they are directly affected by the offence and in most cases directly witness its commission. The statement taken by JPO will become the permanent record of events as seen by the witness. Any other persons whose statements are likely to lead to the manifestation of the truth may be summoned by JPO for the recording of statement while others appear spontaneously. In cases of offences committed flagrante delicto JPOs may constrain persons they suspect may be useful for the manifestation of the truth from leaving crime scenes. Unlike in preliminary inquiry proceedings where witnesses are required to take oath, the recording of statements of witnesses at the level of police investigation does not call for such formality.

Procedurally, after the identification of the witness and his relationship with the parties, the witness is invited by the JPO to give an accurate, relevant and concise account of the events as he saw, heard or perceived, that is material to the case. At the end of his narration the JPO may ask him questions to clarify any

[158] Section 335 CPC

[159] This rule promotes the importance of eyewitnesses to that of witnesses whose testimonies are based on hearsay. This law is against the admission of hearsay evidence which cannot be considered as valid evidence.

doubts. The witness is caused to read over his statement, ascertain its accuracy before signing. In cases where a witness cannot read, his statements are read over to him before he appends his signature thereon. The formalities are more stringent and compelling when it comes to the interrogation of suspects.

2. The suspect and preliminary (police) investigation

A suspect has been defined as "a person against whom there exists any information or clue which tends to establish that he may have committed an offence or participated in its commission"[160]

The suspect during police investigation benefits from a series of prerogatives that guarantees his right to a fair trial prominent among which is the right to the presumption of innocence. The respects of these rights are mandatory. Its violation can render the whole procedure null and void. The respect of the rights of the suspect is an imperative step prior to interrogation.

1.1. The Rights of the Suspect at the commencement of Investigation

The suspect, defendant or the accused persons occupy an important place in criminal procedure. It is against them that the judicial machinery is deployed. The suspect must be treated with much regard, despite the information or clue or better still charges against him. It is not a question here of making things extremely easy for him because criminal procedure puts in conflict individual liberty and the need imposed by society to punish offences, an actual threat to public peace. It is against this backdrop that the CPC has consecrated considerable guarantees to the right to fair trial beginning from the suspect to the defendant as well as the accused. It is in this regards that the law provides that as soon as investigations are opened the judicial police officer shall under the penalty of nullity inform the suspect of:

- His right to counsel;

---

[160] Section 9(1), CPC

- His right to remain silent, emphasising that the said information must be made in the police report[161].

a. Suspects Right to Counsel

Cameroon is a signatory of several international legal instruments protecting the rights of suspects notably the right to counsel which constitutes a right to defence. Such is the case with the International Covenant on Civil and Political Right[162] and the African Charter on Human and Peoples' Right[163]. This right guarantees to all suspects the possibility of being assisted by counsel of his choice as early as during police investigation. According to an author[164]this right in essence as conceived in international legal instruments is not only limited to the suspect's right of his choice of counsel but an obligation to the State as well to provide one to suspects who cannot afford. In the words of the African Commission on Human and Peoples' Right[165] the right to freely chose counsel is fundamental for the guarantee of the right to fair trial, giving the Court the right of veto on the choice of counsel to enter appearance constitutes an unacceptable violation of this right. In other cases, the Commission held that remanding a suspect in custody in a secret destination without any contact with his lawyer constitutes a violation of the right to defence[166]. The Cameroonian lawmaker while spelling out the right to be assisted by counsel however fails to precise the content of the said right. How and under what conditions can the said rights be exercised are not stated. Considering the importance of this right however, its violation is sanctioned by nullity as provided for in the provisions of section 3 of the CPC[167]. Such is the case with the right to remain silent.

---

161 Section 116(3) and (4) CPC.

162 Article 14(3) (d).

163 Article 7(1) (c).

164 ETEME ETEME, « Le droit au procès équitable : Considération générale sur un droit qui donne sens et essence au droit », in *Miroir de droit,* juillet, aout et septembre 2010, p.18.

165 Communication N° 48/90, 50/9, 52/91, 89/93, Amnesty and ORS v. Sudan.

166 Communication N° 143/95 and 150/96, Constitutional Right Project and Civil Liberties Organisation v. Nigeria.

167 Section 3(1) CPC « The sanction against the infringement of any rule of criminal procedure shall be an absolute nullity when it is;

(a) Prejudicial to the rights of defence as defined by legal provisions in force;

(b) Contrary to public policy

b. Suspects Right to Remain Silent

According to E. Duga Titanji[168] the right to remain silent is a corollary to the right of the presumption of innocence. Otherwise referred to as the MIRANDA Warning, he traces the origin of this right from the case of ***Miranda v. Arizona***, while relating the facts of the case. Section 116 above while making provision for the notification of the right to remain silent, does not however lay down the format. Within the American context a typical Miranda would be as follows "You have the right to remain silent. Anything you say can and will be used against you in a court of law. You have the right to speak to an Attorney or have an Attorney present during any questioning. If you cannot afford a lawyer, one will be provided for you at government expense." The last part does not however apply to Cameroon. What can be the attitude of a court faced with the option of silence as a means of defence both at the level of preliminary investigation and during hearing?

It is only after the notification of the rights that the JPO can proceed with the interrogation of the suspect.

c. Interrogation of suspects

The CPC does not lay down a procedure to be followed during interrogation of the suspect. It simply states that the suspect is informed of the allegations against him and treated humanely both morally and materially with reasonable time of full rest[169] without any further emphasis. In most cases the JPO present the facts as contained in the complaint of the victim or in his statement after which he is given the opportunity to present his defence if he so desires. He may opt to make a statement in his defence or make use of his right to remain silent. When he chooses to make a statement in his defence, he gives the investigator the opportunity to ask him questions relevant to the discovery of the truth. On the contrary where he opts for silence,

---

[168]Duga Titanji (E), «The right to defence under the Criminal procedure code of Cameroon: The consecration of International Human rights norms under Cameroonian law? », *Juridis périodique* N° 75, Juillet, Aout et Sepetembre, p. 94.

[169] Section 122 (1) CPC.

he cannot be asked any question. In the course of investigation and more precisely interrogation the suspect must not be subjected to any physical or mental constraint or to torture, violence, threats or any pressure whatsoever, or to deceit, insidious manoeuvre, false proposals, prolonged questioning, hypnosis, the administration of drugs or to any other method which is likely to compromise or limit his freedom of action or decision or his memory or sense of judgement[170].

Apart from the recording of statements and interrogation of the parties, the JPO can as well recourse to confrontation.

3. The judicial police and confrontation

The principle of confrontation is an ancient one dating back to at least Roman times[171]. Today, it is a prevalent feature of the world's major justice systems and an integral component of international fair trial standards. Derived from national constitutionalism and international human rights together with other long-established fair trial guarantees[172], the right to examine the accuser is universally reflected in Regional and Multilateral Treaties the world over. Such is the case with the International Covenant on Civil and Political Right, which stipulates that "in the determination of any criminal charge against him, [the accused] shall be entitled...in full equality...to examine, or have examined, the witnesses against him[173]. This statute has been adopted almost in identical terms in the European Convention for the Protection of Human Rights and Fundamental Freedom[174], the International Military Tribunal for former Yugoslavia[175], the International Military Tribunal for

---

[170] Section 122(2) CPC

[171] Kweku Vanderpuye, «Traditions in conflict: The internationalization of confrontation», *Cornell international law journal*, vol 43, p. 514

[172] See U.N. Sub-Commission on prevention of discrimination and protection of minorities, report of the sub-commission on the Prevention of Discrimination and the Protection of minorities on its 46th session, The Administration of Justice and Human Rights of Detainees, U.N. Doc. E/CN./Sub 2/1994/24 (June 3, 1994), p.85, (noting that fair trial rights have been an international human rights norm for over 40 year, giving right to a substantial body of interpretation in its elaboration and construal)

[173] Article 14(3)(e), ICCPR

[174] Article 6(3)(d), ECHR

[175] Article 21(4)(e), ICTY

Rwanda[176] as well as the African Commission on Human and Peoples Right[177].

According to Kweku V. prior to the twentieth century, the principle of confrontation in continental Europe was uncommon. It had been greatly attenuated during medieval times, during which the procedure of the inquisition took hold. These were dependent on anonymous and secret evidence to preserve social order and uproot dissidence. Evidence in criminal cases was thus received "under 'a veil' of secrecy, and the door was left "wide open to mendacity, falsehood, and partiality". Suspects were not afforded the opportunity to confront such evidence. Given this historical underpinning, it is hardly surprising that the role of the parties in modern continental trials is relatively reduced and subsidiary to that of the judge.

He contends that the adversarial systems generally regard the right to confrontation as an indispensable component of the fair administration of trial, a position that Courts in the U.S have consistently held[178]. In an earlier case[179] the court described confrontation as a fundamental [guarantee] of life and liberty. The Courts [180] noted that the purpose of confrontation is "to augment accuracy in the fact-finding process". In yet another decision [181] the court held that "the central concern of the confrontation clause[182] is to ensure reliability of the evidence... by subjugating it to a rigorous testing in the context of an adversary proceeding".

Whatever the case, the place of pride given to confrontation by international legal instruments and the fundamental norms of some countries notably the United States, as an element of the right to due process, is not universally observed. The Cameroonian constitution does not explicitly make

---

[176] Article 20(4)(e), ICTR

[177] Resolution on the Right to Recourse and Fair Trial, Res. 4(xi) 92 of 9 March 1992

[178] See Chambers V Mississippi, 410 U.S. 284, 294 (1973) (" The right to confront and cross-examine witnesses...have long been recognized as essential to due process")

[179] See Kirby V United States, 147, U.S. 47, 55 (1899)

[180] See Ohio V. Roberts, 448, U.S. 56, 65 (1980)

[181] See Maryland V. Craig, 497, U.S. 836, 845 (1990)

[182] In the U.S the right to confrontation is enshrined in the sixth amendments to the Federal Constitution, which provides that in all criminal cases the accused shall "enjoy the right to be confronted with the witnesses against him", referred to as the confrontation clause.

mention of confrontation even though it guarantees the right to every person to a fair hearing before the courts. One would have expected the CPC to deal with this subject extensively. Unfortunately, one of the rare and perhaps lone instance the Code makes allusion to confrontation is in the course of preliminary inquiry, wherein it states inter alia that "Except in case of force majeure, which must be recorded in the report, there shall be confrontation of witnesses and the defendant, after the witnesses have given evidence for the prosecution, even when the defendant indicates that he shall say nothing during the confrontation"[183]. From a perusal of the afore cited provision, one notes that the lawmakers have made confrontation at the level of preliminary inquiry mandatory and surprisingly even when the defendant indicates that he shall say nothing. Ironically, if the defendant or any of the parties have nothing to say there will obviously be no confrontation.

In the absence of any explicit provision on confrontation, the unanswered question remains, can JPO's logically rely of the provisions of section 180(2) of the CPC to carry out confrontation in the course of police investigations? In other words, can the provisions of the CPC on preliminary inquiry be conveniently applied in the course of police investigations?

Logically, and on a practical node, it's a practice of investigation, a smart judicial police officer confronted with contradictions in the course of investigations is left with no option but confrontation "to augment accuracy in the fact-finding process", in the words of the Court in the case of ***Ohio v. Roberts***. More so, owing to the fact that it has not been overtly prohibited by law. Furthermore, preliminary investigations just like preliminary inquiry have a common objective and almost a similar procedure, though with some disparities. It will be quite unfair to interpret the oblivion of the lawmaker *stricto sensu* to unambiguously mention confrontation during preliminary investigation as a prohibition.

In the absence of a procedure to be followed, an author[184] has cautioned that confrontation should never be general i.e.

---

[183]Section 180(2), CPC

[184] Mbunja (Y.), op.cit, p.128

confronting the suspect with all the witnesses at the same time. The difficulty here is that there is risk of "contamination" of the other witnesses by the response of a witness. It is advisable to confront the suspect or the victim with a witness separately for a more objective outcome. We recommend that any future amendment of the CPC should take into consideration confrontation at the level of police investigation, expressly defining it, as well as specifying the procedure to be followed and sanctions in case of violation. It will be quite interesting elevating confrontation to the level of one of the rights of the suspect at the same level as the right to counsel, right to medical examination, right to feeding etc. A neighbouring notion of confrontation which has been legislated upon elaborately is cross-examination and re-examination during trial before law courts in Cameroon.

Such is the case with regards to search and seizure, prerogative of the JPO which has been properly and elaborately regulated by lawmakers as well

4. The power of Search and seizure of judicial police officers

A search is a process conducted by authorised agents of law going through part or all of individual property, looking for specific items that are related to crime that they have reason to believe have been committed. A seizure is the forcible taking of property by a government law enforcement official from a person who is suspected of violating or is known to have violated the law. A search warrant must usually be presented to the person before his property is seized or in its absence, the explicit consent of the person to be searched.

The importance or pertinence of this requirement in the course of preliminary investigation is highlighted in the fourth amendment of the constitution of the United States of America[185]. This amendment makes mention of the need for the existence not only of a warrant or consent of the person implicated but to the

[185] « The right of the people to be secure in their persons, houses, papers, and effects, against unreasonable search and seizures, shall not be violated, and no warrant shall issue, but upon probable cause, supported by oath or affirmation, and particularly describing the place to be searched and the persons or things to be seized

existence of probable cause[186] as well. According to this notion an officer is said to have probable cause to perform a search and seizure if there is evidence from a crime present or the officer has the reasonable belief that a crime has been committed. Such is the case where an officer pulls an individual for over speeding and smells marijuana, he then has reasons to believe there is an illegal substance in the car.

In our context, the right to privacy which is a basic human right is guaranteed in the preamble of the constitution, wherein it is stated "the home is inviolate; no search may be conducted except by virtue of the law". This provision protects citizens against arbitrary, unreasonable police intrusions. This prescription by the fundamental law of the nation has adequately been taken care of in the CPC, which provides in principle that searches and seizures shall be carried out by judicial police officers who possess search warrants[187]. A search warrant has been defined as an order given to a JPO by the State Counsel, an Examining Magistrate or a Trial Court to enter any public or private place and search it for the purpose of seizing any article or documents used in committing an offence or which appears to be the product of an offence[188].

a) Search and Seizures: Places prone to these measures

The law to this regard does not give an exhaustive list of the said "public and private places" wherein searches and seizures can be carried out. It makes mention of "a house or premises"[189] and... A house has been defined by the Supreme Court[190]as "a permanent or temporal habitation occupied by the owner or otherwise by third parties with his consent and includes; a building as well as its closest attachments, such as parking stores, and its yard protected by the fence" or better still, "a place a person can call his home whether he resides therein or not and irrespective of the

[186] « Facts are apparent and obvious to a reasonable person »

[187] Section 90(1) CPC.

[188] Section 16 CPC.

[189] Section 92(2).

[190]CS, arrête du 27 aout 1968 as narrated by M. Mbella Mbappe Robert, Procureur General of the said Court, in his submissions on the occasion of the solemn opening of the Supreme Court held on the 20th November 1980, see Guy Roger Eba'a , *Les grands moments de la justice au Cameroun* de 1958 a 2010, Presses de l'UCAC, juin 2010, p. 74

legal status of his occupation or the purpose of occupation"[191]. Exceptionally however the chambers of advocates and the office of advocates have been singled out considering the specificities involve in the conduct of searches in the said offices. In the United States apart from houses, Federal Supreme Courts have held that searches can be conducted on cell phone[192], computer, tablet computer or other electronic devices[193], cars[194] etc.

b) Body search

The CPC provides for body search. Body search which consist in manually exploring the body or the dresses of an individual, have as main objective, ensuring that individuals do not carry on them dangerous objects which are perilous to the security of others. The minimum requirement of such an operation is that it should be done in strict respect of the right to human dignity, with decency and by a person of the same sex. Such is the case with suspects handed over to JPO by individuals, suspects arrested by JPO who must be searched or caused to be searched[195]. The exigency of body search equally has a preventive undertone. In fact section 87 authorises JPO to make use of this operation in public places or places opened to the public as soon as he suspects that an individual is bearing arms or any object that can serve for the commission of offences or which constitutes the product of the commission of an offence.

c) Procedure of search and seizure

Procedurally, the conduct of searches and seizures as provided for in the CPC relatively guarantees the right of house owners or occupants. It provides that searches and seizures shall be conducted in their presence and in case of their absence, their representatives and two witnesses taken from the neighbourhood present[196]. More importantly the law provides for a prior search of JPO by occupants or persons in possession of objects to be

---

[191] Crim, 24 juin 1987, Bull.crim n° 267.
[192] Riley v. California (2014) 134 S.Ct. 2473,2482.
[193] Schneckloth v. Bustamonte (1973) 412 U.S.218,219.
[194] People v. Carter (2005) 36 Cal.4th 1114, 1141.
[195] Section 35(1).
[196] Section 93(2) CPC.

seized or their representatives[197]. This is a very laudable initiative which avoids the planting of evidence by some unscrupulous JPO on scenes of crime to implicate suspects. All seized articles must be shown to the suspect, his representatives or persons in possession of them so that they may identify and initial them where necessary[198], with an inventory made at the spot, described in full detail and kept under seal. It is worth noting that occupants, house owners, representatives or witnesses must be informed of such rights before the commencement of the operation and mention of such information explicitly made in the report. This report which is drawn up in respect of the provisions of section 90 of the CPC must be signed by the occupant of the place and the person in possession of the article and in their absence their representatives, witnesses and other persons who took part in the search.

In the conduct of search and seizures the protection of privacy is paramount. The law specifies the period within which searches and seizures can be conducted. It provides that no search may be conducted on a private premise between six (6) pm and (6) am. However, it can exceed six (6) pm provided it was commenced earlier on the authorisation of the State Counsel[199] or exceptionally without such authorisation where it is difficult to get in touch with the State Counsel. This does not however stop a JPO from conducting search in connection with a specific offence from carrying out seizure in connection with another offence, provided it attracts an imprisonment sentence[200]. Where he intends to proceed to seizures, he alone has the right to examine the contents of documents to be seized and is bound by professional secrecy[201].

Even though the law makes the availability of a search warrant mandatory prior to the conduct of searches and seizures, the mandatory existence of this document is not absolute in nature.

Exceptions to the warrant requirement exist for:

---

[197] Section 93(3) CPC.

[198] Section 96 (1) (3) CPC.

[199] Section 99 CPC.

[200] Section 95 CPC.

[201] Section 97 CPC.

- Searches and seizures done with the consent of the occupant, house owner or persons in possession of objects to be seized[202]. Within the context of the CPC the law expressly provides that in the absence of a search warrant, searches and seizures of exhibits may be carried out only with the consent of the occupant or of the person in possession of objects to be seized[203]. An occupant or a person in possession of objects waives his right to challenge the legality of searches and seizures each time he consents. Considering the severe consequence of such a decision, the law has taken measures to ensure that the consent is given freely and voluntarily. Consequently, instances of fraud and coercion and even undue duress may constitute illegal searches. It is for this reason that the CPC goes a step further by providing that consent must be written, signed or thumb printed by the persons concerned[204]
- Searches and seizures Incident to lawful arrest, where the police is looking for weapons that might have been used against them or for criminal evidence that may otherwise be destroyed[205]. Such is the case with offences committed *flagrante delicto* as well during which the JPO have as mission , ensuring the preservation of evidence that may be used for the discovery of the truth[206], seizing any articles or documents used in committing or which appears to be the product of the felony and to conduct searches in the houses of persons suspected of either keeping documents or articles relating to the particular

[202]Schneckloth v. Bustamante, Supra " it is equally settled that one of the specifically established exceptions to the requirements of both a warrant and probable cause is a search or seizure that is conducted pursuant to consent"

[203]Section 94(1) CPC.

[204]Section 94(2) CPC.

[205]Chimel v. California (1996) 395 U.S 752, 764-63 "A similar analysis underlies the 'search incident to arrest' principle in law of search and seizures and marks its proper extent. When an arrest is made, it is reasonable for the arresting officer to search the person arrested in order to remove any weapon that the later might seek to use in order to resist arrest or effect his escape. Otherwise the officer's safety might well be endangered, and the arrest itself frustrated, it is entirely reasonable for the arresting officer to search for and seize any evidence on the arrestee's person in order to prevent his concealment or destruction…"

[206]Section 93(2) (3).

offence or of having participated in the commission of the felony[207]

- Inspection searches such as those at international borders[208];
- Searches and seizures in emergency situations that is necessary to prevent physical harm or serious property damage or to locate fleeing suspect[209]. Such is the case with arrest in cases of a felony or misdemeanour committed flagrante delicto contained in the provisions of section 93(1) of the CPC.
- Searches of vehicle when police have "probable cause"[210]to believe the vehicle contains evidence about a crime (this is known as "automobile exception" to the warrant requirement). The CPC in line with this exceptional search without warrant states that JPO shall be empowered to check the identity and situation of any suspected person in accordance with the provisions of section 32, where necessary may detain him in a special cell for not longer than 24hours [211]. The notion of «probable cause», as used in the CPC suits perfectly well in this context considering the definition of the said notion.
- Searches of obviously incriminating items that are in «plain view»[212]while law enforcement is conducting an otherwise lawful search[213]. The CPC makes mention of

---

[207]Section 104(c) (d) (f) CPC.

[208] United States V. Arnold (9th Cir. 2008) 523 F.3d 941, 945 (" Courts have long held that the searches of closed containers and their contents can be conducted at the border without particularized suspicion under the Fourth Amendment").

[209]People V. Ray (1999) Cal. 4th 464, 472.("This justification (emergency exception to the warrant requirement for searches and seizures) requires specific articulable facts indicating the need for swift action to prevent imminent danger to life or serious damage to property…")

[210]Probable cause means that the officer must possess sufficiently trustworthy facts to believe that a crime has been committed. In some cases, an officer may need only a reasonable suspicion of criminal activity to conduct a limited search. Reasonable suspicion means that the officer has sufficient knowledge to believe that criminal activity is at hand.

[211]Section 86(1) CPC.

[212]'Plain view' evidence is left in the open for everyone to see, it is considered incriminating on the face value and requires no warrant.

[213] Horton V. California (1990) 496 U.S 128, 136 (" what the 'plain view' [search and seizure] cases have in common is that the police officer of each of them had a prior justification for an intrusion in the course of which he came inadvertently across a piece of evidence incriminating the accused".)

this notion when it provides in its section 87(1) that "a judicial police officer may whether in a public place or a place open to the public search or caused to be searched…".

Whatever the case it should be noted that the regime applied on certain professionals is different.

d) The Special Regime of Search and Seizure

For certain professions, the law has provided a special regime of search and seizures. In the absence of a straightforward explanation as pertains to this special treatment it can be deduced from a close reading of the wordings of the provisions of sections 106-108 that the safeguard of professional secrecy as well as the dignity of the professions concerned is at the origin of the said exceptional treatment. Such is the case with searches conducted in advocate's chambers, the chambers of Physicians and notary public. It is not a coincidence that the professionals implicated here are bound by the obligation of professional secrecy.

In concrete terms, the law provides that searches in the chambers of the aforementioned professionals shall be conducted sorely for the following reason;

- Seizing of documents or objects connected with legal proceedings;
- Where the professional is being investigated or;
- Where the document or object is unrelated to the practice of his profession.

This provision[214] which particularly focus on advocates is simply a repetition of the provisions of article 22 of Law N° 90/059 of 19 December 1990 organising practice at the Bar. This article reiterates the principle of the inviolate nature of the advocate's chambers.

According to an author[215] the three conditions laid down in the provisions of Section 106 can be summarised into an important question to wit; what are the items that can be seized in

[214] Section 106(1) CPC.

[215] Mbunja (Y.), op. cit., p.135

a lawyer's chambers? This puts in conflict three important aspects namely professional secret, the right of defence and the exigencies of the manifestation of the truth. Conclusively, he argues that the first two aspects overshadow the last one, thus we can summarily agree that a search in an advocate's chamber cannot have as main objective the seizure of documents or objects having a link with a proceeding for which he has been briefed and more precisely correspondences exchanged between an advocate and his client.

On the other hand, objects not related to the exercise of the profession are liable to seizure, which is perhaps why section 106 in its paragraph 2 recommends the safeguard of professional secrecy and the maintenance of the dignity of advocates.

This author equally makes mention of searches in other domains notably as regards Law N° 97/19 of 07 August 1997 on drugs which in its Article 117 exceptionally permits the operation of searches to be conducted at night for a limited number of offences. This law in its article 119 equally provides for a special form of body check that involves the testing of blood samples, in cases where there exist serious reasons to presume that drugs have been dissimulated in one's organism.

e) Sanctions against the violation of rules of searches and seizures

Searches and seizures conducted in violation of the provisions of Section 93 to 99 are null and void. Such is equally the case with the violation of rules as regards searches and seizures in the chambers of advocates and all other professionals bound by the obligation of professional secrecy. Section 106(3) provides that such a search is null and void.

As regards the fate of documents obtained from searches and seizures, it is in principle destined for the law courts as evidence. When it is legally and regularly obtained, it constitutes non-rebuttable evidence before law Courts. When a person arrested is released, any property seized from him which may not be used as an exhibit shall be returned to him immediately in the presence of witnesses, if any and against signature. A report of the restitution shall equally be made[216]

In the United States, illegally obtained evidence is sanctioned by the exclusionary rule. The exclusionary rule is a judicially created remedy used to deter police misconduct in obtaining evidence. Under the exclusionary rule, a judge may exclude incriminating evidence from a criminal trial if there was misconduct in obtaining the evidence. The rule provides some substantive protection against illegal search and seizures. The exclusionary rule applies not only to evidence that was discovered during an illegal search but also to evidence that police found as an indirect result of an illegal search. This is known as the "fruit of the poisonous tree" doctrine. The "poisonous tree" is the unlawful search or seizure and the "fruit" is any evidence that the police manage to uncover as an indirect result of the unlawful search or seizure. The Black laws dictionary (9th ed. 2009) defines the poisonous-tree doctrine as "the rule that evidence derived from an illegal search, arrest, or interrogation is inadmissible because the evidence (the fruits) was tainted by illegality (the poisonous tree) of the initial search and seizure". Under this doctrine for example, a murderer's weapon is inadmissible if the map showing its location and used to find it was seized during an illegal search.

However, under the CPC which does not explicitly makes use of the exclusionary clause or of the fruit of the poisonous tree, where a search has been declared null and void, the articles seized in the course thereof may be admitted as exhibit if they are not contested[217]. They overt use of "may" in the construction of this provision means, objects seized during an illegal search will be admitted in evidence if it is not contested. Contestation thus is the only remedy against the use of illegally obtained evidence. In other words, the exclusionary clause applies in our context whenever evidence illegally obtained is contested.

---

[216] Section 35(3) CPC.
[217] Section 100 CPC.

5. **The Power of Judicial Police officers to Request the Assistance of Experts**

In the conduct of investigation, the JPO has been attributed the power of requesting the assistance of any expert or of any person capable of assisting him in any given phase of the investigation.

The CPC has not given a definition of an expert. However expertise in this context can be defined as a measure of investigation by which a JPO solicits a person with avowed knowledge and mastery in a given domain to clarify him on a technical issue whose solution is primordial to the manifestation of the truth. According to Yawaga[218], it does not refer to all acts accomplished by a technician, he emphasizes that not all the acts of a technician can be qualified as expertise. It must be a question of technical order which requires not only a simple observation, but a response based on an interpretation.

According to Mbunja Y.[219] the technical question that calls for expertise must require from an expert an interpretation of data submitted to him which can vary from expert to expert, it would not be resolved by a simple material observation. Consequently, questions which in the actual state of scientific and technical progress can be resolved by the accomplishment of simple material or mechanical acts cannot be taken for expertise. Such is the case with the determination of blood group, the issuing of medico-legal certificates etc. He considers as expertise a ballistic test that seeks to identify the arm used in the commission of a felony, psychiatric analyses which is aimed at determining whether the author of an offence is mentally stable, autopsy on a corpse etc.

At the level of police investigation, the law is not explicit on the moment and authority on whom the choice of an expert is incumbent. Generally, the decision to resort to expert opinion can be taken on the initiative of the JPO, one of the parties or the Legal Department. It must be in writing. As regards the choice of experts, it should be noted that a national list of experts is still being waited. In the meantime, JPO can always resort to the list

---

[218] Yawaga (S.), *L'information judiciaire dans le code camerounaise de procédure pénale*, PUA, 2007, p.129

[219]Mbunja (Y.), op. Cit. p.178-179.

of certified experts at the level of Courts of Appeals. Expert certification a given Court of Appeal does not limit their activities within the jurisdiction wherein they are certified. Once certified their jurisdiction is national. However, it will be advisable for every JPO to seek the opinion of the State counsel when it comes to issues of such sensitive nature.

At the level of police investigation who bears the cost of expertise and how does the entire operation unfold? The CPC which gives some guidelines on this subject as regards preliminary inquiry is however silent when it comes to preliminary investigation. It will thus be hazardous navigating in such troubled waters.

If it is true that the judicial police officers are endowed with necessary powers to carry out their duties effectively and efficiently, it is equally true that the powers are curtailed by a more rigorous control of the State Counsel in cases of offences committed flagrante delicto.

CHAPTER IV
JUDICIAL POLICE OFFICERS AND THE INFRINGEMENT OF THE RIGHT TO FREEDOM OF MOVEMENT: REMAND IN POLICE CUSTODY

Literally, remand in police custody means detaining without ceasing to put an eye on the person detained. It is a measure restricting liberty, taken by judicial police officers, with the goal of maintaining at their disposal and within structures provided for, within a given duration, a person whose detention is necessary for a proper investigation already commenced[220]

The "Vocabulaire Juridique", published under the supervision of Doyen Cornu defines remand in police custody as "a police measure by which persons who are neither defendants, nor accused, are retained in certain non-penitentiary structures and must remain therein for a limited variable duration, depending on the type of offence at the disposal of judicial police officers for the purpose of investigation".

According to Jean Pradel, remand in custody is "the detention of a person (generally a suspect) for the purpose of questioning within a judicial police structure[221].

Frederick Djakba[222], Philippe Keubou[223] and Spencer Yawaga[224] see remand in police custody, as a police measure by which a judicial police officer retains a suspect within a judicial police structure, generally a cell, for the purpose of investigation.

The criminal procedure code[225] defines police custody as « a measure whereby for the purpose of criminal investigation and the establishment of the truth, a suspect is detained in a judicial police cell wherein he remains for a limited period

---

[220] Ibid.

[221] Pradel (J.), *Procédure pénale,* 6 éditions Paris, Cujas, (1992).

[222] Djakba (F.), « Droit pénal général et procédure pénale », *Miroir de droit*, N° 02, avril-mai-juin 2010, p.105.

[223]Timtchueng (M.) et Assontsa (R.), « Le nouveau visage de la garde à vue dans la procédure pénale Camerounaise », *Annales de la faculté des sciences juridiques et politique, édition spéciale*, CPP, T.11, p.95

cited by Keubou (Ph.), op. cit., pp.36

[224] Yawaga (S.), *La garde à vue, Les tendances de la nouvelle procédure pénale Camerounaise*, vol.1, PUA, 2007, p. 55, cited by Keubou Ph.), op. cit., p.36.

[225]Section 118(1), (2) and (3) of the CPC.

available to and under the responsibility of a judicial police officer».

It further states that "except in cases of felony or misdemeanour committed flagrante delicto and unless strong corroborative evidence exist against him, a person with a known place of abode may not be remanded in police custody", emphasizing further that "save in cases provided for in sub section (1) and (2) above, no person may be remanded for the purpose of criminal investigation without the written approval of the State Counsel.

Remand in police custody is exercised within the context of police investigation and for the purpose of the manifestation of the truth, in the case of the commission of an offence different from remand in prison custody under section 218 of the Criminal procedure code[226].To this regards "*garde à vue pression*"[227] or better still remand in custody for civil debts as Michel Mahouve et Hermine Kembo [228] puts it, has been proscribed [229] . The provisions of section 118-125 of the Criminal Procedure Code, spells out the regime of remand in custody notably, its definition, conditions or better still modalities of execution as well as the rights of the suspect remanded in police custody.

This regime must not however be confused with related notions of remand in custody which for the purpose of this study will be referred to as special remand in police custody or better still neighbouring notions to remand in police custody.

This chapter thus seeks to examine, not only the various forms of remand in police custody as provided for by the provisions of the criminal procedure code and other special text, it equally highlight the authors vested with the powers to remand in custody..

---

[226] « Remand in custody shall be an exceptional measure which shall not be ordered except in the case of a misdemeanour or a felony. It shall be necessary for the preservation of evidence, the maintenance of public order, protection of life and property or to ensure the appearance of an accused before the examining magistrate or court ».

[227] « Garde à vue pression », refers to irregular remand aimed at forcefully ensuring the execution of a civil or contractual obligation.

[228] Ibid.

[229] Ibid. p.176.

I. REGIME OF REMAND IN POLICE CUSTODY

Remand in custody as seen by Rose Djila[230] consist of detaining an individual against his or her will in the cells of the police or gendarme units for surveillance, which infringes individual liberty. This restrictive measure of liberty, which though indispensable in some circumstances according to her must be realistically made use of,[231]such that it should not be considered as a banal instrument of procedure but as a grievous act which must remain exceptional [232].It is with this in mind that the Cameroonian lawmakers within the context of the Criminal Procedure Code legally framed this measure with guarantees, defining it [233] as a police measure whereby for purposes of criminal investigation and the establishment of the truth, a suspect is detained in a judicial police cell, wherein he remains for a limited period available to and under the responsibility of a judicial police officer. It further states that except in cases of felony or misdemeanour committed flagrante delicto and unless strong corroborative evidence exists against him, a person with a known place of abode may not be remanded in police custody.

A. Common Regime of Remand in Police Custody

This provision lays down the criteria and conditions for a classical remand in police custody. It provides that it's a police measure executed in the course of police investigation and for the purpose of the establishment of the truth. It further emphasizes that it can only be executed where there exist "strong corroborative evidence".

While observing that the said notion of strong corroborative evidence has not been defined by the legislator, Michel Mahouvè and Hermine Kembo[234]define same through a related term "soupcons plausible" as used by the European

[230]Ibid. p.13.

[231] Address of the First President of the Supreme Court at the occasion of the solemn opening of the judicial year of the 26 February 2009, cited by Djila (R.).

[232]Déclaration of the French Prime Ministre, Mr François Fillon on Humann Right : les droits fondamentaux et les libertés publiques, avec les prise en compte des règles d'habeas corpus dans « la réforme de la procédure pénale des mineurs », paris le 21 juillet 2009, cited by Djila (R.).

[233]Section 118 of the CPC.

[234]Ibid. p.189.

commission on Human Rights[235] as "the existence of elements or Information, liable of persuading an objective observer that the suspect may have committed the offence».

A classical remand in police custody limits the measure to "cases of felony or misdemeanour committed flagrante delicto" defined in section 103 of the criminal procedure code[236] perhaps due to the freshness of the evidence which facilitates the establishment of the truth. It should be noted, however, that it is not an easy task to draw a line between preliminary investigation and investigation within the framework of a flagrante delicto offence in our Cameroonian context. Judicial police officers apply the flagrante delicto rule to offences committed years back.

The exceptionality of remand in custody can as well be seen in the restriction or prohibition of the said measure as regards "a person with a known place of abode" which have as goal ensuring the appearance of the suspect. It is an important element that can be used to trace a suspect who has jumped bail. In fact, as regards remand in police custody flagrante delicto offences is the principle and non-flagrante delicto offence the exception.

The notion of "a known place of abode" which has not been defined by the legislator is not only delicate but poses a serious difficulty. Should it be assimilated to the notion of domicile of civil law, which is the place where someone is principally established? An author terms it "*rigoriste*" [237], indicating in essence that the notion of known place of abode poses a practical problem, considering the fact that urbanization in the Cameroonian setting is anarchical and does not facilitate

---

[235]CEDH ,30 aout 1990, Fox. Campbell et Hartley C. Royaume Uni, cité in F. Sudre et al. Les grands arrêts de la cour européenne des droits de l'homme, cited by Mahouvè (M.) and Kembo (H.T.), op.cit.p.189

[236] (1) Felonies and misdemeanour are deemed to be committed flagrante delicto when they are in the course of being committed or when they have just been committed

(2) shall also be classified as felonies or misdemeanour committed flagrante delicto when;

(a) after the commission of the offence the suspect is pursued by public clamour;

(b) soon after the commission of the offence the suspect is caught in the possession of an article or shows a sign or trace which tends to suggest that he took part in the commission of the felony or misdemeanour

(3) There shall equally be flagrante delicto where a person requests the state counsel or a judicial police officer to investigate a felony or misdemeanour committed in a house which he occupies, or over which he has charge.

[237]Ibid. p. 189.

the tracing of a suspect subject of investigation, the raison d'être of the notion. Joseph Emmanuel [238]after an interview of a judicial police officer observes that practically, judicial police officers always consider the profession exercised, matrimonial situation. A person, who enjoys a social status considered respectable by judicial police officers, who is married and has children, will easily, be granted bail, unlike a bachelor without employment. This flaw created by the absence of a clear-cut or precise definition of the aforementioned term has led to a haphazard application left at the whims and caprices of judicial police officers, who define same depending on the circumstances, the interest at stake and above all almost always for their benefit.

That notwithstanding article 9 of the Covenant on Civil and Political Rights, while emphasizing on the principle of liberty[239], summarily spells out the rights of suspect[240], specifying as well and more importantly the duration of any measures of restriction of liberty[241].Interpreted *stricto-sensu*, this provision is irrefutably intended to limit the duration of both remand in police custody as well as remand in prison custody. To this regards the duration of this measure has been fixed at 48 hours (2days) renewable once[242]. According to Frederic Djakba[243], it is not different from what prevailed in the former law notably the "*Code d'instruction Criminelle*" passively noting that it does not offer any advantage to the suspect comparatively. The duration of 48 hours can, however, be extended exceptionally with the written approval of the state counsel twice (8days). This is an unfortunate extension, considering the humanitarian and liberal context of the present code and the fact that the said extension is largely beyond the promptness evoked by the international covenant on civil and political rights. In the French positive law

[238]Ibid. p. 26.

[239] 9(1) « everyone has the right to liberty and security of person. No one shall be subject to arbitrary arrest or detention. No one shall be deprived of his liberty except on such grounds and in accordance with such procedure as are established by law ».

[240] 9(2) « Anyone who is arrested shall be informed of the reasons of such arrest and shall promptly be informed of any charge against him ».

[241] 9(3) « Anyone arrested or detained on a criminal charge shall be brought before promptly before a judge or other officer authorise by law to exercise judicial power and shall be entitled to trial within a reasonable time or to release….. ».

[242]Section 119(2) (a) of the CPC.

[243]Ibid. p. 108.

on the contrary, the duration has been reduced to 24 hours renewable once for offences other than terrorism in the course of which the duration can be extended up to and not more than 4days[244].

This already deplorable situation is further compounded by extension with regards to distance. According to the provisions of section 120(1) (2) of the criminal procedure code, for every 50 kilometres between the place of arrest and the police station or the gendarmerie cell, the extension shall be 24hours.

The foregoing constitutes the regime of remand in custody as well as its constitutive elements. Besides the common or classical regime there exist other notions related to remand in police custody, referred to as special remand in custody, distinguished from remand in prison custody, worth evoking as well, so as to avoid any confusion while bringing out the complexity of the notion that most often infringes on the same rights that the legislator sought to avail.

B. Special Remand in Police Custody

As mentioned here above there are other notions which are akin or can be likened to remand in police custody executed by judicial police officer in the course of police investigation or during routine controls, with almost similar characteristics as remand in police custody, but with some peculiarities that differentiate them from same. Related notions of remand in custody include, detention in section 104(4) of the criminal procedure code, detention for the purpose of verification of identity[245], detention for the purpose of control or verification of situation[246], as well as detention within the context of the execution of a bench warrant ordered by an Examining Magistrate out of the jurisdiction. To the aforementioned can be added administrative remand in custody, as well as remand ordered by the military court in the course of investigations for offences that falls within the jurisdiction of the Military Tribunal and more especially as pertains to the offence of terrorism.

---

[244] Ongolo (J.E.), Ibid, p.31.

[245] Section 32 CPC.

[246] Section 86 CPC.

C. Remand in Police custody for Simple Offences

Any officer or agent of the judicial police may in a public place or a place open to the public and subject to the provisions of section 82(3) of the CPC, arrest the author of a simple offence who either refuses to disclose his identity or discloses an identity suspected to be false and where necessary detain him for not longer than 24hours [247] .Under normal circumstances, the commission of a simple offence under Section 21(1) c[248] of the Penal Code , due to its nature does not give room to either arrest or detention.

A judicial police officer faced with such an offender has two options; either he request the payment of the fine fixed by law and depending on the category of the offence as laid down by regulation[249]or he makes a report to be forwarded to the Legal Department on the grounds of which the offender may likely be prosecuted.

The principle of individuality commands that prosecuted persons must be rigorously identified in order to avoid any confusion[250].As such inability to identify an offender due to his refusal, gives room to detention as well as an identity suspected to be false. Such a detention is, however, limited in duration (24) hours. He can only be remanded in police custody beyond this duration if during interrogation another offence of a gravity that warrants remand is discovered. It is similar to remand in custody for verification of identity even though the conditions under which the said measures are taken are not the same.

D. Remand in Police Custody for Verification of Identity and Situation

Judicial police officers have been empowered to check the identity and situation of any suspected person in accordance with the provisions of Section 32 of the CPC and where necessary

---

[247] Section 32 CPC.

[248] « A simple offence shall mean an offence punishable with imprisonment for up to 10 (ten) days or with fine of up to 25000 (twenty-five) FCFA ».

[249] 362 -370 of the pénal code.

[250] Kitio (E), *Les délais en procédure pénale Camerounaise : Entre célérité et droit à un procès équitable*, édition recherche scientifique universelle (R.S.U), p. 100-102.

may detain him in special police custody for not longer than 24 hours[251]. The hypothesis presented in the provision of this Section, is that of a person intercepted by judicial police authorities, who cannot justify his identity or who refuse to justify same. He is thus, remanded in custody for a proper investigation on his identity and his situation within a remand period that must not exceed 24 hours. Such a remand if not justified by other legal causes must cease failure of which the judicial police officer or agent can be prosecuted for false arrest[252]

E. Remand in Custody by Assimilation

During the execution of a bench warrant out of the jurisdiction of a court, the regime applied to the concerned suspect in case of transfer is that of remand in police custody.

Such is equally the case where in the course of hearing of a witness in the course of rogatory commission, a judicial police officer remands the said witness for a period of 48 hours, after finding out that he is likely to be charged as co-offender or an accomplice to the offence which is subject of the rogatory commission. This duration which can be renewed with the written approval of the State Counsel can only be executed in compliance to the provisions of section 119 of the criminal procedure code. This section requires that the suspect be informed of the ground of suspicion and invited to give an explanation with mention made in the police report. It should, however, be noted that the duration of remand is more extensive when it comes to administrative remand in custody (*garde à vue administrative*)

F. Administrative Remand in custody (Garde à vue administrative)

According to an author[253], remand in custody(a restrictive measure of individual liberty under normal circumstances[254] and

---

[251] Section 86(1), CPC.

[252] Section 291, Pénal code.

[253] Edouard Kitio, « La garde à vue administrative pour grand banditisme et respect de droit de l'homme au Cameroun, Application de la loi N° 90/054 du 19 décembre 1990 sur le maintien de l'ordre», in *Juridis Périodique* N° 30, avril-mai-juin 1997, p. 47-56.

within the framework of maintenance of public order) under the provisions of section 2(4) of law N° 90/054 of 19 December 1990,drifts from the classical regime of judicial remand in custody, even though it is applied to a notion of criminal law "grand banditisme", defined as;[255]

> *"l'activité des bandits, ceux-ci étant des malfaiteur dangereux, des brigands ou des hommes sans scrupules; le grande banditisme selon ce dictionnaire est l'ensemble des actions répréhensible*" or beter still;
> *"l'ensemble d'action criminelles commises dans une region; c'est la criminalité. Le bandit est donc l'individu qui se livre à des actions criminelles. C'est un individu malhonette et sans scrupule"*[256].

Remand in custody in this context has as objective the fight against "*grande banditisme*"[257] although crime is unavoidably inseparable with justice. As such, this remand was supposed to be ordered by judicial police officers in compliance with the provision of sections 118 to 124 of the criminal procedure code.

The legislator within the scope of administrative remand has made provisions for a much longer duration of remand[258], 15 days renewable for an unlimited duration and without any clear-cut conditions nor prior authorisation to such extension or prolongation. As regards the authority vested with jurisdiction to take such measures the above cited articles accord same to administrative authorities who include the minister of territorial

[254] That means at a time when the institutions of the republic are functioning normally, thus the action of the administration is merely preventive.

[255] *Dictionnaire Universel, Hachette*. Edicef.58.rue Jean-Bleuwen, F.92178 VANVES.1988.

[256] Dictionnaire, Petit *Larousse illustré*, 1983, Librairie Larousse, 17, Rue Mont parnasse et boulevard Raspail, 114 Paris vi.

[257] The aforementioned dictionary defines « grande banditsme», as an assembly of criminal or iniquitous activities carried out by armed or highway robbers within a region

[258] « les autorité administrative peuvent, en tout temps et selon les cas, dans le cadre des opération de maintien de l'ordre prendre de mesures ci-après…..prendre des mesures de garde à vue d'une durée de 15jours renouvelables dans le cadre de la lutte contre le grand banditisme ».

administration, governors, senior divisional officers, divisional officers, district heads and even certain chief of services[259].

The enlargement of the authorising personalities leaves us with the impression that the law on the maintenance of order under normal circumstances is more rigorous than the law applied during exceptional circumstances[260]. Commenting on this, an author observes that administrative detention has always been an arm in the hands of administrative authorities to punish whoever infringes their rules. The purpose of such measures according to the said author is most often far from corresponding with the preoccupations of the legislator. As such,

> *"outrage à l'autorité administrative, outrage au chef d'état[261],les manifestation collective de mécontentement même non accompagnées de violence[262] ainsi que le refus d'exécuter un ordre verbal d'une autorité administrative (....) sont susceptible d'entrainer la garde à vue administrative"[263],*

adding to this list Edouard Kitio cites the example of a call by a citizen for the candidature of Owona Nguini for the 2018 presidential election that led to his remand by the governor of the central Region for "*trouble à l'ordre public et incitation à la rebellion*"[264].Due to the lack of precision of the law, measures of administrative remand in custody are executed both within

---

[259] François Anoukaha, «Droit pénal et démocratie en Afrique Noire Francophone : L'expérience du Cameroun (suite et fin)», *JURIDIS INFO*, N° 23 juillet-aout-septembre p.73-76.

[260] Law N° 90/047 of 19 December 1990 on the state of emergency; Official Journal of the Republic of Cameroon

[261] L'arrêté préfectoral N° 64/AP/L 11/BP du 22 Mars pris par le préfet du département de l'Océan portant garde à vue administrative de monsieur P.J. pour, cited by Edouard Kitio, Ibid.

[262] Arrêté préfectoral N° 250/AP/L 11/SP du 03 mars 1996 portant garde à vue administrative de certaines personnes (23 au total), cited by Edouard Kitio, Ibid.

[263] According to this author the use of insulting language against an administrative authority and most especially the president of the Republic, though not within the context of armed or highway robberies are motives for administrative remand. Such is equally the case with peaceful manifestations and the refusal to execute a written or verbal order of an administrative authority.

[264] Affaire MP C/ Patrice Sohna, reported in the journal Kalara, in its N° 137 edition of the 29 February 2016, p.1, therein, it is reported that Patrice Sohna was remanded in administrative custody, for disturbance of public order and for inciting rebellion. This was due to fact that he called for the candidature of Owona Nguini for the 2018 presidential elections.

penitentiary structures and in the police or gendarmerie cells. This measure escapes from the control and supervision of both the judicial police officers and state counsel respectively, originally vested with the power to remand in custody.

G. Authorities Empowered to Remand

As regards the authors vested with the power to remand in police custody the criminal procedure code has maintained the power of judicial police officers in case of offences committed flagrante delicto, a power that has been extended to the state counsel who can order a remand in police custody as well. Exceptionally the Examining magistrate can as well remand in police custody.

H. Judicial Police Officers as Authorities Empowered to Remand

Judicial police officers as defined by the provisions of Section 79 [265] are among other things [266] responsible for investigation of offences, collecting of evidence, identifying offenders and accomplices, and bringing them before the legal department.

Michel Mahouvè and Hermine Kembo notice that under the «*Code d'instruction Criminelle*» remand in police custody was regulated only in the cases of offences committed flagrant delicto .They further explain that remand in police custody was the sole prerogative of the judicial police officers, who could solicit the authorisation of the state counsel only for the purpose of extension, a practice that was extended to cover the cases of non-flagrant offences as well[267].Under the criminal procedure code, the provisions of section 118-126 are quite instructive. The prerogative of the judicial police officer to order remand in police

---

[265] « The following shall have the status of judicial police officers;

(a) Officers and non-commissioned officers of the gendarmerie;
(b) Gendarmerie in charge even in an acting capacity of a gendarmerie brigade or gendarmerie post;
(c) Superintendent of police;
(d) Deputy superintendent of police;
(e) Gendarmes and inspectors of police who have passed the judicial police examination and taken the oath;
(f) Public servants even if they are temporally performing the functions of head of external service of national security.

[266] Section 82 CPC.

[267] Ibid., p.178.

custody has been limited to the cases of offences committed flagrant delicto as defined in the provisions of section 103 of the criminal procedure code. Joseph Emmanuel[268] notes that the quasi generalisation of flagrance even when the offence was committed years back has become the order of the day in most police and gendarmerie units. This rather curious attitude is justified by the fact that it offers very extensive powers, especially coercive powers that they do not possess in cases of preliminary investigation[269]. It should be noted that except in cases of flagrante delicto as explained hitherto, all the other hypothesis of remand are within the jurisdiction of the State Counsel. His role will be discussed subsequently.

II. THE RIGHTS OF SUSPECTS REMANDED IN POLICE CUSTODY

Cameroon in its conception of the criminal Procedure Code adequately took into consideration its conventional engagements as regards the respect of human rights contained in the various international legal instruments to which she is signatory. The good fate of the lawmaker is quite visible as regards remand in custody in the course of which the rights of the suspect have been reinforced. Such is the case with the right to the presumption of innocence, the right to information, the right to medical examination, the right to visits, the right to feeding and upkeep as well as the right to counsel.

A. The Right to Presumption of Innocence

The right to the presumption of innocence is an emanation of doctrine notably Cesare Beccaria in his work *"Traité des delits et des peines"*, 1764[270] as well as section 11(1) of the Universal Declaration of Human Rights wherein it is stipulated that; "everyone charged with a penal offence has the right to be presumed innocent until proven guilty according to law, in a

---

[268] Ibid.

[269] Ibid, p.26

[270] "La justice doit respecter le droit que chacun a d'être cru innocent. Un homme ne peut être considéré comme coupable avant la sentence du juge; et la société ne peut lui retire la protection publique qu'âpres qu'il est convaincu d'avoir violé les conditions auxquelles elle lui avait été accordé", cited by Leumega (E.), Ibid, P.141.

public trial at which he has had all the guarantees necessary for his defence. This legal instrument has been copied by other international or regional texts such as the International Covenant on Civil and political rights in its article 14(2)[271], article 7(1) of the African Charter on Human and Peoples' Rights[272], article 8(2) of the American convention on Human Rights[273] as well as article 6(2) of the European convention on Human Rights[274].A more concrete guarantee of the said right is provided for in the preamble of the constitution in the following words "every accused person is presumed innocent until found guilty during a hearing conducted in strict compliance with the right of defence".

Constructed finely to suit our context, Section 8 of the CPC states that, "any person suspected of having committed an offence, shall be presumed innocent, until his guilt has been legally established in the course of a trial, where he shall be given necessary guarantees for his defence. This right which applies to the suspect, defendant and accused, is constructed not only to protect individual rights notably the reputation of the suspect[275], but is a principle according to which the burden of prove is on the prosecution. As Montesquieu put it, "quand l'innocence des citoyens n'est pas assurée, la liberté ne l'est pas non plus"[276]. Fortunately, this right is guaranteed suspects remanded in police custody by the provision of section 8 of the CPC. The importance of this right was highlighted by the African commission on Human and Peoples' Rights in the case of **Abdoulaye Mazou C/ Etat de Cameroun**[277] wherein the commission ruled that ***«une detention fondée sur le seule suspicion qu'un individu pourait***

---

[271] « Everyone charged with a criminal offence shall have the right to be presumed innocent until proved guilty according to the law ».

[272] « Every individual shall have the right.......to be presumed innocent until, proved guilty by a competent court or Tribunal".

[273] « Every person accused of a criminal offence has the right to be presumed innocent so long as his guilt has not been proved according to the law ».

[274] Everyone charged with a criminal offence shall be presumed innocent until proved guilty according to law

[275]Ngono S., «l'application des règles internationale du procès équitable par le juge judiciaire», in *Juridis Périodique* N° 63, avril-mai-juin 2005.p.44, cited by Lemeuga (E.), Ibid., p.139.

[276] This assertion by Montesquieu can be translated to mean that when the innocence of citizens is not ensured, liberty is not as well.

[277] The commission in this case ruled that a remand based solely on the suspicion that an individual may be at the origin of an offence constitutes a violation of the right to the presumption of innocence.

être à l'origine d'une infraction, est une violation du droit à la presumption d'innocence»[278]. The commission is still to arrive at such a conclusion as regards failure to inform suspects of their rights prior to their remand.

B. The Right to Information

The right to information of a suspect as regulated by the code can be situated at two levels. Initially, as soon as investigations are opened, the judicial police officer must under the penalty of sanction, inform the suspect of his right to counsel and his right to remain silent, with mention of same made in the police report.[279]

However, subsequently in the course of investigation, the law provides that[280] where a judicial police officer intends to remand a suspect in custody, he shall inform him of the grounds of suspicion against him and invite him to give any explanation he deems necessary, with mention made in the police report as well. As far as our research is concerned, our interest is on the second case. The information to the suspect of the decision to put him under police custody is of primordial importance for two reasons; firstly, it infringes on individual liberty, that is, freedom of movement and secondly, any explanation given by the suspect before such a remand is liable of clarifying some doubts and changing his fate. If the explanation given clarifies the strong corroborative evidence that existed, he may probably be dispensed of remand in police custody.

C. The Right to Medical Examination

The right to medical examination is provided for in the provision of Section 123 of the CPC[281]. According to Michel Mahouvè and

---

[278]Op.cit., p.144.

[279] Section 116(3) CPC.

[280] Section 119(1) CPC.

[281] (1) The person remanded in police custody may at any moment be examined by a medical officer appointed by the state counsel, of his own motion. Such medical officer may be assisted by another chosen by the person on remand at his expense.

(2) The state counsel may order such medical examination at the request of the person concerned, his lawyer or a member of his family. Such medical examination will be carried out within 24 hours after the request.

Hermine Kembo[282], this measure permits the verification of the health situation of the suspect at the beginning, in the course of investigation and at the end. This measure permits an evaluation of the quality of treatment given a suspect, which can serve as grounds for allegations of torture or poor treatment. The attribution of the prerogatives to the State Counsel, however, poses a problem as regards the right to a fair trial, considering the fact that the State Counsel is a party to the investigation as well as to the proceedings wherein he is a principal party. This worry has been addressed by the legislator who has given the suspect's counsel as well as members of his family, the possibility of requesting a medical examination coupled with the possibility of choosing a medical officer to assist in such check-up with the right to countersign the report and making observations .In spite of its importance the right to medical examination happens to be among the least used rights by suspects remanded in police custody in the course of investigation. The right of family members to apply for medical examination can only be made possible if the said family members are given access to pay regular visits to the suspect under police custody.

D. The Right to Visits

The rights to a fair trial, through access to justice warrants that every suspect, defendant or accused, be given the opportunity to prepare and present his defence under acceptable conditions, receive material as well as moral support from family members and others. Such rights are stipulated in Section 116(3) of the criminal procedure code. As regards counsel more particularly, this right can only be practically implemented if counsel chosen by a suspect is given access to a suspect remanded in police custody. It is within this context that section 122(3),was conceived and states inter alia "the person remanded in police

---

(3) At the end of custody, it shall be obligatory to medically examine the suspect at his expense and by a doctor of his choice on condition that either the suspect himself, his counsel or family members so request. In all cases he shall be informed of his discretion.

(4) The report of the commissioned medical officer shall be put in the suspect's case file and a copy thereof given to him. It may be counter signed by the medical officer chosen by the person so remanded who may where necessary endorse it with his view.

[282]Nkengue (J.P.S.), « L'OPJ, l'enquête de police et la torture », cited by Mahouvè (M.) and Kembo (H.T.), in, *Les tendances de la nouvelle procédure pénale camerounaise* , p. 234-236.

custody may at any time within the period of detention and during working hours, be visited by his counsel, members of his family and by any other person following up his treatment while in detention". Such visits are limited within the duration of working hours. It gives family members the opportunity to take care of the upkeep of suspects notably, by supplementing their feeding which is the prerogative of the state.

E. The Right to Feeding

Feeding is among the rights to which the suspect remanded in police custody is beneficiary, considering its importance to human existence. This right is made possible by the provisions of Section 122(4) of the CPC, which provides as follows; "the state shall be responsible for feeding persons remanded in police custody. However, such persons shall have the right to receive from members of their families or from their friends the means of subsistence and other necessaries". While it engages state responsibility fully, it equally makes provisions for supplementary sources, which has become the main source in the absence of state subvention to police and gendarmerie units to this effect.

F. The Right to be Treated Humanely and Freedom from Torture.

The absence of subvention does not however stop judicial police officers from treating Suspects remanded in custody with humanity. The prohibition against torture, cruel, inhumane or degrading treatment as stipulated in Article 5 of the universal declaration of Human Rights[283], Article 7 of the International Covenant on civil and Political Rights[284] and Section 5 of the African Charter on Human and Peoples' Rights [285] is a fundamental right which the suspect benefits from in the course

---

[283] « No one shall be subjected to torture or to cruel, inhuman and degrading treatment or punishment. ».

[284] « No one shall be subjected to torture or to cruel, inhuman and degrading treatment or punishment. ».

[285] « Every individual shall have the right to the respect of the dignity inherent in a human being and to the recognition of his legal status. All forms of exploitation and of degradation of man particularly slavery, slave trade, torture, cruel, inhuman or degrading punishment or treatment shall be prohibited. ».

of police investigation. The Cameroonian legislator while penalising torture[286], has as well guaranteed the respect of the moral and physical integrity of a suspect remanded in custody in the provisions of Section 122(2) of the CPC in the following words; "the suspect shall not be subjected to any physical or mental constraints or to torture...", it goes further by adding to the list the following elements not provided for by international legal instruments to wit "...threats, or any pressure whatsoever, or to deceit, insidious manoeuvre, false proposals, prolonged questioning, hypnosis, the administration of drugs or to any other, method which is likely to compromise or limit his freedom of action or decision or his memory or sense of judgment"[287] .The aforementioned right can only be properly ensured to the benefit of the suspect in the presence of counsel.

G. The Right to Counsel

The right to counsel is provided for in the international Covenant on Civil and Political Rights[288], the African Charter on Human and Peoples' Rights[289], the American Convention on Human Rights[290].Even if the presence of counsel at the level of police investigation is aimed at ensuring the regularity of the procedure, the legislator highlights the importance of such a presence when he provides that "...as soon as investigations are opened, the judicial police officer must under the penalty of sanction, inform the suspect of his right to counsel...". The right is of such importance that the penalty for its violation is nullity as provided by Section 3 of the CPC. Even if counsel cannot proceed with examination and cross examination, his presence during interrogation is dissuasive and prevents the judicial police officers from making use of unorthodox means to extort evidence.[291]The respect of rights provided by legal instruments

---

[286]Section 132(bis) of the Penal Code.

[287] The aforementioned rights can only be properly ensured in the presence of counsel.

[288] Article 14(3) (d).

[289] Article 7(1) (c).

[290] Article 8(2) (d).

[291] Mani Ayong (F.E.), « L'égalité des parties au procès pénal : Fiction ou réalité », *Miroir de droit* N° 04, octobre-novembre-décembre 2010, p.43.

can only be guaranteed and its effectiveness ensured if and only if a good control mechanism is put in place.

III. THE CONTROL OF THE REGULARITY OF REMAND IN POLICE CUSTODY

One of the key phases in a criminal proceeding during which the rights of suspects are more likely to be violated, and with grievous consequences is the police investigation phase and more especially by way of remand in police custody. Such consequences, as raised by Biboum Landry [292] citing an author[293] may include

> *la perturbation du travail ou des loisirs, l'impossibilité de regagner son domicile pour déjeuner ou diner même l'obligation de coucher à la geôle du poste de police.."* [294] ,while emphasizing that" *l'atteinte à la liberté est en elle seul suffisamment grave pour que l'organisation du contrôle de l'activité policiers s'impose comme une nécessité fondamentale*[295].

A necessity reiterated by the European Commission on Human Rights[296] as cited by Michel Mahouvè et Hermine Kembo in the following words

> ***Seul une prompte intervention judiciaire peut effectivement conduire à la détection et à la prévention de mauvais traitement qui risquent d'être infligé aux personnes détenues***[297].

---

[292] Ibis, p.51.

[293] Merle (R.), « Le problème du contrôle juridictionnel de la garde à vue », in *Détention provisoire, contrôle judiciaire et garde à vue, les problèmes soulevés par leur contrôle juridictionnelle*, XIIe journées franco-Belgo-luxembourgeoises, Poitier, 11 et 12 décembre 1970, PUF, 1971.

[294] According to Biboum Landry some of the upsetting effects of remand include the disruption of work and leisure, impossibility to return home for breakfast or launch as well as the obligation to pass the night in a cell.

[295] Biboum Landry emphasizes that the infringement of liberty is sufficiently serious to warrant the imposition of control of the said activity by the police.

[296] CEDH, 6 février 2003, Zeynep Avic c. Turquie§ 46, et 3 juin 2004.

[297] The European Commission on Human Rights in the case cited above stated that only a prompt judicial intervention can effectively lead to the discovery and prevention of poor treatment liable of been inflicted on persons remanded in custody.

To this regard, the criminal procedure code has provided for a hierarchical control that can be carried out by the State Counsel, superior judicial police officers from superior units, by the persons remanded as well as by judicial measures.

A. Hierarchical Control by the Judicial Police

According to Edouard Kitio[298], the direct hierarchy of judicial police officers can as well proceed with control of regularity of remand in police custody, citing as an example the case of a commissioner of a central police station who can proceed to the control of the public security units within his area of competence[299]. The Regional Delegate for National Security can as well carry out surprised or announced controls of police units within his jurisdiction at the Regional level. It is governed by article 12(1) of Decree n° 2002/003 of 4 January 2002 on the organisation of the General Delegation of National Security, which confines the duty to the General Inspectorate. However, such controls are more recurrent within the gendarmerie wherein hierarchy proceeds regularly with cell controls or inspections. Such controls are destined to ensure respect of the duration of remand in police custody as well as the conduct of investigation. This activity is organized by article 6 of decree N° 2001/181 of the 25 July 2001 on the organization of the National Gendarmerie. The aforementioned author opines that such measures can as well help in reducing abuses in the course of police custody, observing that when such measures are announced, judicial police officers always precipitate in emptying their cells in order to avoid problems. A disgruntled suspect can as well engage control measures against remand in police custody.

---

298 Kitio (E.), op. cit., p.178.

299 Article 191(1) (2) Décret N° 2012/552 DU 20 NOV.2012 portant délimitation territoriale de commissariats d'Arrondissement dans certains Commissariats Centraux de sécurité Publique, p.76.

B. Control of the Regularity of Remand by Suspect (Habeas Corpus)

The CPC has given the suspect the possibility of controlling the regularity of remand in custody by way of the writ of habeas corpus before the High court by virtue of Section 584.

The writ of habeas corpus (which literally means to "produce the body"), in Medieval Latin means "we, a court, command that you have the body (of a detainee brought before us)". It is recourse in law through which a person can report an unlawful detention or imprisonment to a court and request that the court order the custodian of the person, usually a prison official to bring the prisoner to Court to determine whether the detention is lawful. Technically, it is only a procedural remedy; it is a guarantee against any detention that is illegal but does not necessarily protect other rights such as the right to fair trial. Habeas corpus has deep roots in English common law. It falls among the historically "prerogative writs"[300], issued by the English courts in the name of the monarch to control inferior courts and public authorities within the Kingdom, notably the writ of mandamus, prohibition, certiorari, precedendo. It is difficult to say exactly where it first appeared in writing but it was most famously codified in the Magna Carter signed by King John, which provided "no man shall be arrested or imprisoned...except by the lawful judgement of his peer and by the law of the land". It originated as an instrument in opposition to the kings "divine right to incarcerate people".

The US constitution, influenced by the Magna Carter explicitly charges: "The privilege of the writ of Habeas corpus shall not be suspended, unless when in cases of rebellion or invasion, the public safety may require it". Many other modern countries have included the writ of habeas corpus in their constitutions. This writ has been given due recognition at the international level as an instrument of protection[301], in explicit

---

[300] A writ is a formal order under seal issued in the name of a sovereign government, court or other competent authority.

[301] International Covenant on Civil and Political Rights

terms[302]. Applied to most British Overseas Territories by virtue of an Act of 1862, this writ according to Dashaco J. and Ewang (S.). was transposed to former Southern Cameroons by virtue of the Southern Cameroon High Court Laws 1955[303].If it is true that this law, globally permitted the reception of English law in West Cameroon, and more especially the mechanism of habeas corpus, it is equally true that it was only by virtue of Law n° 80/019 of 29 December amending the Ordinance of 26 August 1972 on judicial organisation that its application was extended to the entire national territory. However, a harmonised and comprehensive view of this mechanism has only been eased by the CPC, which not only specifies its domain of application but specifies the role of each party as well as the procedure.

As far as the application of this mechanism is concerned, and most especially within the scope of police investigations, the CPC, unlike law N° 80/019 of 29 December 1980, extends the application of this measure to special remand in custody. Such is the case with administrative remand in custody as well as remand ordered by the military tribunal.

Whatever the case, remand in custody irrespective of the remanding authority is subject to control by way of the habeas corpus mechanism, considering its initial goal[304]. This is the logical conclusion one arrives at, after a perusal of the provisions of article 9(4)[305] of the International Covenant on Civil and Political Rights to which Cameroon is signatory. According to the Human Rights Committee (HRC), in its interpretation of this provision[306], this guarantee is opened to all persons, whose liberty has been restricted by way of arrest or remand. Remand in custody within the context of the committee is not limited only to

---

302 Article 9(4), « Anyone who is deprived of his liberty by arrest or detention shall be entitled to take proceedings before a court, in order that the court may decide without delay on the lawfulness of his detention and order his release if the detention is not lawful»

303 See Dashaco (J.) and Ewang (S.)., «Habeas Corpus under the Cameroon Criminal Procedure Code», in *Readings in the Cameroon Criminal Procedure Code*, PUA, 2007, p. 151-177.

304 Habeas corpus has as principal objective the protection of persons against the abusive restrictions of their liberties.

305 Article 9(1) « Everyone has the right to liberty and security of person. No one shall be subject to arbitrary arrest or detention. No one shall be deprived of such of his liberty except on such grounds and in accordance with such procedures as established by law»,
(4)« Anyone who is deprived of his liberty by arrest or detention shall be entitles to take proceedings before a court, in order that the Court may decide without delay on the lawfulness of his detention and order his release if the detention is not lawful»

306 See general comments N° 8: (Right to liberty and security of persons), adopted at the sixteenth session of the Human Rights Committee, 30th June 1982

remand within the frame of criminal offences but covers an extensive domain including mental illness, vagrancy, drug addiction, educational purposes, immigration control, remand linked to public or state security as well as house arrest. This is the substance of section 584 of the CPC, which in our opinion is applicable to all arrest or remand be it civil, military or administrative.

The said section enumerates the following as grounds for such application; illegality of arrest or detention or failure to observe the formalities provided for by law.

Substantially, and within the scope of preliminary or police investigation, the Courts in some cases have considered the arrest or remand of persons with a known place of abode as illegal. In one of such cases the High Court of Wouri, while nullifying an arrest and remand in police custody held that the suspect in question was arrested in his house[307]. The same Court in yet another case held that the office of a civil servant as regards the public service is a substantial clue in the determination of place of abode. As such, a civil servant who serves in a particular town and who provides a certificate of residence will be considered to have fulfilled the requirement of a known place of abode[308].

Procedurally, the absence of a warrant (arrest or remand) has been one of the predominant causes of illegality of arrest or remand in custody for which the President of Courts readily grants an order for Habeas corpus. The absence of a warrant as an author[309] puts it can be initial or subsequent. It is said to be initial when the said warrant never existed prior to the arrest or remand. On the other hand, it can as well be subsequent when it actually existed, but in the course of the procedure, expired and was never renewed. A typical case will be a remand warrant which violates

---

[307] See Ord. n° 698/PTGI/W/DLA du 29 Aout 2007 du Pres. Du TGI du Wouri, Jacques Makaké C. Ministère public (where the suspect was arrested in his home), cited by M. Mahouvé and H. Kembo in Le droit de l'homme..op cit. p. 253

[308] See Ord. N° 001/ORD du 14 Décembre 2007 du Prés. du TGI de la valée du Ntem, Zogo Ongolo Abraham C. Ministère public (the suspect was a civil servant of the taxation department of the locality and furnished the Court with a resident certificate), cited by M. Mahouvè and H. Kembo, op cit. p. 253

[309] Ibid. p. 254

the provision of section 119(2) (a) and (b)[310]. He cites the case of a suspect who was remanded in custody and later transferred to the Legal Department. After realising that there was need for further investigation the case file was re-transmitted alongside the suspect for further investigation. Due to logistic and distance problem, the suspect was abandoned at the Gendarmerie Company where he spent about 24 days in custody. In spite of the contention of the Legal Department to the effect that the police report of the arrest and its decision returning the file for further investigation constituted a remand warrant and an extension respectively, the Court held that the remand was illegal[311].

Similarly where such warrant is issued by an authority other than the one designated by law or in violation of rules laid down by the said law, the disregard of this rules vitiates the legality of the warrant and is an open door for the application of the mechanism of habeas corpus. This position is corroborated by Anoukaha Francois[312] who states that there is violation where the remanding authority did not have the *locus standi* to remand single handedly, whereas, Pougoue Gérard [313] is of the opinion that the absence of a warrant refers to the hypothesis where an individual is remanded or detained arbitrarily without any warrant. Such was the case of a remand warrant issued out of the context of flagrante delicto, where the Court noted ***«qu'en l'absence des éléments de flagrance tels que cernés par l'article 103 [du CPP] […], la mise en détention sur l'ordre de Procureur de la République est dépourvu de toute fondement juridique»[314].***

---

[310] 119(2)(a), «The time allowed for remand in custody shall not exceed 48 hours renewable once»;
(b), « However, the period may with the written approval of the State Counsel be exceptionally extended twice»

[311] See Ord. N° 003/ORD du 19 mars 2009 du Prés. du TGI de la valée du Ntem, Zo'o Engo Charles, Bekoung Mba Philibert, Mba Mba Fils et Zo'o Zo'o Charles Materne, cited by M. Mahouvé and H. Kembo in Le droit de l'homme..Op cit. p. 254

[312] Anoukaha (F.), « Droit pénal et démocratie en Afrique Noire : l'expérience camerounaise », in *juridis info* n° 23, p. 79.

[313] Pougoue (G.), « Protection des droits fondamentaux et systèmes juridiques (rapport de droit camerounais) », p. 1, in *production des membres du groupe de recherche des droits de l'homme de l'institut Catholique de Yaoundé.*

[314] See Ord. n° 698/PTGI/W/DLA du 29 aout 2007 du Pres. Du TGI du Wouri, Jacques Makaké, placé en détention provisoire pour complicité d'enlèvement de mineur, Ibid.

Procedurally, the President of the High Court who has been given the jurisdiction to hear such matters is seized by way of an application[315]. According to an author[316], the law has not fixed any dateline within which an aggrieved party can seize the Court. It suffices that at the moment of seizure the suspect should still be deprived of his freedom of movement.

After seizure, the law has mandated him to take the following steps;

- Order the custodian of the person remanded or detained to produce him on the day and hour mentioned in the order with documents authorising the arrest or detention,
- Forward a copy of the application and the order to the Legal Department for its submission, this in the interest of the law,

In most jurisdictions, hearing is done in chambers in the presence of all the parties. In fact, the law is mute on the genuine procedure to be followed in the course of hearing in matters of Habeas corpus. However, one can deduce from a perusal of the provision of section 585(5) that there is room for oral evidence before the President during which the parties and probably their witnesses will obviously testify and be subjected to cross examination. According to this section the President of Court only rules on the documents before him in the absence of the applicant and after considering the reasons of such a non-appearance. This position is corroborated by the provision of section 586(1) which provides that "When the President gives an interlocutory ruling on a preliminary issue; such ruling shall not be subject to appeal". The inference drawn from the preceding provisions is that the President in ruling on matters of habeas corpus is not limited to the documentary evidence submitted by the applicant and the submissions of the State Counsel.

Considering the primordial role of the Legal Department in the process of arrest and remand in custody, its role in matters

[315] Not only is the application, made in four copies supposed to be supported by an affidavit, it must as well mention the following elements, the identity of the applicant if necessary, the identity of the arrestee or detainee, the place of arrest or detention as well as a summary of the facts of the alleged illegality.

[316] Tankoua (E.), «La libération immédiate, " un jeu de ping-pong dans certaines juridictions "», in *juridis périodique* N° 48, octobre-novembre-décembre, p. 113

of habeas corpus has been viewed with much scepticism. However, far from just intervening for the interest of law, the said interference has equally been justified by the provision of Section 128 of the CPC[317]. This position however poses a problem of the nature of the habeas corpus procedure. Is it a civil or a criminal procedure? An author has qualified it as a procedure of a special nature "sui generis"[318].

That notwithstanding, far from the scepticism that surrounds the involvement of the Legal Department in such procedures, the Legal Department in some cases has surprisingly been very objective and rational. In one of such cases the applicants Nchuafane Daouda and Mballa Bénédicte argued that they were remanded in prison custody by the Commissioner of Government of the Military Tribunal of Yaoundé on the 10th of December 2010 wherein they have spent six months. In an interesting submission, the State Counsel recalled to the President of Court that Law n° 2008/015 of 29 December 2008, organising military justice was violated, emphasizing that as per the provisions of section 12 of this law, the dateline for remand has been fixed at 20 days, urging the President of Court to grant the application. The application was consequently granted[319]. In yet another case, Fatouma seized the President of the High Court of Mfoundi by way of habeas corpus soliciting her release. Her application was contemplated on the fact that on the 20 day of April 2011, her son was arrested and remanded on the instructions of the commissioner of Government of the Yaoundé Military Tribunal. She stated that when she paid him a visit, she was equally apprehended and remanded. The Legal Department while revealing that the applicant is charged as an accomplice to the offences of aggravated theft and falsification and remanded on the instructions of the Commissioner of Government, submitted that the remand was blatantly illegal as per the

---

317 (1) The Legal Department shall be a principal party in a criminal trial before the Court and shall always be represented at such trials under pain of rendering the entire proceedings and the decision null and void.

318 Mahouvè (M.) et Kembo (H.T.), op. cit., p. 271

319 TGI du Mfoundi, Ordonnance n° 76/HC du 28/07/2011, aff. Nchuafane Daouda et Mballa Bénédicte c/ MP, (inédit), cited by Kitio (E), op. cit., p.280

provision of Section 12 of the Code of Military Justice, urging the President grant her application[320].

We however observed that the Legal Department is prompt in urging the Court to grant the application of the applicant in the face of illegal arrest and detention for matters emanating from the Commissioner of Government. As regards applications from common law Courts it's rare to find the Legal Department so readily urging the Court to grant the application even in the face of flagrante violation. Such is the case with the suspects who spent over 24 days in police custody as cited by M. Mahouvè and H. Kembo[321].

That notwithstanding, when the President of Court is satisfied with both the documentary and oral evidence adduced in the course of hearing he delivers a judgment on the merits. Contrary to preliminary rulings on preliminary issues in the same matter, which are not subject to appeal, judgments on the merits are subject to appeal in accordance with the provisions of section 274 of the CPC. Such appeal must be lodged five (5) days with effect from the date following the day on which the decision was given[322]. Such appeals are forwarded to the President of the Court of Appeal within five (5) days following the notice of appeal[323]. The President of the Court of Appeal or any other Judge of the Court appointed by him must hear and determine the appeal

---

[320] TGI du Mfoundi, Ordonnance n° 132/HC du 15/09/2011, aff. Fatouma épouse Abdouramane c/MP, cited by Kitio (E.), ibid., p.281

[321] See Ord. N° 003/ORD du 19 mars 2009 du Prés. du TGI de la valée du Ntem, Zo'o Engo Charles, Bekoung Mba Philibert, Mba Mba Fils et Zo'o Zo'o Charles Materne, cited by M. Mahouvé and H. Kembo in Le droit de l'homme..Op cit. p. 254

[322] Section 274(1) CPC, « The appeal shall be made by way of an unstamped application in four (4) copies and addressed to the President of the Inquiry Control Chambers. A copy of the ruling appealed against shall be attached to his application.

(2) The application for appeal shall, under pain of its being declared inadmissible, clearly state and argue the grounds of appeal.

(3) The report acknowledging receipt of the application and a copy of the application shall be served on the Procureur General of the Court of Appeal.

(4) The Procureur General and other parties shall have a time-limit of fourty eight (48) hours to file their submission.

(5) Subject to the cases referred to in section 252 and 253, the President of the inquiry control chambers shall cause shall cause the duplicates if the inquiry file to be forwarded to him

(6) The Procureur General and parties shall be informed in writing of the hearing date»

[323] Section (287),(1) CPC

within the time-limit of ten (10) days as provided for under section 275(2) of the CPC[324].

Apart from control carries out by the victim, his relative or counsel on his behalf, violation of individual liberty through abusive remand can be sanctioned judicially by nullity.

C. Judicial Control of Remand in Police Custody (Nullity)

This control is provided for by the provisions of section 124 of the CPC which states inter-alia that:

1) The judicial police officer shall mention in his report the reasons for remanding the suspect in police custody, the length of time within which he was subjected to questioning, the interval of rest during questioning, the day and hour when he was either released or brought before the state counsel;
2) The suspect shall sign the said entries and in the manner prescribed in section 90(3),(4),(5) and (7) of the CPC, where he refuses to sign the judicial police officer shall mention that fact in his report.
3) These entries shall be made in a special register kept in all judicial police stations where suspects may be remanded. The said register shall be submitted to the state counsel for inspection and control.
4) The non-observation of this section shall lead to the nullity of the police report.

The nullity within the context of this section which is visibly prejudicial to the rights of defense is sanctioned by absolute nullity as provided for in section 3 of the CPC .The said nullity cannot be overlooked and can be raised at any stage of the criminal procedure by any party. The legislator has not left out the author of such a violation who must not be allowed to go free.

[324] Section (287),(2) CPC

D. Control of Regularity by Punishment of Defaulting Judicial Police Officers.

Paragraph 4 of Section 124 of the CPC states that, the non-observation of the provisions of the said section shall lead to the nullity of the police report as well as all subsequent acts, without prejudice to disciplinary action against the judicial police officer concerned.

While emphasizing that the sanction evoked here is specific to infringement of liberty, notably criminal sanctions, Michel Mahouvè et Hermine Kembo add that such sanctions linked with irregularity, which can vitiate a procedure of remand in police custody, must be arbitrary. They note that section 291 of the penal code punishes false arrest with an imprisonment term of from five to ten years and with a fine of form twenty thousand (20,000) francs to one million (1,000,000) francs. The offence is aggravated where the deprivation last for more than a month, or where it is accompanied with physical or mental torture or where the arrest is effected with the aid of a forged order or from a public authority or of a uniform unlawfully worn, or pretending an appointment not held. Whatever the case, the practical implementation of remand in police custody, be it in the police and gendarmerie cells, in application of the provisions of the criminal procedure code, is of primordial interest to us.

CHAPTER V
JUDICIAL POLICE OFFICERS AND OFFENCES COMMITTED FLAGRANTE DELICTO

In principle, in the case of a felony committed flagrante delicto the State Counsel shall be competent to carry out investigations. When he arrives at the scene of the commission of the offence, the powers of the judicial police officers to carry out investigations ceases immediately unless the State Counsel decides otherwise[325].

Felonies and misdemeanours are said to have been committed flagrante delicto when they in the course of being committed, when after the commission of the offence, the suspect is pursued by public clamour, or when soon after the commission of the offence the suspect is caught in possession of an article or shows a sign or trace which tends to suggest that he took part in the commission of the felony or misdemeanour. There shall equally be flagrante delicto where a person requests the state counsel or a judicial police officer to investigate a felony or misdemeanour committed in a house which he occupies or over which he has charge[326].

I. SPECIAL PREROGATIVES OF JUDICIAL POLICE OFFICERS IN CASES OF FLAGRANTE DELICTO OFFENCES

Every duty conscious and professional JPO who is duly informed of an offence committed flagrante delicto, immediately informs the State Counsel after which he visits the locus instantly.

A. Obligation of Information

Considering the fundamental role of the State Counsel as regards offences committed flagrante delicto, the law provides that a JPO informed of an offence committed flagrante delicto must immediately inform the State Counsel of it. Not only is such information made mandatory, its written nature is mandatory as well. Any information initially given by telephone or any other

[325] Section 111 CPC.

[326] Section 103 CPC.

means of communication must be explicitly stated in the police report[327]. The law provides that after informing the State Counsel the JPO shall without any delays visit the crime scene.

B. Visit to the Locus Inquo

The information of the State Counsel, of all offences committed flagrante delicto which precede a visit to the *locus inquo* is of utmost importance. It is geared primarily towards attaining the following objectives:

- Prevent any person likely to supply useful information from leaving the place without his permission subject to punishment provided in the penal code for defaulting witnesses. This measure is not however expected to last more than 12 hours, under pain of prosecution for false arrest;
- To where necessary remand in police custody any suspected person. It should be noted that remand in police custody in a classic case of police investigation is subjected to the existence of strong corroborative evidence, the absence of a known residence or inability to fulfil the conditions of bail of the provisions of section 246(g). In the case mentioned hereabove remand in police custody does not take cognisance of any of the conditions. It is instantly executed for any suspect;
- Ensure the preservation of evidence that may be used for the discovery of the truth;
- Seize any article or document used in committing the offence or which appear to be the product of the felony;
- In case of urgency carry out his duties outside his territorial jurisdiction. This intrusion into another jurisdiction is subject to information of the State Counsel of the said jurisdiction by the State Counsel of the place of commission of the felony or misdemeanour deemed to have been committed flagrante delicto. He is assisted by the JPO serving within the area into which he has entered[328]

[327] Section 104 CPC.
[328] Section 88 CPC.

- Conduct searches in the houses of persons suspected of either keeping documents or articles relating to the particulars of the offences or of having participated in the commission of the felony. Just like remand, searches and seizures in cases of felonies committed flagrante delicto are not subject to the requirement of search warrant.

Among the rights of the Judicial police officer in cases of felony committed flagrante delicto features predominantly the right to arrest and the right to intercept record or transcribe all correspondences sent by means of telecommunication and take any photographs at private residences[329].

C. The Judicial Police Officers and Arrest in Cases of Offences Committed Flagrante Delicto

Arrest consists of apprehending a person for the purpose of bringing him without delay before the authority prescribed by law or by the warrant[330]. From the wordings of this provision, it can be deduced that an arrest which in essence is an infringement of the right of freedom of movement, can only be executed on the instructions of specifically limited judicial authorities[331] or by warrant. An arrest warrant has been defined as an order given to an officer of the judicial police to arrest a defendant, an accused or a convict and bring him before the judicial authority cited in section 12 of the CPC[332]. The law makers omitted suspects within the list of those subject to arrest, erroneously giving the impression that State Counsel do not have jurisdiction to issue. An arrest warrant should not be confused with a bench warrant though they have a similar mission. A bench warrant has been defined as «an order given by a court to any officer of the judicial police to bring immediately before it the person named therein...»[333].

Procedure of Arrest

[329] Section92(3) CPC.
[330] Section 30(1) CPC.
[331] Section 12 CPC.
[332] Section 18 CPC.
[333] Section 14 CPC.

A JPO effecting an arrest must disclose his identity and inform the person to be arrested of the reason for the said arrest and where necessary allow a third party to accompany the person arrested in order to ascertain the place to which he is been detained. In the instant case he simply orders the person to be arrested to follow him and in the case of refusal, use reasonable force necessary to arrest him. No bodily or psychological harm must be caused on the person to be arrested. The specificity of the powers of JPO in cases of offences committed flagrante delicto is that the JPO carries out arrest without necessarily respecting the formalities. The said arrest deviates from the regular principles and rules of arrest.

As regards magistrates the law provides that any magistrate who witnesses a felony or misdemeanour being committed flagrante delicto may order the arrest of the offender or his accomplice; after disclosing his identity and informing the person to be arrested of the reasons thereof[334].

The law equally attributes almost similar but reinforced powers to "any person" to arrest in case of felony or misdemeanour committed flagrante delicto without any precondition of disclosure of identity or the motive of arrest[335].

Whatever the case the peculiarity of the powers of the JPO in cases of misdemeanours and felonies punishable with at least two years of imprisonment is evident when it comes to the interception, recording or transcription of all correspondences sent by means of telecommunication as well as taking of photographs at private residences.

D. The Powers of Interception, Recording or Transcription of Correspondences

The law provides that in cases of felonies and misdemeanours punishable with at least two years imprisonment, the judicial police officer may on the written authorisation of the State Counsel and under the control of the later, in accordance with the conditions laid down in section 245 of the CPC in the course of investigations;

---

[334] Section 31 CPC.

[335] Section 30(3) CPC.

- record or transcribe all correspondences sent by means of telecommunication;
- Take any photographs at private premises.

This power which before the coming into force of the CPC was not explicitly attributed by any text was mentioned in the preamble of the constitution which states inter alia that «the privacy of all correspondences is inviolate. No interference may be allowed except by virtue of decisions emanating from the judicial power».

Henceforth the interception, recording or transcription of correspondences is regulated by the provisions of section 245 of the CPC. This provision should not however be confused with the recording of a conversation by an individual with a third party, which is in essence not prohibited by law and can be used as exhibit in court. Within the context of investigation the law provides that any such interception, transcription or recording of communication can only be authorised by the State Counsel in cases of police investigation[336], the Examining Magistrate in the course of preliminary inquiry[337] as well as the inquiry control chambers in the course of further inquiry[338].

Within the context of police investigation, such operations cannot be carried out on the initiative of the judicial police officer. It must be authorised and controlled by the State Counsel. It should be noted that unlike the Examining Magistrate whose jurisdiction in this domain is not materially limited, the interception of communication by the State Counsel is limited to cases of felonies and misdemeanours punishable with imprisonment of at least two years. The authorisation of the State Counsel does not have a judicial character and thus not opened to appeal.

The CPC[339]formally includes lawyers within the frame of this operation. It states that unless the President of the Bar Council is informed, no interception can be effected on the

[336] Section 92(3) CPC.
[337] Section 248(4) CPC.
[338] Section 267 CPC.
[339] Section 245(4) (h).

telephone line of a barrister's office or residence. An author[340] in the same line emphasizes that the interception or transmission shall not under any circumstance be done on the conversation between a lawyer and his client who are protected by the principle of confidentiality and inviolability. However, interception, transcription or recording must be distinguished from an operation of verification of the origin of a telephone conversation which is not submitted under any formalities by the CPC.

On the contrary it excludes members of a public institution provided for by the constitution benefitting from immunity from prosecution. Such persons in our opinion will obviously include the President of the Republic, members of parliament and the Constitutional Council. This privilege ceases whenever the immunity of the personalities above are uplifted by the bureau of the national assembly for example in case of offences committed flagrante delicto.

The delicate nature of the operation calls for a precision on the elements of identification of the means of communication to be intercepted, the offence which motivated the authorisation of the measure as well as its duration. As regards its duration the maximum, period is fixed at four months renewable under the same condition and formality. The law does not limit the number of times this measure can be renewed. It simply provides for renewal each time the four months elapses but not after the close of police investigation.

Technically the operation of interception, transcription and recording requires not only a certain degree of technical know-how but the putting in place as well, of a technical platform which permits the JPO to accomplish this mission. As such the law provides that the commissioned JPO may order the installation of an interceptive device by any qualified agent of a service or institution placed under the authority or supervision of the ministry of telecommunications or any qualified agent of the operator of a telecommunication network or provider or authorised telecommunication services. The law lays more

---

[340] Kenmoe (E.), *La pratique de l'information judiciaire dans le code de procédure pénale du Cameroun*, édition véritas, 2013, p.168

emphasis here not only on the qualified nature of the agent but on the supervisory authority as well. Its role however is limited to the installation of the interceptive device. It does not participate in the listening transcription or recording properly speaking which is in essence the sole prerogative of the commissioned JPO. The operation of interception, transcription or recoding can be carried out both within the jurisdiction of the Unit of the JPO or throughout the national territory

The Examining Magistrate or the JPO commissioned by him or by the State Counsel shall transcribe the correspondences relevant to the case and shall make a report thereof. As regards correspondences in foreign languages the law provides that it shall be transcribed either in English or French with the assistance of a translator requisitioned for that purpose most probably after having taken oath. The JPO must make a report of each of the operations of the interception and recording stating the date and hour that the operation started and ended and shall be kept under seal. Such measure is geared towards preventing third parties from getting access to the content of the report.

Any action taken in violation of the above section shall be null and void. In the absence of the nature or type of nullity made mention of here, E. Kenmoe[341] opines that since the operation here is destined at protecting private interest the nullity referred to in this section is relative nullity. This author is however worried about the fate of facts revealed in the course of an interception, transcription or recording, which while constituting offences are foreign to the initial procedure. He holds the view that just like in seizures a separate report is supposed to be drawn up and transmitted to the State counsel who reserves the right of engaging prosecution against offenders depending on the nature of the offence.

On the expiry of the prescription period of the criminal action, the recordings must be destroyed at the instance of the State Counsel or the Procureur General and a report of the destruction drawn up. What about the taking of photographs.

---

[341] ibid., p.169

E. Judicial Police Officers and the Power to Take Photos in Private Premises

As pertains to the taking of photographs by JPO, the provision of section 245 subjects it to the regime of authorisation of the State Counsel or the Examining magistrate only when it concerns private premises. The conditions and procedures are like those of interception, transcription and recording of correspondences. In principle, the taking of photographs in public places or places opened to the public is not subjected to prior authorisation. It is within this context that surveillance cameras are littered in public places such as streets, banks, airports, hospitals and more recently in some offices. Such is equally the case with places which are private in nature but opened to the public such as supermarkets and restaurants. The essences of the protection of private premises by the law makers can be justified by the need to individual liberty and the private life of citizens.

The result of police investigation either in preliminary investigation or in cases of offences committed flagrante delicto is summarised in what is referred to as a "*procés verbal*" better known in English as a police report.

CHAPTER VI
POLICE REPORT

Record keeping is one of the most important functions of law enforcement officers World over. Judicial police officers are trained to document their observations and actions whenever they are called upon to perform their duties and they do so in police reports. These reports become official records and they are carefully kept for the benefit of the public. Police reports are generated just about every time a law enforcement officer responds to a call. This includes motor vehicle accidents, arrests, investigations, and several other situations. Police reports are entered in criminal court proceedings and they are also used by insurance companies when they investigate claims. Although police reports are rarely admitted in civil court cases, they can help lawyers to identify witnesses as well as grasping a mastery of a lawsuit.

In French, Belgian and Dutch laws, police report can be defined as a detailed authenticated account drawn up by a magistrate, police officer, or other person having authority of acts of proceedings done in the exercise of his duty. In a criminal charge, a "process verbal" can be defined as the statement of the facts of the case.

An author[342]defines *procès-verbal* (PV) as "*des actes sur lesquels les agents de police judiciaire rendent compte des infractions qu'ils ont constatées, des opérations qu'ils ont faites et des renseignements qu'ils ont obtenus*"[343]

The investigation of offences, the collection of evidence, identification of offenders and their accomplices and bringing them before the Legal Department is the sole responsibility of JPOs. The results of their findings are contained in a police report. The drawing up of such reports is an exclusive obligation of judicial police officers. Those with the status of judicial police officers within the context of the CPC it should be recalled include; officers and non-commissioned officers of the

[342]Ndjere (E.), op. cit. , p.76

[343]Tranlated to mean " PVs are documents on which judicial police agents report offences they observed, operations carried out as well as information gathered.

gendarmerie, gendarmes in charge even in an acting capacity of a gendarmerie brigade or post , superintendent of police, deputy superintendent of police, gendarmes or inspectors of police who have passed the judicial police officers examination and taken oath and public servants even if they are temporally performing the functions of head of an external service of the National Security.

The Court of Appeal of the North West Region[344], operate a clear cut distinction between a police report and the special register of Section 124(3) of the CPC, which is prone to uncertainty in the following excerpts:

"Section 124(1) clearly states that the judicial police officer shall mention in his report such entries. His report constitutes the police case file which in the French version of section 124(1) is translated "process verbal". Besides these entries being mentioned in the police report, section 124(3) also demands that same entries be mentioned in a special register kept at the police station for the purpose of control and inspection by the State Counsel. Again, the French version of section 124(3) states it even clearer when it says, "les mêmes mention doivent figurer sur un register special", which means the same entries as made in section 124(1) shall be made in the special register. The entries are only made in the special register as the learned Substitute General wants this court to understand, then which is the case file that is sent to the State Counsel for action and subsequent prosecution of the matter? This is so because the special register as per section 124(3) is kept in the police station since it is for controls and inspections which should be carried out at anytime unannounced. Conclusively, the entries as per the cited sections are supposed to be entered in the police report which is forwarded to the State Counsel for action and which is exhibit "A", the basis of this appeal, and in the special register which is kept at the police station".

The court in the instant case was responding to one of the issues raised for determination by the court, to wit; whether the

[344] Ndi Tangiri and 54 others Vs The People of Cameroon, Suit n° CANWR/MS/60C /2012 SLR 4 , (2016),p.63-66

police report envisaged in section 124(1) and (2) is the same as the special register mentioned in section 124(3) of the CPC.

I. FORM OF A POLICE REPORT

The code while giving a vivid description of what should be the elements that constitute a police report fails to precise the form that this content should take. Consequently, the form of a police report varies depending on the investigating unit. The form of police reports from public security police units and those of the gendarmerie units are slightly different though with a similar content.

A. The Form of a Police Report

A police report is composed of a heading, the preamble, the body, and a conclusion.

1. The heading

The heading of a typical police report from a Gendarmerie unit presents the following elements chronologically in the heading; the address of the investigating unit and a space reserved for the authority to whom the report is destined (Legal Department), the nature or type of investigation (flagrance or preliminary investigation[345]), the report number and the date of closure. Other elements of the heading include the name of the head of the investigating unit and his rank, the investigating officer who always features as an assistant to the unit head for all investigations. Lastly, the provisions of the CPC empowering the JPO, to carry out investigations, as well as the identity of the suspect and the offence for which he is investigated.

The heading of a police report from a Public Security post is presented as a mail, addressed to the State Counsel, with the address of the unit on the left hand and on the right hand in a

[345] Investigations carried out in cases of offences committed flagrante delicto as defined in section 103 and executed under conditions laid down in section 104-115 of the CPC is not the same as preliminary investigation. Judicial police officers are empowered to receive complaints and reports and carry out investigation according to provisions of section 116 to 120 of the CPC. Investigations carried out under the conditions laid down in section 116-120 are called preliminary investigation.

typical French style it specifically mentions that the mail is from the head of the investigation unit, to the State Counsel whose address is equally specified. Below this, on the left hand side and in sequential order is the police report number, the subject (referring to the offences investigated), the identity of the suspect, reference (reference here refers to the origin of the order to investigate. It can result from a complain made directly at the unit or transmitted through the Legal Department with specified instructions) and lastly a list of the documents that makes up the complete report.

2. The preamble

The preamble as an element of a police report is unique to police reports from gendarmerie investigating units. It states the date and time the complaint was received at the unit, mentions if the complaint was accompanied by the suspect or not. If the complaint was transmitted for investigation from the Legal Department, it is mentioned alongside any specific instructions contained on the transmission document.

3. The facts

The third element of a police report is the summary of the facts of the matter. In this part of the report, the investigator states the date the complaint was received and its origin; relate the facts as contained in the complaint or the report in case of an oral complaint as well as the offences cited in the complaint. If the complaint was transmitted through the Legal Department, the JPO mentions the instructions received from the legal department.

4. The investigation

This part of the report relates in details the various operations undertaken by the JPO in the course of investigations. These operations may include the parties from whom statements were recorded. He mentions if other operations such as searches and seizures were carried out, if there was a visit to the *locus in quo*, if the suspects were arrested, if there was confrontation etc. Each of these operations are materialised by a report which must be annexed to the final report.

5. Conclusion

The conclusion of a police report is a sort of personal appraisal of the matter by the investigating officer. After relating the various operations carried out, he gives his personal opinion of the complaint based on facts gathered from the various operations carried out. It can conclude that based on the elements gathered, the suspected can be prosecuted for the offences listed by the complainant or for other offences. It can as well conclude in the inexistence of the constitutive elements of the offence alleged to have been committed. Whatever the case the State counsel is not always bound by the conclusion of the JPO.

II. THE CONTENT OF A POLICE REPORT

Unlike the form, the CPC has provided for the various elements that must feature in a police report. It provides that a police report shall state the date and time each phase of investigation started, the full name and status of the investigator, where necessary authorisation to carry out part of the investigation out of the jurisdiction.

Persons from whom statements are required can either chose to dictate it to the investigator or write by themselves[346]. Each sheet of the original of the report must bear the signature of the investigator; idem with statements recorded from the parties. Each sheet of such statements or reports of confrontations must bear the initials of all the parties who took part in the process, including interpreters. The obligation to sign or initial, equally apply to the statement register which should not be confused with the statement sheet. Apart from the statement sheet, all gendarmerie units equally keep statement registers wherein statements are initially recorded prior to transcription into the statement sheet[347].

In case of inability to sign, the investigator must cause the party concerned to affix his right thumb print on the document

[346]90(8) CPC.
[347]90(2) (3) (4) CPC.

and in case of inability, any other fingerprint. In case of refusal to sign mention of the refusal is made in the report[348].

The signing of a report sheet or register is not absolute, in as much as parties can out rightly refrain from signing them, a more human rights friendly option will be to sign but with reservation. The reservation which is written must be explicit and unambiguous.[349]

III. THE LEGAL NATURE OF POLICE REPORTS

Documents drawn up by legal officers and experts in the course of criminal proceedings are considered not only to be legally binding, but to be authentic as well until a counter expert opinion proves the contrary. Such is the case with various reports established by bailiffs, medical doctors etc.

Within the same context an author[350] opines that all the reports drawn up by the Examining Magistrate as well as the orders made are authentic acts which are legally binding. Their authenticity can only be compromised if it is established that it was not regularly established i.e. by fraud or forgery.

One would have expected a similar treatment of reports which originates from investigative units, established by JPO who like other judicial authorities, such as bailiffs and notaries take oath before service and even by other experts who are not direct auxiliaries of justice such as medical Doctors. Unfortunately, the law unequivocally provides that reports written by JPO shall serve only as mere information[351]. If it is admitted that this provision applies to statements recorded from the witnesses and suspects, what about the various reports drawn up by the same officers after searches and seizures, visits to the locus in quo or even in the course of rogatory commissions?

A. Nullity of Police Reports

Judicial Police Officers in the course of police investigation are liable to commit a variety of procedural errors. While some can

---

[348] 90(5) (6) CPC.
[349] 90(7) CPC
[350] Mbunja (Y.), op. cit., p.46.
[351] 91 CPC

be overlooked, others have far reaching consequences on the outcome of the procedure. Such is the case with exclusion of certain evidence by the trial court or nullification.

1. Definition and types of nullity

Nullity is the concept or doctrine that deprives legal acts of their effects, in common law terms; it is the concept of voidness or voidability.

After distinguishing two types of nullity i.e. absolute and relative nullity, an author[352] has defined absolute nullity as nullity that violates a rule of public order with permanent defects while relative nullity only violates a rule established for the protection of a private person with a temporal defect. According to him, though there is a tendency to think that an absolute nullity is something more serious than relative nullity, no one seriously posits this as a criterion for distinction.

Within the same context the CPC while not providing a definition of nullity state some pointers in the following words "the sanctions against the infringement of any rule of criminal procedure shall be an absolute nullity when it is:

(a) prejudicial to the right of defence as defined by legal provisions in force;
(b) Contrary to public policy.

It further provides that the said nullity shall not be overlooked and can be raised at any stage of the criminal proceedings by any of the parties and shall be raised by the trial court of its own motion[353].

In the same manner the law makers while skilfully evading a definition of relative nullity deduces cases of relative nullity from the pointers of absolute nullity, emphasizing however that they shall be raised by the parties *in limine litis* before the trial court[354]. Going by these pointers, the CPC within the scope of police investigation clearly spells out circumstances of infringement that can lead to one of the nullities.

---

[352] Ronald J., «Rethinking the doctrine of nullity» in *Louisiana law review*, vol.74, number 3, Spring 2014, p. 687-691

[353] Section 3(1) (2) CPC.

[354] Section 4 CPC.

2. Police reports and absolute nullity

Unlike in the course of preliminary inquiry where the rules of nullity and at times procedure are explicitly elucidated[355] with a possibility of nullification in the course of the proceedings, the CPC barely mentions circumstances of nullity without any further precision.

A classic case of absolute nullity deduced from the pointers of Section 3 of the CPC is provided for in Section 116(3) which states inter alia that "as soon as investigations are opened the JPO shall under penalty of nullity inform the suspect of:

- His right to counsel;
- His right to remain silent".

It is important to emphasize that mention of this information shall be made in the report. Judges have been fast to hold that the nullity mentioned hereabove is absolute, initially because it violates the rights to defence of Section 3(a). In such cases the police report is wholly nullified. What can be the attitude of the Court in a case where the rights were notified but the JPO simply omitted to mention same in the police report? Or where it was simply stated that the suspect was informed of his rights under Section 116(3) of the CPC, without any trace to that effect. Most JPO have adopted an explicit form of information after which suspects are expected to expressly append their signatures on a space reserved for such information. The format is presented thus:

We equally inform him of his right to remain silent and his right to Counsel.

Suspect	**interpreter**	**Assistant**	**Judicial police officers**
…………	………………	…………	………………………

Considering the written nature of police investigation, it is our considered opinion that such substantial formality cannot simply be left at the mercy of suggestions or conjecture; it is

[355]Sections 251 and 254(1) CPC.

supposed to be done with traceable evidence. A mere mention that suspects were informed of these rights without evidence thereof will not meet the test of Section 116(4), and in case of contestation will be difficult to establish. However, where the violation does not affect a substantial formality, the violation thereto is relative.

The violation of the provision of Section 90(3) (4) (5) and (7) as regards the remand in custody notably the signing of entries is sanctioned surprisingly by absolute nullity. Section 124 in its paragraph 4 explicitly provides that the non-observation of the provisions of this section shall lead to nullity of the police report as well as all subsequent acts, without prejudice to disciplinary sanction against the JPO concerned.

In Suit N0.CFIB/40P/2009; ***The People & ANOR Vs Njina Kevin Ndango***[356], the Court of First Instance Buea adjudicating on the interpretation to be given to section 124(4) and whether failure to comply with it renders the entire trial a nullity, the Court held as follows:

"***Now, there is no doubt that the CPC attaches a high premium on the rights of the Accused persons. PWs 2 and 4 both admitted under cross-examination that in the process of recording Exhibits "D", "D1" and "E", not all the mandatory provisions ordained in Section 124(4) of the CPC were complied with. These violations must lead to the nullity of the Reports, the Accused statement and "all subsequent acts" of the Judicial Police Officer concerned. This however, to my mind cannot be given an interpretation of such latitude as would include the nullity of the entire trial. What that section refers to are subsequent acts of the Judicial Police Officer concerned, who could even be visited by disciplinary section. If for instance the JPO, who in interrogating the suspect violates the provision of Section 124(4) of the CPC, decides in the course of investigation to conduct a search in a given premises, whatever is discovered as a result of a search will be vitiated by nullity, if it were the intention of the legislator that non-compliance with the provisions of Section 124 of the CPC would lead to nullity***

[356]CCLR, PART 14, p. 68-69

of the entire trial and judgment, it would have been so mentioned expressly, as is the case with Section 367 of the CPC which categorically states that failure to comply with the provisions of section 366 (CPC) " shall render the trial and the judgment null and void". Such is not the language of Section 124(4) of the CPC. Besides, it is trite law that what is not mentioned in a piece of legislation is excluded. "Expressio unius est exclusion alterius". I now say, with increasing confidence, that this trial and judgment are not a nullity.

This was the position of the **Court of Appeal** of the North West region[357]; where the court held that "***Exhibit "A", the police report, never stated the reasons for remanding the appellant despite the fact that they passed the night in custody. The length of time they were subjected to questioning is not stated notwithstanding the fact that the exercise dragged too long extending to late hours. The day they were brought before the State Counsel is not stated. The investigator; the PW1; counsel for the appellants submitted; confirmed all these facts under cross-examination. Most of the appellants range between the age of fifty (50) to eighty-four years, which called for special attention; and ought to have been stated in the police report... As a sum total of the above analysis, it is our considered opinion that the trial magistrate indeed erred in ruling that Exhibit "A", the police report is not a nullity. This court therefore upholds the appeal of counsel for the appellants and declares Exhibit "A", the police report, a nullity".***

On whether the nullity of the police report leads to the nullity of all subsequent acts including the trial, the Court ruled ***"This court therefore upholds the appeal of counsel for the appellant and declares Exhibit "A", the police report, a nullity. The matter is returned to the trial court, the Court of First Instance Bamenda, for continuation of the trial".***

Though the nullity in this case is absolute, by ordering the continuation of the trial, the Court of Appeal limited the interpretation of the word «subsequent acts» to acts done in the course of investigation sorely.

---

[357]Op.cit.

In another ruling the **North West Court of Appeal**[358], responding to whether the nullity of the investigation report leads to all subsequent acts including the trial, embarrassed by the position of the trial Magistrate using its jurisprudence abusively or erroneously, the court stated inter-alia ***"The trial Magistrate relied on suit N° CANWR/MS/60/2012 of the 12/11/2012: Ndi Tangiri James and 53 ORS Vs The People to declare the rejected case file an absolute nullity and with it, the direct summons as well as the ensuing trial. The accused was accordingly discharged. The two cases are glaringly distinguishable. In fact, one is like day and the other like night. The matter handled by the Court of Appeal was on the no observance of the provisions of Section 124 of the CPC. It hinged on what the judicial police officer is expected to do in drawing up a case file when a suspect is in their custody. On the contrary in the instant case we are dealing with the admissibility of a case file. The trial Magistrate grossly misconceived the Court of Appeal ruling. He erroneously relied thereon in declaring the case file and the entire proceedings so far recorded an absolute nullity. It was really bizarre. How could the trial magistrate reject the case file and with the same breath declare it as an absolute nullity?*** Holding further that ***"… it was premature for the trial court to have discharged the accused when the prosecution had not closed their case…"***

3. Police report and relative nullity

The CPC[359] has clearly spelt out the elements of a classical police report. Among the formalities laid down whose violation may lead to nullity is the initialling or signing of all reports by all the parties involved (suspect or witnesses, interpreters if any, judicial police officers or their assistant). Such will be the case with reports of recording of statements or interrogations, reports of confrontations, reports of seizures[360], search reports[361]etc

[358]The People of Cameoon and Dr. Yoh Peter Tingem Vs Tume Evelyne Mainsah, Suit N°. CANWR/MS/52C/2013 SLR 4, (2016), p. 82-85

[359] Section 90 CPC.

[360] Section 94-96 CPC.

[361] Section 98 CPC.

The violation of these formalities renders the police report null. Every police report drawn up in contravention of these formalities Section 90, 93-99 as per the provisions of section 100 of the CPC shall be null and void. Nullity within this context will be relative and as such only the police report is affected and not the entire proceedings. The relativity of the nullity is further highlighted when the law makers authorises the admission of exhibits from searches declared null and void, if such exhibits are not contested.

PART III

THE DEPARTMENT OF PUBLIC PROSECUTION AND POLICE INVESTIGATION

The commission of offences may lead to the institution of criminal proceedings and, as the case may be, to a civil action. While the institution of criminal proceedings aims at procuring a sentence or a preventive measure against the offenders as provided by law, civil actions are intended to provide compensation for damages resulting from an offence[362].

The Legal Department is the public prosecutor of all criminal matters be it simple offences, misdemeanour or felony committed against public or private interest. The Department is counsel for the community acting on behalf of society. State Prosecutors have with the Ministry in charge of Justice the discretion whether to prosecute or not.

One of the fundamental roles of the Legal Department is to institute and prosecute criminal proceedings[363]. Without prejudice to the civil party who is always free to constitute himself a civil party in a criminal case, the Legal Department also investigates and record offences in the course of which the state counsel has the right to issue court processes, order any measure of investigation, notably searches, seizures, visit to the *locus inquo*, and expert appraisal.

[362] Section 59 CPC.

[363] Section 60 CPC.

CHAPTER VII
THE LEGAL DEPARTMENT: SUPERIOR JUDICIAL POLICE OFFICER AND COURT PROCESSES

Court processes have been defined as written documents by which a magistrate or a court orders either;

- the appearance or production of an individual before them;
- the remand in custody of a suspect, a defendant or an accused;
- a witness suspected of hindering the search for evidence;
- the imprisonment of a convict;
- the search of objects either used for or procured by the commission of an offence.[364]

Generally, court processes are constituted of summons, bench warrants, remand warrants, production warrants, search warrants, warrants of arrest and imprisonment warrants.

I. THE STATE COUNSEL: AUTHOR OF WARRANTS IN PRELIMINARY INVESTIGATION

Unlike the Examining Magistrate, in the course of investigations the State Counsel has been attributed the powers of issuing a limited number of court processes: summonses, warrants of arrest, search warrants. To this list is added a production warrant in the course of prosecution[365].

A. Summonses

A summon has been defined as an order requesting a person to appear before the State Counsel, Examining Magistrate or a trial court on a date and hour mentioned on the summons. The purpose of summonses is to command the person named therein to appear before one of the authorities here above. Summonses in principle are void of any constraining aspect even though non-appearance, refusal to testify or false evidence most especially for a witness can be punished by law. An individual summoned by

[364] Section 11 CPC.
[365] Section 12(1) CPC.

any of the authorities above is free to present himself or not. It is like a form of convocation for the suspect, defendant, or witnesses. Summonses are issued at the request of the State Counsel, any aggrieved party, or any other interested party.

Service which consists of delivering of a summons to the persons named therein is effected by an officer or agent of the judicial police or by any such persons assigned the duty. Apart from summonses, the State counsel can in the course of police investigation issue warrants of arrest

B. Warrant of Arrest

An arrest warrant is an order given to any officer of the judicial police to immediately bring before it the persons named therein. Its execution completely leaves out the regular process server (bailiff) due to its nature which requires the use of force. Whatever the nature of the offence that motivates arrest, the purpose of warrant of arrest is not remanding in police custody. It is aimed at bringing the person mentioned therein before the signatory of the warrant for the purpose hearing. A person can only be considered to have been remanded after having been arrested on the strength of a warrant of arrest in the course of transfer, if he was arrested outside the territorial jurisdiction of the authority that issued the warrant of arrest.

Considering the serious nature of arrest warrants which are liable to infringing the freedom of movement, it can only be issued against suspects in the course of police investigation, Examining magistrates during preliminary inquiry against defendants or by a trial court against an accused. Witnesses are not subject to arrest. Exceptionally however the provision of Section 188(2) of the CPC gives the Examining Magistrate the possibility of delivering a warrant of arrest against defaulting witnesses. Responding to the question whether such an arrest is supposed to have been preceded by a summons or not, an author[366] is of the opinion that the warrant can be issued against a witness who had not initially been summoned. He is of the opinion that Section 13(4) of the CPC does not make it

[366]Mbunja (Y.), op. cit., pp.146.

obligatory, concluding that if the Examining Magistrate suspects that a convocation or a summon will have as effect alerting the defendant who can escape, an arrest warrant will be acceptable. It is our considered opinion that this procedure will not be proper considering that default is the element that justifies the use of an arrest warrant against a witness. The Examining Magistrates suspicion even if grounded will under no circumstances replace default which is not synonymous to suspicion.

A JPO charged with the execution of a warrant of arrest may be accompanied by enough law enforcement officers to prevent the person from escaping. Warrants of arrest can only be executed after 6am and before 6pm[367]. If a person against whom a warrant is issued cannot be found after careful search a copy of the warrant shall be left at his last known place of abode or with the village head or quarter head. A report of the steps taken to execute the warrant shall be made and forwarded to the authority that issued it. The report shall be signed and stamped by the head of the administrative unit, village chief or quarter head[368]. Such is not the case with search warrants.

C. Search Warrants

A search warrant is an order given to a judicial police officer by the State Counsel, an Examining Magistrate or trial Court to enter any public or private place and search it for the purpose of seizing any articles or documents used in the commission of an offence or which appears to be the product of an offence[369].

The court processes which are issued at the instance of the State Counsel and executed by judicial police officers having been adequately dealt with here above, it is worth noting that the state counsel is a superior JPO.

II. THE LEGAL DEPARTMENT AS A SUPERIOR JUDICIAL POLICE OFFICER

Apart from receiving written information, written or oral complaints or written reports from competent authorities, the

[367] Section 23 CPC.
[368] Section 20 CPC.
[369] Section16 CPC.

Legal Department directs and controls the operations of the officers and agents of the judicial police. On the strength of this prerogative, he is endowed with the power of wholly substituting judicial police officers in the course of investigations with regards to particular offences and to ensure the regularity of all remands.

A. Judicial Police Officer of Felonies Committed Flagrante Delicto

For the purpose of refreshing our memory, felonies and misdemeanours are said to have been committed flagrante delicto when they in the course of being committed, when after the commission of the offence, the suspect is pursued by public clamour, or when soon after the commission of the offence the suspect is caught in possession of an article or shows a sign or trace which tends to suggest that he took part in the commission of the felony or misdemeanour. There is equally flagrante delicto where a person requests the State Counsel or a judicial police officer to investigate a felony or misdemeanour committed in a house which he occupies or over which he has charge[370].

1. The Obligation of Information of the State Counsel in Cases of Offences Committed Flagrante Delicto

In principle and considering the primordial role of the State Counsel in the investigation of offences committed flagrante delicto, a judicial police officer informed of a felony committed flagrante delicto must immediately inform the State Counsel. Its mandatory nature is emphasized by the use of the adjective "shall" by the lawmaker[371], an obligation which is closely followed by another obligation of the materialisation of the said information in writing[372]. This compulsory provision which is almost an injunction is grounded on the premise that in the case of a felony committed flagrante delicto, the State counsel is the competent authority to carry out investigations[373].

---

[370]Supra.
[371]Section 104(1) (a) CPC.
[372]Section 104(1) (b) CPC.
[373] Section 111 CPC.

2. The State Counsel and Investigation

When the State Prosecutor arrives at the scene of the commission of the offence the powers of the judicial police officer to carry out investigation ceases instantly unless he decides otherwise. To further elucidate the powers of the State counsel in cases of felonies committed flagrante delicto, the law provides that even in cases where JPO proceed with the arrest of suspects, such suspect must be brought before the State Counsel who personally proceeds to identify and interrogate them though summarily[374] and if he decides to prosecute can remand in custody[375]. All the measures taken by the State Counsel within the scope of his investigation are summarised in a report which in our opinion contain all the elements of a police report as laid down in the provisions of section 90 of the CPC. JPO can only carry out any operation such as searches, seizures, and arrest on his instructions and following his directives. We are of the opinion that reports of the delegated operations are contained in the report made by the State Counsel, on grounds which he can chose to prosecute the suspects.

B. The Prosecution of Suspects Arrested Flagrante Delicto by the State Counsel

The law has given the State Counsel quite several options as regards prosecution of suspects arrested flagrante delicto. He may prosecute him in the nearest court session under the conditions laid down by law[376]. The law equally provides for direct summons as a mode of prosecution opened to the State Counsel. We suppose that this mode of prosecution applies in the case where upon arrival at a crime scene he decides to delegate his

[374] It should be noted that suspects arrested flagrante delicto are accompanied by a properly mounted police report, which serve as the base of interrogation of the State Counsel. The difference here has been that in non-flagrante delicto proceedings, the case file is handed to the State Counsel who treats same in chambers and does not proceed to interrogation. Suspects in this case are prosecuted by way of direct summons if the offence committed is a simple offence or misdeameanour. In some cases however, as was the case in Edea between 2010-2014, it was common to find the State Counsel personally conducting investigations in cases of offences committed flagrante delicto..

[375] 114(1) CPC.

[376] Section 298-301 CPC.

powers to investigate to JPO. The wordings of the law to this regards are quite instructive as it states "the provisions of the present section shall not prevent the State Counsel from instituting prosecution against the suspect by way of a direct summons or after preliminary investigation"[377]. The modes of prosecution only apply in cases of misdemeanours committed flagrante delicto. Felonies committed flagrante delicto are exempted from the aforementioned modes owing to the fact that preliminary inquiries are obligatory in cases of felonies [378] wherein the Examining Magistrate is seised by a holding charge preferred by the State Counsel[379].

Apart from its role of investigation of offences notably felonies committed flagrante delicto as well as misdemeanours, the State Counsel enjoys extensive prerogatives pertaining to remand in custody over which he has control, supervises, and regulates.

III. THE EXTENSIVE ROLE OF THE STATE COUNSEL AS REGARDS REMAND IN CUSTODY

At a time when the role of the Legal Department as regards the restriction of individual liberty is under serious scrutiny on the international scene, an author[380]notes that such measures (remand in police and prison custody at the request of the Legal Department) are not only hostile to the right to a fair trial[381]but illogical as well[382].That notwithstanding, the Legal Department

---

[377] 144(3) CPC.

[378] Section142(1) CPC.

[379] Section 143 CPC.

[380]ETEME ETEME, «Le parquet et la privation de liberté : Mauvais ménage ? Réflexion sur le devenir d'une relation antinomique», *Miroir de droit*, N° 02, avril-mai-juin 2011, p.14.

[381] L'un des ingrédients du procès équitable réside dans l'égalité des armes entre les parties .Or, le pourvoir dévolu au parquet d'intervenir dans la privation de liberté à celui qui sera peut-être son adversaire devant le juridiction ou même devant le juge d'instruction soulève le problème de l'équité.

[382] Le ministère public a non seulement un statut de dépendance hiérarchique, mais, au procès pénal, c'est l'une des parties, au même titre que la personne poursuivie et la partie civile. Au terme de l'article 128 du CPP, en effet, il est « partie principale au procès devant toute juridiction répressive » et doit d'ailleurs, « à peine de nullité, poursuit ledit texte, être présent à toutes les audiences. » Comment comprendre dés lors que l'une des parties ait déjà, bien avant le procès, la possibilité de museler l'autre par la possibilité soit de garde à vue, soit d'une détention provisoire ?

under section 127(2) of the CPC[383]has been accorded extensive rights as regards remand in police custody, contrary to the formal provisions of the «*Code d'instruction Criminelle*», wherein, the initiative of remand was the sole prerogative of the judicial police officer, with the State Counsel's intervention limited only to extension. As such, under the Criminal Procedure Code, remand by judicial police officers has been limited to cases of offences committed flagrante delicto. All other cases of remand are subject to the authorisation of the State Counsel[384]. Such is the case with non-flagrant offences defined[385] as "*l'enquete d'usage, prealable aux poursuites par voie de citation directe...une procedure de caractere policier, diligentée d'office ou sur les instruction du Procureur de la Republique par un officier de police judiciaire ou un agent de police judiciaire*"[386], in the course of which a judicial police notices that the conditions of a known place of abode and the gravity of the offence is not met. Such is equally the case with the extension of remand initially authorised by judicial police officers at expiration.

While exhorting the exorbitant power of the state Counsel as regards remand in custody, Landry Biboum[387] is of the opinion that section 111 of the criminal procedure code [388] is a solution to the bad faith and inertia of judicial police officers. In the absence of precision on the procedure of extension by the legislator, divergent views from legal luminaries persist.

While Joseph Emmanuel[389]thinks that extension is carried out by the competent state counsel when the suspect has been brought before him by the mechanism of "*soit fait retour*", which

---

[383] « ...the Legal Department shall as provided for in this section, comprise the magistrates in the Legal Department of the Supreme Court, of the Court of Appeal ,of the High Court and of the court of First Instance ».

[384] Section 118(3) CPC.

[385] Biboum (L.), «Le procureur de la république et la privation de la liberté », *Miroir de droit*, N° 02, avril-mai-juin 2011, p. 44.

[386] Investigations carried out in the case of non-flagrante offences are initiated by the State Counsel and executed by Judicial police officers under his control, prior to prosecution by way of direct summons.

[387] Ibid.

[388] « In the case of felony committed flagrante delicto, the state counsel shall be competent to carry out investigation. When the state counsel arrives at the scene of the commission of the offence, the powers of the judicial police officer to carry out the investigation shall cease immediately, unless the said state counsel decides otherwise.

[389] Op.cit., p.28.

returns the suspect to the cell for complimentary information, within a specified duration. On the contrary Landry Biboum D.[390] in his capacity as State Prosecutor, holds that authorisation of extension can be given in writing, after seizure, either by "message" or by correspondence wherein the facts motivating the extension are presented. He emphasizes that practically the authorisation given in writing consist in the inscription "accord" on the said message or correspondence. It should be noted however that irrespective of who orders remand in police custody, the code has guaranteed respect of the rights of the suspect even while in custody.

IV. CONTROL OF REMAND IN POLICE CUSTODY BY THE LEGAL DEPARTMENT

The control of the regularity of remand in police custody as provided for in the Criminal Procedure Code is regulated by the provision of Section 78 (1) [391]as read with Section 137[392]. The control which can be carried out at any time in a police investigation unit concerns both ordinary remand as well as administrative remand. [393] While in some Legal Departments ordinary cell controls are organised, supplementary controls can be carried out as well after a denunciation from a litigant.

Practically, cell controls are mostly carried out by Deputy State Counsels, who verify among others the remanding authorities who under section 118 of the CPC, must be judicial police officers and in the case of administrative remand who according to Edouard Kitio [394] include; the Governor, Senior Divisional Officers, Divisional officers, chief of services, chief of

[390]Ibid., p.47-48.

[391] (1) « The duties of the judicial police shall be performed under the super vision of the state counsel.... »

[392] (1) « The state counsel shall direct and control the operations of the officers and agents of the judicial police.

(2) He may, at any time visit the police post of gendarmerie brigade in order to verify the conditions of persons in custody provided for in section 124 (3).In the course of such control the persons whose release he orders of his own motion or by virtue of an order of habeas corpus, must immediately be set free, under pain of prosecution for unlawful detention against the judicial police officer in charge of the police post or gendarmerie brigade where the custody takes place »

[393]Ibid.p.49.

[394] Ibid.

bureau. They equally control the nature of the offence that motivated the remand, the nature of the investigation (flagrant or not) and the duration of remand. This control is initially done by way of registers[395] held at the units as well as daily remand statistics; subsequently he proceeds with the physical control of detainees, confronting them with the information contained in the register. In case of irregularities or abnormalities of a very serious nature, suspects can be released instantly as well as those whose release has been ordered by way of habeas corpus.

The passage of the State Counsel or his Deputy is materialised by the signing of the register of remand in police custody as well as signing the cell control sheet with the head of the unit in question, a precision made by Biboum Landry[396]. According to Philippe Keubou[397], cell control can equally be carried out by the Procureur General of the Court of Appeal, in his capacity as the hierarchical superior of the State Counsel and who according to the CPC[398], supervises the activities of the judicial police officers within his jurisdiction. It is our opinion that such controls can be carried out by the State Counsel on the instruction of the Procureur General who must not necessarily do it personally.

Joseph Emmanuel[399], however, notes that in his capacity of hierarchical superior, the State Counsel is judge and party, found in the delicate situation wherein he controls himself, making self-sanction not only difficult but illusory as well. This assertion is confirmed by Rose Djila[400] who cites with nodding approval the Kribi case in ***Ordonance N° 1/HC/PTGI/Kribi of the 13 February 2009***. In this matter the State Counsel did not only condone an irregular remand in police custody from the 30th of January to the 13th of July 2009, but vehemently refused to execute a release order obtained by way of habeas corpus.

In the same context most Departments have cultivated the habit of refraining from executing Court decisions immediately

---

395 Section 123 (3) CPC.
396 Ibid, p.53.
397 Ibid, P.40.
398 Section 134 (2) (a) CPC.
399 Ibid. p.33.
400 Ibid, p.13.

where they feel aggrieved. Responding to the question as to whether the Legal Department has any discretion on whether to execute an order of the Court granting bail to an accused person, the Inquiry Control Chambers of the Appeal Court of the South West Region[401] had this to say ***"My understanding of the above section of the law (Section 545(1) (2)) is that it behoves the Legal Department to execute court decisions whether they are in agreement with it or not. The Legal Department cannot refuse to execute a court order merely because they are aggrieved by it and have filed an appeal. To hold otherwise would mean that the Legal Department can review decisions of the court, thereby usurping the prerogatives of the Court of Appeal. Even if the law makes them a party, the Legal Department is only a party in a criminal action and nothing more...".*** To emphasize on the clear and unambiguous nature of this legal provision, the court had this to say:

"The catchwords in the above section of the law are 'subject to'. When something is said to be subject to another, it means it imposes a condition or an exception. The provisions of Section 545(2) of the CPC and Section 22 of the penal code are therefore exceptions to the provision of Section 547 of the CPC. It is therefore the position of the law that Court Orders especially decisions granting bail, should be executed immediately at the instance of the Legal Department whether they intend to file an appeal or not. I am emboldened in taking the stance considering the views expressed in a compilation by the Ministry of Justice captioned "Solutions proposed for some legal difficulties relating to the implementation of the CPC". On page 52, to that question the Ministry proposed the following answer: "pursuant to the provisions of Section 545 of the CPC, Presidents of all Courts shall ensure that the orders and judgments of their Courts are enforced. Once the documents to be enforced have been issued, they must be immediately signed, and forwarded to the Legal Department which shall execute them forthwith. The Legal Department shall not question the validity of the Documents issued".

[401]Lorencea. M. &1OR Vs. The People of Cameroon, (2016)1, CCLR PART 18, p. 34-36

Contained in the above answer is the official position of the Ministry of Justice, which I think, clinches the matter. And the choice of the word, 'forthwith' which connotes 'immediately' is also very instructive.

Since the Legal Department is supposed to represent the interest of the State and pursue the Nation's Judicial policy, it must be seen to respect the official prescription of the Ministry of Justice in given areas of the law.

Furthermore, I think it is necessary for the proper administration of justice and for the Court to efficiently play its adjudicatory role in the society to ensure that lawfully made orders of the Court are not rendered nugatory by action or conduct of the parties.

And as held in the Nigerian case JIM NWABODO V JOHN NWOBODO (2002) 2 A RR page 142- "

It is a serious matter for anyone to flout a positive order of a court and proceed to taunt the Court further by seeking remedy in a Higher Court while still in contempt of the lower court. I couldn't agree more!".

This instructive warning by the Inquiry Chambers to overzealous State Counsel though within the context of bail in the course of PI, equally applies to the excesses observed in cases of remand in police custody as was the case with the Kribi case. The State Counsel as many of his colleagues takes pleasure in flouting the very rules whose enforcement they are supposed to ensure.

In spite of the laudable measures put in place to ensure the respect of the rights of suspects in the course of investigation, challenges like the one above persists.

CHAPTER VIII
CHALLENGES TO THE RESPECT OF THE RIGHTS OF SUSPECTS

While admitting that the respect of the rights of persons remanded in police custody is far from been satisfactory, we observed that the unsatisfactory mark stemmed from structural institutional, instrumental as well as implementation obstacles. Such impediments can be classified into internal and external challenges.

I. INTERNAL CHALLENGES TO THE RESPECT OF THE RIGHT OF SUSPECTS

Internal obstacles referring to obstacles created by the JPO, that Impedes the respect of the rights of persons remanded in custody and external challenges referring to challenges which are independent of the will of legal practitioners thus incumbent to the state or other actors.

The internal challenges to the respect of the rights of persons remanded in police custody are caused by the lack of proper mastery of the provisions of the code as pertains to remand in custody, laxity by the hierarchy in control missions aimed at ensuring respect, corruption which has been deeply rooted in most sectors of the administration.

A. Reticence of Judicial Police Officers towards the CPC

Reticence has been observed as one of the causes of the non-respect of the rights of the suspect remanded in custody. Prior to the adoption of the CPC which is humanitarian in nature, the JPO under the "*Code d'Instruction Criminelle*" had exorbitant powers in thc conduct of investigations, be it through the flagrante delicto procedure or by way of investigations commenced by way of a complaint. With the coming into force of the CPC, which dissected the attributes hitherto recognized sorely to the JPO into two, giving a greater part of it to the State Counsel, the powers of the JPO to remand has been limited only to cases of offences committed flagrante delicto and conditioned as well. The old habit of the old procedure manifested by remand on the initiative of JPO in flagrant violation of the provisions of Section 118 (2 and 3) of the CPC has been difficult to do away with. Resistance in the words of an author[402] has taken a more violent form in some cases resulting to assault of Deputy State counsels who attempt to check excesses. Such was the case at the Third District Police station Yaoundé[403]. At times the reticence has taken the form of outright resistance of court decisions obtained by way of habeas corpus ordering the immediate release of persons illegally remanded as was the case in ***Ordonance N° 1/HC/PTGI/KRIBI of the 13th of February 2009***[404], as cited by Rose Djila[405]. This reticence can be attributed not only to the old habit that dies hard but to the absence of mastery of the procedure due to the absence of continuous training to this regard.

B. The Absence of Mastery of the Code in General

After more than a decade of the application of the CPC we observe with much consternation the reticence put up by the elements of investigating units with regards to the application of some provisions of the code, violating in passing the rights of the suspect. Such is the case with the ordering of remand in almost all offences irrespective of the gravity and nature of the offence. We came to the conclusion that the reticence observed was not only due to the procurement of undue gain but was justified by the lack of mastery of the provisions of the code, especially as regards the notion of remand in custody and the rights of the suspect attached thereto. This situation would have been salvaged if there was a rigid control of the activities of the elements especially as regards the respect of the rights of suspects remanded in custody.

---

[402] Ngai (C.), « La loi n° 2005/007 du 27 juillet 2005 portant code de procédure pénale : Excursion autour de la garde à vue », in *juridis périodique* n° 71 du Juillet – Aout – Septembre 2007, p. 114.

[403] Affaire MP et Olama Hubert c / Six policiers, TGI/Mfoundi , jugement N° 122/crim. Du 1er mars 1996.

[404] In this case the elements of the Public security station Kribi utterly refused to liberate the alternate member of parliament of the Ocean Division, remanded in custody for the 30th of January to the 13th of January 2009.

[405] Djila (R.), «Panorama de la jurisprudence des Cours et Tribunaux Camerounais en matière de libération immédiate », in, *Miroir de droit* n° 02 du Juillet – Aout – Septembre 2009, p. 14.

C. The Absence of Rigid Control

In spite of the reticence and the non-mastery of the provisions of the code as regards the rights of suspects remanded in police custody, we are of the opinion that the situation of the respect of the rights of suspects remanded in police custody would have been better off if the hierarchy with a better mastery, rigorously controlled the activities of their elements to this regards. It is surprising to note that with the institution of cell control, violations as regards exceeding the maximum duration of remand still exist. More surprising is the fact that most abusive remands are carried out during the weekends, with no records to this regard. Little or nothing has actually been done to eradicate such practices. It is no secret that a majority of cases are motivated by the urge of undue gain.

D. Corruption

Lack of mastery of the provisions of the CPC, reticence and lack of a rigid control only cannot justify the violation of the rights of the suspect remanded in police custody. It is common knowledge that over the years, the Customs Department, the Taxation Departments, and the Judiciary have been indexed as the most corrupt departments. Within the judiciary, the police have always been pointed as corrupt. The corruption is manifested not only by the harassments of transporters on our highways but in the course of investigations as well. A practical case is the exercise of illegal detention which is not only caused by reticence but by the desire to reap some financial benefits from same. It is evident that the ordering of remand in offences such as non-possession of identity card as well as the assaulting and sequestration of a Magistrate, cannot be justified by reticence or lack of mastery exclusively. Most of the cases of violation are motivated by the egocentric desire of the JPO which is none other than the extortion of sums of money.

Far from being internal, the causes of the violation of the rights of suspects remanded in police custody are external as well.

II. External Challenges to the respect of the rights of suspects during police investigation

It will be quite unfair to attribute the entire blame for the non-respect of the rights of the suspects remanded in police custody as provided for in the CPC, to the excesses of the JPO. The violation of the rights of suspects remanded in police custody can equally be ascribed to factors independent of their will. Such is the case with the lack of infrastructure, the absence of feeding, the absence of medical examination, etc.

A. The Absence of Adequate Infrastructure

Infrastructure plays a non-negligible role in the respect of the rights of suspects remanded in custody. The respect of the right to physical integrity entails not only that suspects should be remanded in structures which respect a minimum of comfort, but that gender and age should be respected as well. To this end, the law outrightly prohibits the remand of minors of 12 to 14 years of age except in cases of capital murder[406]. Where such measures are unavoidable, it must be executed in a borstal institute or in the case of remand in prison custody, in a special section of the prison meant for the detention of minors[407].The second paragraph of this section emphasizes on a separation between the minors and adults. By extension, one would have expected same treatment as regards the separation of minors and adults at the level of preliminary investigation. Surprisingly, in most cells in the country not only are minors detained in the same cell as adults, but in cells with reduced space as well. The cells lack basic facilities such as toilets. Detainees spend 8 days in custody without taking a single bath, defecating and urinating in buckets in the same cell at times while others eat. Such treatment is not only dehumanizing but equally fall below the minimum standard of human dignity as propounded by the Criminal Procedure Code. The poor infrastructural facilities are further compounded by the absence of a guaranteed source of feeding as ensured by the code.

---

[406]Section 704(1) of the CPC.
[407]Section 706 of the CPC.

B. The Non-Compliance of the State to its Feeding Obligation

Feeding is one of the essential and fundamental needs of every human being, whose supply must not be suspended in case of remand in custody. It is in line with this reasoning that the CPC in its humanising perspective made the provision of feeding to suspects an obligation of the state.[408] This provision, however, authorises friends, relatives to supplement the said supply. Unfortunately, this laudable legislative act is still to be concretised by a modification of the budget of the Police or the Gendarmerie to meet up with the obligation. Feeding has become the sole prerogative of friends, family members and well-wishers. Detainees without relatives or friends are left at the mercy of good will Cameroonians and co-detainees. Some go for days without eating.

C. The Absence of Medical Examination

The rights to medical examination of persons remanded in custody has as objective among others to ensure the quality of treatment reserved for persons remanded in custody, considering the fact that by virtue of the provisions of section 122, suspects are supposed to be treated humanely. The law provides that persons remanded in custody may at any moment be examined by a medical officer appointed by the state counsel of his own motion. It further provides that this officer can be assisted by another chosen by the person on remand at his own expense[409]. Paragraph 4 of the same provision makes it obligatory for medical examination to be carried out at the end of remand but curiously this provision makes the person remanded liable for the expenses of the examination. For a measure which is so fundamental, since it helps in evaluating the quality of treatment given to persons remanded in custody, one would have expected that it be done systematically and at the expense of the state. The absence of this measure which constitutes a violation of the rights of suspects makes it very difficult for persons remanded in police

---

[408]Section 122(4) of the CPC.
[409]Section 123 of the CPC.

custody to show evidence of degrading and inhuman treatment as in the case of torture.

D. The controversial Role of the State Counsel in the Control of Regularity of Remand in Custody

As aforementioned, the State Counsel is at the same time one of the authorities endowed with the power of ordering the remand in custody of persons. At the same time, he has been vested with the powers to control the regularity of same, coupled with the fact that he is a party to the procedure. In his capacity of hierarchical superior[410], the State Counsel becomes at the same time Judge and party. He is placed in the delicate position where he has to control himself. An author[411] notes that no matter his great capacities and human qualities, such control renders auto-sanction very difficult and even illusory. The author[412] in the same line of reasoning thinks that considering the implication of the State Counsel in the work of the JPO, it is necessary to oust him from the control of regularity, proposing that the said control would have been better off with the Examining Magistrate, who is more independent than the former. The pertinence of the observation of these authors was evident in the Kribi case cited above wherein the state counsel connived with JPOs, to obstruct the execution of "*Ordonance*"[413] N° 1/HC/PTGI/KRIBI of the 13th of February 2009 ordering the immediate liberation of one Mbonga Mauger by way of habeas corpus. The urgency of a more independent organ of control is justified by the constant and flagrante violation of the rights of persons remanded in custody by the ambiguous mechanism of "*soit fait retour*". A measure over which nobody has control, and which renders the duration of remand almost limitless. A measure which according to Edouard Kitio[414], calls for regulation by the legislative power.

---

[410]Section 78 (2) of the CPC.

[411] Ongolo (J.E.), op. cit., p.33.

[412]Dountsop (Ph.R.), « La flagrance des crimes et délits dans le code Camerounaise de procédure pénale », in *Les tendances de la procédure pénale camerounaise*, Yaoundé, Presses Universitaires d'Afrique, (novembre 2007), p.50.

[413] An « ordonnance » within the common law context is a ruling.

[414]Ibid. p.109.

E. The Ambiguous Notion of "known place of abode"

The notion of known place of abode is an open gate of violation. The lawmakers, inspired from the western system in its conception of this notion, did not take into consideration the chaotic nature of our urbanisation. Streets and houses are not named and numbered. As such tracing a suspect in such a context is an uphill task. To further compound issues the CPC does not give any definition of the notion of known place of abode. The imprecision created by the absence of a definition as well as the impossibility of its application in the present state of our urbanisation has created a vacuum which is exploited negatively by JPO to order remand even for offences such as renting fraud[415].

F. The Ineffectiveness of the National Commission of Human Rights and other NGO's

The National Commission on Human Rights created by Decree N° 90/1459 of the 8th day of November 1990 has as main mission the defence and promotion of human rights. Article 2 of the Decree cited above, gives it the possibility of proceeding with investigations in all places where persons are remanded, proceeding with interrogation and confrontation. However, this control is subject to the authorisation of one of its author i.e. the State Counsel who happens to be a main actor as regards remand. One wonders how this is possible, considering the fact that no right-thinking State Counsel will authorise the commission to control its excesses. Whereas, the proper implementation of this text would have considerably contributed to the protection of the rights of suspects in the course of investigations. On the field, its role and that of other NGO's assigned the same mission is almost absent in spite of the grievous violations registered daily and nationwide. This situation is worsened by its very fragile set up which in essence has no means of constraint on defaulters. Its role is limited to recommendations and proposals which always end up in the drawers. This is quite evident in what has been referred to as the Anglophone crises. After the visits of the

[415]Section 322(1) of the Penal Code.

commission led by its Chairman, to the North and South West Regions with a lamentable situation of violation of human rights, a report of its mission was forwarded to the presidency with proposals on the way forward. It is worth noting that the commission was not granted access to some cells and penitentiary structures and was not even given audience to some of the suspects arrested. The government has been silent over all the reports submitted.

CHAPTER IX
THE LEGAL DEPARTMENT AND PROSECUTION

According to Carlson A. [416] the philosophy underlying prosecution is that anti-social conduct must be punished. Since anti-social behaviour threatens the very fabric of society, the suppression of such conduct is a matter of public interest for society as a whole. Consequently, the right to exact punishment or to refrain from doing so is the sole prerogative of the society or the state. But since society or the State can only act through natural persons, it has delegated its powers to prosecute offenders to certain qualified persons in the community styled "public prosecutors" or "State prosecutors" or better still State Counsels within the context of the CPC.

To this regards the Legal Department enjoys a seemingly absolute monopoly in the institution and prosecution of criminal proceeding. It is perhaps by dint of this monopoly that all police reports are destined to the said Department, excepting police reports of investigations within the jurisdiction of the military Tribunal. On the grounds of the said police reports the Legal Department alone prepares the charge, initiate criminal proceedings, and conduct prosecution. The monopoly of the Legal Department is more evident by its discretion as regards prosecution.

I. THE LEGAL DEPARTMENT AND PROSECUTORIAL DISCRETION

Prosecutorial discretion or better still "*opportunité de poursuite*" is one of the fundamental principles of prosecution. The rationale behind this principle according to Carlson A.[417] stems from the conviction that no society will tolerate a rule of compulsory prosecution which is absolute and so relentless that the State Prosecutor was required to institute criminal proceedings in each and every case, no matter how weak the incriminating evidence. The State Prosecutor must therefore have the power to evaluate the evidence in advance of instituting a prosecution. If he is

[416]Anyangwe (C.), op.cit. p.85.
[417]Ibid., p.86

convince that a suspect's conduct did not violate the criminal law or that the evidence cannot persuade the court of the suspects' guilt, he serves the social interest by not wasting resources on a futile and frivolous criminal trial and by not subjecting the defendant to its many discomforts.

Just like every human endeavour the State Counsel in the execution of his prosecutorial discretion is not immune from error, which according to an author[418] is a routine hazard of decision making, not liable to calling to doubt the wisdom of the State Counsel in the exercise of discretion which is necessary and desirable.

The discretion of the State Counsel to prosecute or not is derived from the facts contained in the police report. He must not prosecute all charges for which there is sufficient evidence. Likewise, he may with absolute impunity decline to prosecute even in case of provable criminal liability. In principle a prosecutor is expected to prosecute where he is convinced there is sufficient evidence to sustain the prosecution.

Still it remains true that the State Counsel is free to select and does in fact select among cases those he shall prosecute and those not. He in fact picks and chooses which law he will enforce against which violators. Much depends on the degree of social harm done. It may be either small or significant[419].

A. The Materialisation of Prosecutorial Discretion "l'opportunité de poursuite"

The prosecutorial discretion of the Legal department is materialised by the faculty of the legal Department to either close a matter in chambers or by the procedure of "*correctionalisation*".

1. Closure of matters in Chambers

The Legal Department after receiving a police report wherein there is sufficient ingredients of the commission of an offence can either proceed with the identification of the offences contained therein and preferring a charge or close same in

[418] Ibid.
[419] Ibid.

chambers. Closing a police report entails initially that one, two or more offences could be identified, and the suspect brought before the Court. It equally entails that for some personal reasons the State Prosecutor single handedly decides not to prosecute. In recent practice, closure of police reports in chambers are supposed to be grounded in substance and in law, with a copy of the decision notified on the complainant through the investigating unit. The legal nature of this decision of closure however raises some legal issues. Can an aggrieved party appeal against such a decision? Can an aggrieved party after having been duly notified set in motion criminal action by private prosecution? If a judgment against which an appeal can be lodged is defined as a decision by a court or other tribunal that resolves a controversy and determines the rights and obligations of the parties, then the decision of the Legal Department is not a judgment and cannot be appealed against, it simply serves as information to the parties. It is not covered by the principle of res judicata as laid down in the provisions of Section 62(e) of the CPC. If it is established that it is not a judgment, it goes without saying that an aggrieved party can alternatively make use of private prosecution. The idea of motivation of closures in our opinion reduces the prosecutorial discretion of the Legal Department since such closures must be reasoned henceforth. If aggrieved parties can alternatively detour this discretion, then its raison d'être is gradually being eroded.

2. Prosecutorial discretion and "correctionalisation"

According to an author[420] the prosecutorial discretion of the Legal Department is equally materialised by the possibility of "*correctionalisation*". "*Correctionalisation*" is a procedure by which the prosecutor overlooks the aggravating circumstance of a felony[421] for the purpose of transforming samc into a misdemeanour[422]. One of the consequences of this act of

[420] Mpinda (F)., *Le procureur de la république au Cameroun*, PUA, 2016, p.31

[421] Section 21(1) (a) of the penal code "a felony shall mean an offence punishable with death or with loss of liberty for a minimum of more than 10 (ten) years and a fine where the law so provides"

[422] Section 21(1) (b) of the penal code " a misdemeanour shall mean an offence punishable with loss of liberty or fine, where thc loss of liberty may be for more than 10 (ten) days but not for more than 10(ten) years and a fine of more than 25000 FCFA (twcnty-fivc thousand).

prosecutorial discretion is relieving the Examining Magistrate of jurisdiction of a matter and prosecuting same by way of direct summons. While stating that this attribute is not *ex nihilo*, thus contestable, Ferry Armand cautions that the tolerance of the State Prosecutor must be justified by elements such as the personality of the suspect, his sincerity, the singular as well as the comprehensible nature of the offence, provocation by the victim.

B. Reasons for Prosecutorial Discretion

The reasons for the attribution of the powers of prosecutorial discretion to the state counsel Stated by Carlson Anyangwe[423], as listed by Ewang Sone[424] in its diversity can be summarised in, the need for efficient management of resources, the safeguard of public function, the need for objectivity as well as the preservation of public policy and diplomatic ties

1. The need for efficient management of resources

According to his analyses no prosecutor has available sufficient means to prosecute all offences brought to his knowledge. Realistically there are insufficient investigating units to investigate and prosecute every criminal act that occurs.

In the same line the triviality of the offences committed may equally account for the uses of prosecutorial discretion by the State Counsel. Triviality in this case refers to petty offences which by nature do not involve a high degree of moral guilt and the social harm done is generally slight. In this case the prosecutor serves general interest. He however emphasizes that public interest will require that even the petty offences committed with exceptional frequency be prosecuted or if the suspect is a recidivist.

[423]Carlson A. op.cit., pp.92-93.

[424]Ewang (S.), Can a State Prosecutor discontinue a private prosecution by entering a nolle prosequi? E.NEKO V. Sam Mofor (1971) Appeal N° WCCA/11/71, unreported-judgment per O'Brien Quinn. in jurisdis périodique N° 31, p.41-42

2. **The safeguard of public functions**

Matters in which high personalities are implicated such as members of government, diplomats, members of parliament, member of the judiciary (magistrates). Such cases require leave of the Minister of Justice to prosecute.

3. **The pursuit of objectivity**

A State prosecutor would refuse to prosecute an offence which falls within the classes of offences for which prior complaint of the victim is required. Such is the case of offences such as invasion of residence, abuse, incest, adultery, and desertion.

The need to evaluate each case on its merit, account for the enormous power, given to the Prosecutor. Public interest is best served, and justice is best dispensed not by mechanical application of the letter of the law, but by a flexible and individualised application of its norms through the exercise of a prosecutor's thoughtful discretion.

The fear of being charged for malicious prosecution can equally hamper the prosecution of offences. Malicious prosecution is the most common form of tort of abuse of legal procedure which is available against persons who deliberately abuse the legal process in order to harm another.

The Prosecutor will probably not prosecute where the offender had acted out of a particularly laudable motive, although as a general rule motive does not affect criminal responsibility. If the commission was motivated by compassion or praise worthy motives, the State Prosecutor may not prosecute.

4. **Preservation of Public policy and diplomatic ties**

It is doubtful if prosecution would be instituted where it is clear that such an action would lead to public indignation and riot.

Diplomatic or even economic considerations certainly weigh in the prosecutor's mind when deciding whether to prosecute or not in certain cases. More harm than good may be done to the public in attempting to prosecute in certain circumstances. If an offence had already been punished in a foreign country or if prosecution might jeopardise foreign relations, the Prosecutor would most likely not prosecute.

Likewise, if prosecution would require divulging state secret or if it would endanger national security.

The state counsel in his monopoly in the institution and prosecution of offences does not monopolise discretion to prosecute or not to prosecute.

II. THE DISCRETION OF THE MINISTER IN CHARGE OF JUSTICE TO DISCONTINUANCE OF CRIMINAL PROCEEDINGS (NOLLE PROSEQUI)

The principle of hierarchical subordination imposes on the State Counsel the obligation of reporting prior to prosecution in certain matters. Prosecution in such cases is subject to the explicit approval of the minister. All State Counsels are under obligation to inform the Minister via the PG of all matters of a certain importance notably:

(a) matters relating to the security of the state and to repression of subversive activities;

(b) all matters involving;

  i. Parliamentarians, ex-parliamentarians, Mayors, and traditional rulers

  ii. Senior Divisional Officers, Sub-Divisional Officers and all high-ranking civil servants as a whole;

  iii. Law officers as a whole and those with the status of law officers

(c) Matters which though falling under the common law jurisdiction, present an exceptional character or gravity (i.e. mutiny among different ethnic groups)

The discretion of the Ministry of Justice in this domain is not only mandatory but extensive as well. The law makers in the construction of the ministerial discretion as regards prosecution in the CPC[425] simply copied the provisions of section 73-75 of the former Criminal Procedure Ordinance which deals with the power of the prosecutor to enter a nolle prosequi in criminal matters at any stage of the proceedings before judgement.

[425] Section 64(1) The Procureur General of a Court of Appeal may by express authority of the Minister in charge of Justice, enter a nolle prosequi at any stage before judgment on the merit is delivered, if such proceeding could seriously imperil social interest and public order.

The North West Court of Appeal[426], responding to the issue on whether a defendant can be granted bail after restituting the corpus delicti, highlighted the importance and extent of the ministerial discretion in the following words ***"In the instant case, the appellant has restituted the money misappropriated. Section 18(2)new of the 2012 Law states that where the corpus delicti is restituted, the territorial competent Procureaur General subject to a written authorisation by the Minister of Justice, may enter a nolle prosequi against prosecution prior to committal order before the trial court. By this section it does not mean that when the corpus delicti is restituted, the normal procedure to be followed shall automatically come to an end. No!! The accused shall remain in custody. The prosecution of the accused can only come to an end, when the Procureur General enters a nolle prosequi. The nolle prosequi is at the discretion of the Minister of Justice. It implies that one could even pay back the misappropriated funds and he might not authorise the entry of a nolle prosequi in that person's favour. Furthermore, subsection (1) and (2) of that section are for the time being in abeyance. This is because the modalities for the restitution of the corpus delicti have not yet been put in place by rules and regulations as provided in subsection (3). So, it was wrong of the Examining Magistrate to twist the law in favour of the respondent and grant him bail".***

Furthermore, the CPC does not give that latitude to the State Counsel to withdraw a matter for which hearing has already been opened. The PG has been empowered to do so at 'any stage' before judgement on the merit, on the express authorisation of the Minister and where social interest and public order are at stake. Keubou sees this incursion through the mechanism of nolle prosequi as a means of stifling judicial powers and serving egoistic interest. Questioning why such powers when the Ministry of Justice disposes of prosecutorial discretion[427]. The consequence is that if the State Counsel who is on the field notices traces of peril of social interest or public order as per this

---

[426] The People of Cameroon Vs Tanoh Lawrence Ndangoh, Suit NO.CANWR/ICC/6C/2012 SLR, 4 (2016),p. 14

[427] Keubou (Ph.), op.cit., pp. 89.

provision, he cannot act, he simply informs the minister through the PG and wait for instructions.

Apart from the incursion of the Minister in charge of Justice into the prosecutorial discretion of the Legal Department, the CPC has greatly limited the discretional powers of the Legal Department by the institution of privileged proceedings wherewith the Legal Department must henceforth conform, without any possibility of swaying.

III. OTHER LIMITS TO THE PROSECUTORIAL DISCRETION OF THE STATE COUNSEL

The prosecutorial discretion of the Legal Department cannot be exercised over privileged proceedings, offences over which only victims can set in motion criminal proceeding and private prosecution as well as complaints with civil claim.

A. Privileged Proceedings

Privilege proceedings is not new to the Cameroonian legal framework; it existed in the CIC applicable in the French parts of the country prior to the promulgation of law N° 2005 of the 27 July 2005 instituting the CPC. This privilege which was limited to magistrates[428], has been extended to administrative authorities. The rationale behind the extension is the protection of State representatives within a global context and not just Magistrates, with the inconveniences that it covers both offences committed in the execution of their duties and that committed out of this context.

1. Magistrates and Privileged Proceedings

The CPC far from just identifying protected officials, lays down rules of procedure to be followed which drifts from the regular investigating and even prosecuting canon instituted by law. The CPC as regards magistrates in its part X titled, "privileged proceedings" explicitly provides that "where a judicial or legal officer is likely to be charged with committing an offence, the competent PG shall request the President of the Supreme Court to

---

[428] Article 479 CIC.

appoint an investigation Magistrate as well as three Magistrates of a grade at least equal to that of the magistrate incriminated and they shall, if necessary, hear and determine the matter at first instance"[429]. Paragraph 2 stresses on the fact that in addition, he shall indicate the town wherein the case shall be heard.

The jurisdiction of the Magistrate so appointed extends throughout the national territory[430], and in the event of appeal, the matter is heard by the judges of the Supreme Court appointed by the president of the said court and sitting as a collegiate bench[431].

When the Magistrate prosecuted is the most senior in the highest grade, his case shall be heard by a joint session of the Bench of the Supreme Court[432]. As lofty as this provision may seem, its implementation poses a serious problem.

On the 20th of February 2017 at the heart of the Anglophone crises an Advocate General of the Supreme Court, Justice Ayah Paul still on duty was whisked off his residence *manu- militari,* by elements of the Gendarmerie. He was remanded in police custody at the Secretariat for Defence where he spent hundreds of days in gross and flagrante violation of the aforementioned provisions[433]. However, prosecutorial discretion was later applied in his favour including Barrister Agbor Balla, Dr. Fontem Neba and 52 others arrested under similar circumstances. Proceedings at the Military Tribunal against them were stopped by the use of nolle prosequi[434].

2. Administrative authorities and privilege proceedings

Where the Governor of a Region has committed a felony or misdemeanour, within or outside the performance of his duties, the PG at the competent Court of Appeal addresses a report to the President of the Supreme Court who transfers the matter to a competent court[435].

---

[429] Section 629 CPC.
[430] Section 631 CPC.
[431] Section 632 CPC.
[432] Section 633 CPC.
[433] Reported in *The Horizon newspaper*, titled: « will Ayah Paul be revoked from Magistracy as he clocks four months in detention?» of May 30, 2017, p.2
[434] Reported by *The Horizon newspaper*; titled « Anglophone crisis : Ayah Paul Abine and 54 other persons freed from detention » of September 25, 2017, p. 2
[435] Section 634 CPC

The same procedure applies to Senior Divisional Officers or any other head of administrative unit or a judicial police officer after the commission of a felony or misdemeanour not connected to the exercise of his duties. The State Counsel transmits the case file to the competent PG, who in turn seizes the President of the competent Court of Appeal. The later designates the Legal Department in charge of instituting prosecution and the competent trial Court to hear the matter.[436] Investigations and trials in the cases mentioned here above are assigned to jurisdictions other than those where they exercise their duties[437]. The Courts have given a strict interpretation to the geographical limits of privileged proceedings according to which it covers only the space where they exercise their duties, meaning an administrative authority (Divisional Officer) can be tried within the same Division but in a subdivision other than that where he exercises his duties[438].

Most practitioners have consistently and erroneously linked privileged proceedings to administrative litigation, submitting same under the same conditions of prior complaint of the victim to the hierarchy of the administrative authority even when it comes to criminal action. The Court of Appeal of the North West Region[439] précised the domain and context of the application of privileged proceedings to administrative officers in the following words:

"The suit that was instituted against 1st appellant was a criminal action for violation of some provisions of the Penal Code. It was not an administrative litigation. According to section 1 of the Penal Code "all persons shall be subject to the criminal law". However, certain persons benefit from immunities. The 1st appellant is not one of these. That notwithstanding, certain persons cannot be prosecuted directly. The 1st appellant is one of such persons. To prosecute him, the procedure laid down in Section 634(2) (3) on privileged

---

[436] Section 634(2) CPC

[437] Section 634(3) CPC

[438] See TPI d'Akonolinga, jug. Du 20 septembre 2007, MP et Ebalo Fombo Emmanuel c. Bissack Emmanuel, n° 239/cor/ADD, cited by Mahouvé (M.) and Kembo (H.T.), Supra. p. 57.

[439] Nguelle Nguelle Felix & Sakiri Usmanu alias Sarkiri usman Balarabe, Suit N0.CANWR/MS/35C/2014 SLR 4 (2016), p .93-95

proceedings must be followed. This is exactly what happened before the 1st appellant found himself in the Court of First Instance Fundong. This (section 3(1) law N° 2006/22 on the organisation and functioning of the administrative Court) provides for the institution of civil suits against decentralised public authorities and local administrative authorities for acts committed by their employees in the course of their employment. However, the matter before the court below was not a civil suit against the administration. It was a criminal action that involved the personal criminal responsibility of the 1st appellant. Moreover, the issue was not raised in the court below, nor was it a ground of appeal. As counsel for the 2nd respondent submitted pursuant to Section 545(1) of the CPC, it is not opened to this court to decide on it because it is a fresh issue that was not raised by the appellant in the lower court. It was not one of the issues raised in the preliminary objections. The issue raised in the preliminary objection were within the competence of the court following section 296(1) of the CPC, the Court had to decide on them. Again the court was not under a duty to as stipulated in section 14(1) of the 2006/022 law, supra, to send the case to the Administrative Bench of the Supreme Court to determine the issues of administrative trespass as appellant's counsel argued".

The Court contrary to the argument of counsel for the appellants that case file in privileged proceedings must be one prepared by the judicial police and forwarded to the State Counsel for the institution of prosecution, held that this position was not only oblique but fallacious as well, stating that everybody is at liberty to choose the mode of commencement of criminal proceedings against an accused person and if a victim opted for direct prosecution he will not obviously pass through the Judicial police officer.

B. The Victim and the Setting in Motion of Prosecution: A Limitation to the Prosecutorial Discretion of the Legal Department

According to Mahouvè Michel and Hermine Kembo[440] the law makers in the construction of the CPC, while focusing on the rights of the suspect, accused or defendant, did not set aside the rights of the victim. The rights of the victim were taken into consideration by the transposition of the Romano-German system which admits the participation of the victim in criminal proceedings, even though with some traces of common law. According to these authors the influence of the victim in criminal proceedings is materialised by the acknowledgement of a right permitting him both to set in motion criminal action as well as bringing same to an end. To this end the law makers have facilitated the victim's access to criminal justice. The victim can henceforth set in motion criminal action either by private prosecution or by the filling of a complaint with a civil claim.

1. Private Prosecution

Private prosecution, just like a complaint with a civil claim gives the possibility to the victims of offences not only to surpass the inertia of JPO and the Legal Department but equally limits the prosecutorial discretion of the Legal Department in criminal matters. In the English speaking Regions of the country, the commencement of criminal action by private prosecution was subject to the approval of the Procureur General who had powers to discontinue any criminal proceedings commenced by whoever at any stage before judgement[441]. Any contravention to this rule could be counteracted by the entering of a nolle prosequi as was the case in F.NEko v. Sam Mofor, WACA/11/71, 1971, (unreported).

Section 290 of the CPC, provides that "criminal proceedings in the Court of First Instance shall be commenced by a committal order of the Examining Magistrate, an order of the inquiry control chambers, by "direct summons" or by application of the procedure relating to offences committed flagrante delicto.

---

[440]Mahouvé (M.) and Kembo (H.T.), op.cit.,.p. 422-433.

[441]S. 10(1) of Law N° 66/LF/3 of the 10th June 1966 as read with Section 73(1) of the CPO.

Criminal action engaged by the civil party in addition to setting in motion criminal proceedings gives him the possibility of choosing the judge in his matter. As a matter of fact, he fixes the date of the court session in the bailiff's act. This mode of commencement is limited to misdemeanours solely.

a. Components of a private prosecution

Direct summons in this context is issued at the request of the aggrieved party, who is the civil party[442], on the person, at his place of work, at his residence, at the mayor's office or the legal Department [443]. A direct summons contains the following elements: the date of service, the full name, affiliation, date and place of birth, occupation, address, residence and where necessary the address for service, the full names and address of the bailiff. It as well, states the full name, affiliation, and full address of the civil party who in this case is the addressee and particularly his residence or place of work. It further states the facts of the case and the provisions of the law under which the accused is charged, the court seized of the matter, place date, hour of hearing[444]. The civil party who institutes criminal action by private prosecution chooses an address for service to himself within the jurisdiction of the court if he is residence elsewhere[445]. Service of direct summons by the Bailiff is effected under the same conditions as ordinary summons[446]. Among the components of a direct summons features the payment of deposit and stamp duty whose presence is not only problematic but ambiguous as well.

b. The ambiguous notions of deposit and stamp duty of direct summons

A court is said to have been properly seized with a direct summons if and only if the following complementary conditions are fulfilled; the payment of a deposit at the registry of the court as well as the stamp duty of the direct summons at the Taxation

[442] Section 40(3) CPC.
[443] Section 40(4) CPC.
[444] Section 41(1) (2) CPC.
[445] Section 42 CPC.
[446] Section 43-542CPC.

Department. If the exigency of the payment of a deposit is well spelt out in the CPC as regards complaint with civil claim[447], such is not the case with direct summons. Even though the payment as well as the obligation of stamp duty is mandatory throughout the National territory there is no legal provision to that effect. In the absence of a similar provision as regards direct summons the legality of the defrayment of the said sum is being contested in the Regions that hitherto applied the CPO, who in the words of Mahouvè Michel and Hermine Kembo [448] are "discovering" this mode of commencement of criminal proceedings.

This difficulty as stated by the aforementioned author was raised by Chief Justice L. Asuagbor during the seminar on "The implementation of the CPC, with reference to the difficulties encountered at the hearing, recovery of fines and cost and the effective functioning of the criminal record index" [449]. They, however, note that in the former laws of the francophone part of the country the payment of the said deposit was provided for by article 151 of decree of 5 October 1920 on the regulation of court fees in felonies, misdemeanours and simple offences. In the absence of a special instrument fixing court fees in respect of felonies, misdemeanours and simple offences as provided for by the provisions of section 744 of the CPC, is the implementation of this decree not repugnant? Section 746 of the same Code which explicitly spells out the legal instruments that shall be considered repugnant does not make mention of the said decree. This list to our mind simply states a limited number of previous provisions that are repugnant among many others. This can be deduced by the use of the phrase "in particular" which in essence does not denote exhaustive. Whatever the case, direct summons just like the complaint with a civil claim breaks the prosecutorial discretion of the Legal Department.

---

[447] Section 158 (1) « The victim who sets the criminal action in motion by virtue of section 157(1) shall at the risk of his complaint being inadmissible deposit at the registry of the court of first instance an amount considered sufficient to defraying the cost of the proceedings »

[448] Ibid.

[449] This presentation was done on the occasion of the heads of courts meeting held in Yaoundé on the 27-30 October 2009 , p.6.

2. Complaint with a Civil Claim, a Limit to the Prosecutorial Discretion of the Legal Department

Any person who alleges that he has suffered injury resulting from a felony or a misdemeanour may when lodging a complaint with the competent Examining Magistrate file a claim for damage. The complaint in which a victim claims damages set criminal action in motion[450].

a. The domain of complaint with civil claim

A complaint with a civil claim expressly excludes certain offences such as simple offences or offences whose prosecution is solely reserved for the Legal Department[451]. The CPC does not state the category of offences that are excluded by this provision. Ferry Armand[452]cites a case wherein the Examining Magistrate of the Bertoua Court of First Instance declared a complaint inadmissible grounded on the argument that article 318(1) of the customs code of CEMAC reserves the setting in motion of criminal action to the Legal Department. In this matter a certain group (Groupement actif des douanes de l'Est) filed a complaint with a civil claim against an unknown for contraband.

Mbunja Yohanes[453] equally brings out the case where a complaint with civil claim is excluded as means of commencement by the text itself. Such is the case with article 147 of Law N° 94/01 of 20th January 1994 on forestry, fauna and fishery which permits the administration of forestry to "cause to be summoned" all offenders of the offences that it sanctions. He cites the case where the Supreme Court held that an Examining Magistrate seized of the matter by complaint with a civil claim by the said administration lacked jurisdiction *ratione materiae*[454]. Pertaining to simple offences, he poses a practical issue raised. What will be the attitude of an Examining Magistrates seized by a complaint with a civil claim whose findings end up with a simple offence? Will he pass an order of refusal or an order of

[450] Section 157 (1) (2) CPC
[451] Section 157 (3) CPC
[452] Mpinda (F.), op.cit., pp.201
[453]Mbunja (Y.), op.cit., p.64-67
[454] CS, arrêt n0 28/P du 27 Mai 2010, Aff. Hazim Marcel et Samir Camil El Chamas c/ MP et Etat du Cameroun (MINFI), inédit.

inadmissibility? We share his opinion on this issue. It will be proper for an Examining Magistrate faced with this impediment to pass an order declaring the procedure inadmissible.[2]

b. Elements of a complaint with a civil claim

In addition to establishing that he has suffered injury, a civil claimant must deposit at the registry of the Court of First Instance an amount considered sufficient to defraying the cost of the proceeding[455], an amount which can be increased in the course of the proceedings. The procedure is however subjected to the approval of the State Counsel who may declare the civil claim inadmissible, order for the commencement of inquiry against a known or unknown person[456]. The transmission of the case file to the State Counsel is an obligation. Whatever the case, it remains a deviation to the prosecutorial discretion of the State Counsel.

[455] Even though the law provides that the deposit is destined to defraying the cost of the proceedings, controversy still persists on the use of the said sum. In most jurisdictions, it is common to find civil claimant who after paying considerable sums as deposit are still constrained to defray supplementary sums for visits to the locus inquo, whereas the deposit which can comfortably support the full cost of the visit is at the registry of the Court untouched. More disturbing is the destination of such sums which are hardly ever used.

[456] Section 160(1) (2)

CHAPTER X
OBSTACLES TO THE INSTITUTION OF CRIMINAL PROCEEDINGS

It is a principle at law that everybody is equal before the law. This principle is not however absolute, there exist limitations to this principle which fundamentally constitutes immunity accorded to certain political personalities and at times obstacles to prosecution are created by the law itself.

I. IMMUNITY

Philippe Keubou[457] defines immunity in this context as facts which while maintaining an offence, renders prosecution inadmissible (not applicable to the civil). He distinguishes the political, judiciary, family, and diplomatic immunities.

A. Political Immunity

Political immunity in this context involves or benefits the President of the Republic and Parliamentarians.

1. The President of the Republic

According to the provisions of Article 53(1) (2) and (3) of the Constitution of 18th January 1996, the Court of Impeachment in respect to acts committed in the exercise of his duties shall have jurisdiction to try the President of the Republic for high treason solely. Acts committed by the president pursuant to Article 5, 8, 9 and 10 of the Constitution are covered by immunity and he is not accountable for them even after the exercise of his functions.

This same provision provides that the Prime Minister, members of government and other persons ranking as such, and senior government official to whom powers have been delegated can be tried before this court for conspiracy against the security of the state. The constitution does not expressly or implicitly grant immunity to these categories of personalities in the exercise of their functions as well.

[457] Keubou (Ph.), op.cit.,, p. 77.

Trial against the President of the Republic for high treason is not instantaneous; it can only be commenced after an indictment by the National Assembly and the Senate deciding through an identical vote by open ballot and by a four fifth majority of their members.

The immunity of the President of the Republic as regards the commission of common law offences is absolute. He can neither be tried for such offences in the course of his mandate or thereafter.

2. Parliamentary Immunity

Parliamentary immunity is governed by the provisions of Article 1 of Ordinance N° 72-12 of 26th August 1972 on the immunity of parliamentarians of the National Assembly. Parliamentarians enjoy immunity for written or oral speech made during parliamentary sessions, seating in plenary session or in commissions. This immunity extends to opinions expressed out of the vicinity of the National Assembly but expressed within the framework of the exercise of his duty as parliamentarian.

Such was the case with the famous resistance speech of the honourable member of parliament of Jakiri special constituency during the plenary session of October 2016. In his speech he accused East Cameroon of gross marginalisation against the west Cameroonians insisting that the administrators of East Cameroon comported themselves in West Cameroon[458] as 'occupational colonial forces'. This according to him was manifested by the violation of basic right, rape, and torture and most significantly by the complete wiping off of the Anglo-Saxon culture through an imposition of the French sub system of education in west Cameroon as well as the adulteration of the common law system by the civil law system. In his famous

[458] It should be noted that following the Douala treaty of 12th July 1884, Germany annexed Cameroon. Thirty years later, in 1916, the Germans were defeated and forced out of the territory by English and French led forces who proceeded to the partition of Cameroon, under the authority of the League of Nations. After the demise of the League of Nations and the birth of the United Nations, the French and British authorities maintained their interest in Cameroon and administered same. After the independence of French Cameroon on the 1st January 1960 and the granting of independence to British Cameroon through reunification on the 1st October 1961, Cameroon adopted a federal system of government wherein French Cameroon was referred to as East Cameroon and British Cameroon as West Cameroon.

statement "**when injustice becomes a law resistance becomes a duty**"[459] he called on all west Cameroonians to resist the "occupational colonial forces".

To many observers, the speech of the honourable Member of Parliament of Jakari was an apology of secession. A warrant of arrest was purportedly issued by the Delegate General for National Security for the apprehension of Joseph Wirba. On the 11th April, the Vice President of the SDF parliamentary group Honourable Joseph Mbah Ndam held a press conference during which he urged the House Speaker to ensure that the parliamentary immunity of his colleague is not tampered with. He also called on the House Speaker to protect the escapee House member and make sure he returns home without being arrested[460]. Honourable Wirba Joseph however resurfaced during the June 2018 session and while addressing the National Assembly, stated that he has come to continue from where he stopped. He accused the President of the House for failing to protect him from the purported warrant, and insisted that he has been in hiding for the past 3 months for fear of being arrested and molested by the 'occupational forces of East Cameroon'[461]. It should be noted that the said warrant has never been executed nor has any criminal proceedings been engaged against the honourable Member of Parliament though he has been conspicuously absent in the last two sessions.

Parliamentary immunity which is personal and does not extend to family members equally means that no member of parliament can be arrested or tried during a session for committing a misdemeanour or a felony. The arrest or trial of a parliamentarian under such circumstances must be preceded by a prior authorisation of the National Assembly. Authorisations in this sense consist in the uplifting of parliamentary immunity. Immunity can be uplifted by the National Assembly, if it is in session or by the Bureau of the National Assembly when the National Assembly is not seating. Parliamentary immunity does

---

459 Citing one of the pioneer American President Thomas Jefferson who is actually the author of the slogan expressed within the context of the declaration of American independence.

460 See, *The horizon newspaper* of April 20, 2017, titled, Anglophone crisis : «SDF MPS disavow Fru Ndi, says Wirba should be protected» , p. 2

461 Reported in The Post weekender, N° 01830 of June 23, 2017.

not cover simple offences, misdemeanours or felonies committed flagrante delicto, out of the ambits of their official duties and the law does not provide for the authorisation of the National Assembly. The National Assembly has on several occasions uplifted the immunity of some of its members. Such was the case with the Member of Parliament of the Balikumbat constituency, Fon Doh Gah Gwanyim, who was prime suspect in the murder case of John Kohtem, the representative of the SDF party, his political adversary. His immunity was uplifted on the 14th February 2005 by the Bureau of the National Assembly. On the 12th April, he was sentenced by the Ngoketunjia High Court to serve a 15 year's imprisonment term. On appeal, he and the co-accused were granted bail and later on acquitted on grounds of procedural irregularities, notably the irregular composition of the Court [462]. Since then other Parliamentarians such as Etonde Ekotto Edouard [463], Booto A Ngon André [464] and Dieudonné Ambassa Zang[465] have had their immunities equally uplifted by the Bureau of the National Assembly.

It should however be noted that all trials against Parliamentarians can be suspended on the submissions of the National Assembly. Does parliamentary immunity suggest that even after his mandate, a parliamentarian cannot be tried?

Responding to a similar question an author[466] opines that the parliamentarian like every other citizen is subjected to the law. In fact, he explains that during his mandate, the prescription period of section 68(2) (b) of the CPC is suspended and prosecution can commence after the running out of his mandate.
Two other state institutions whose members benefit from political immunity are members of the Constitutional Council and ELECAM

[462]Report of the Ministry of Justice on the state of human rights in Cameroon, 2005, p. 54-55.
[463] See A. n° 2006/009 of 6th October 2006.
[464] See A. n° 2006/010 of 6th October 2006.
[465] See A. n° 2009/011/AB/AN of 4th August 2009.
[466]Kenmoe (E.), *La pratique de l'information judiciaire dans le code de procédure pénale du Cameroun*, édition Veritas, 2013, p.54-55.

3. Immunity of Members of the Constitutional Council

The Constitutional Council is one of the newest institutions created by law N° 96/06 of the 18th January 1996 on the constitutional revision of 2nd June 1972(modified by law N° 2008/001 of April 14, 2008).

The members of the Constitutional Council just like parliamentarians benefit from two types of protection of a similar nature i.e. immunity and inviolability.

The immunity of the members of the Constitutional Council is contained in the provisions of article 12 of Law N° 2004/005 of 12 April 2004 establishing the Status of members of the said Council. It summarily stipulates that no member of the Constitutional Council can be prosecuted, arrested, detained, or tried on account of his opinion or vote casted in the course of his duty.

Adversely the provisions of article 10(1), (2), (3), (4) of the same law, lays down the circumstances under which the members of this Council can be prosecuted with or without the authorisation of the bureau of the Council. This is however slightly different from what obtains in ELECAM.

4. Immunity of Members of ELECAM

Elections Cameroon abbreviated ELECAM, is a neutral body appointed to oversee all election matters in Cameroon. Created by Law N° 2006/011 of 29th December 2006 to set up and lay down the organisation and functioning of elections, it is responsible for the organisation and supervision of elections in Cameroon. This body was made operational in January 2010 with the signing and transfer of documents and materials from the Ministry of Territorial Administration and Decentralisation (MINATD).

By dint of its very mission, the Members of ELECAM benefit from two forms of immunity. Just like their counterparts of the Constitutional Council, and by virtue of the provisions of article 3 of the aforementioned law, they can neither be prosecuted, arrested, detained nor tried on the basis of their opinion voiced out in the exercise of their function. Apart from cases of offences committed flagrante delicto, it is prohibited to engage criminal action against members of ELECAM still in office. Immunity from prosecution far from been just political can as well be grounded on diplomatic motivation.

B. Diplomatic immunity

Diplomatic immunity is also called extraterritoriality or ex-territoriality. In international law, the immunities enjoyed by foreign states or international organisations and their official representatives from the jurisdiction of the country in which they are present. Diplomatic immunity extends to foreign states or international organisations as entities and to their heads, delegations, troops in passage, war vessels, mission premises and other assets. It exempts them while within the territory of a foreign sovereign, from local judicial process, police interference and other measures of constraint. The term stems from the fiction that such persons or things are deemed not to be within the territory of the sovereign where they are actually present.

A United Nations conference on Diplomatic intercourse and immunities, held in Vienna in 1961, resulted in the signing of a convention on Diplomatic Relations duly ratified by Cameroon on the 4th March 1961. There appears to be general agreement that the Diplomatic agent during the term of his office is totally exempted from both criminal and civil jurisdiction in the State where he is accredited[467]. According to the Vienna Convention, this immunity extends both to the family of the diplomatic agent and to his staff. The mission[468], person[469] and residential premises[470] of diplomatic agents are immune not only from the process by creditors, but also from being entered by police and other law enforcement officers. Immunity extends to archives, documents, as well as the diplomatic bag of the mission. The receiving State has the responsibility of protecting the diplomatic courier from arrest or detention. This protection extends to correspondences, papers and excepts as provided in paragraph 3

[467] Article 29 of the Vienna Convention of the 18th April 1961.
[468] Article 20 of the Vienna Convention of the 18th April 1961.
[469] Article 27 of the Vienna Convention of the 18th April 1961.
[470] Article 28 of the Vienna Convention of the 18th April 1961.

of article 29[471]. Whether and under what conditions they may be used to grant asylum to outsiders is controversial.

The immunity of its diplomatic agents from jurisdiction may be waived by the sending State. In criminal proceedings, waiver must always be express. In civil or administrative matters, waiver may be express or implied. A waiver is presumed to have occurred if a diplomatic agent appears as defendant without claiming any immunity. The initiation of proceedings by a diplomatic agent shall prelude diplomatic agents from invoking immunity of jurisdiction in respect of counter-claim directly connected with the principal claim[472].

Emmanuel Ndjere [473] however poses a problem of immunity or inviolability of mission premises and the necessity of safeguarding local public order faced with a "force majeur" such as a fire incident, which is perilous both to the mission premises and neighbouring Structures. Apart from the above mentioned scenario used by Emmanuel Ndjere, a more practical scenario could be the case of the Cameroonian embassies in Paris, Brussels and Berlin which were ransacked or shattered by angry demonstrators on Sunday the 27th of January 2019, following a nationwide unauthorised strike action organised by the CRM party. It is reported that this havoc was perpetrated under the watchful eyes of French security forces who had ostensibly been alerted days back of an eminent attack[474].

This situation is akin to the dilemma raised by serious presumption of irregularities faced with the principle which excludes the violation of diplomatic bag. This situation may arise when security services have good reasons to believe that the Diplomatic bag is being used to transport products which have no relation with the diplomatic mission (drugs or arms) and which constitutes an offence to criminal law. In the first three scenarios, the express consent of the diplomatic agent is of absolute necessity. As regards the second scenario, while recognising that

---

[471]Article 22 of the Vienna Convention of the 18th April 1961.

[472]Article 30 of the Vienna Convention of the 18th April 1961.

[473] Ndere (E.), op.cit.,p. 251-252

[474]Reported in *The post newspaper* N° 01978 of Monday, January 28, 2019, p. 2
Reported as well in *The guardian post newspaper* N° 1977 of Monday, January 28, 2019, p. 3

States have been led to take such measures in exceptional cases, where there were serious grounds for suspecting that the bag was being used contrary to paragraph 4 of the aforementioned paragraph and with detriment of the receiving State, the diplomatic bag has on such occasions been opened with the permission of the Ministry of Foreign Affairs of the receiving State, and in the presence of a representative of the mission concerned.

Foreign Consular Officers do not enjoy exemptions from the local administration of justice to the same extent as the staffs of foreign diplomatic missions, and the laws governing consular immunities is less a matter of settled customary international rules than bilateral or multilateral treaties.

This is not, however, the case with family immunity.

C. Family Immunity

Family has been defined as a place where we experience our biggest triumphs and our deepest vulnerabilities, where we have our greatest potential to do good. It is believed that the family is divine in nature and that God designates it as the fundamental building block of society both on earth and through eternity. As such, it becomes the foundation for civilisation and a sanctuary for the individual. It is where we learn the social grace of loyalty, cooperation, and trust. It is where we learn to love ourselves and each other, to bear one another's burden, to find meaning in our life and give purpose to others' lives and feel the value of being part of something greater than ourselves.

The sacredness of this fundamental institution of every society has been considered by the law makers through the protection given to its members, against prosecutorial discretion of the Legal Department. The penal code has enumerated a series of offences for which family immunity applies in a bit to consolidate family ties.

Such is the case with the provision of section 100(2) of the penal code which deals basically with accessory after the fact, defined in paragraph 1 thus "An accessory after the fact shall mean a person who after the commission of a felony or misdemeanour shelters an offender or his accessories from arrest or from investigation, or who has custody of or disposes of anything taken, misappropriated or otherwise obtained by means of the offence". Paragraph 2 emphasises that "This section shall not apply as between husband and wife". Reciprocally couples owe each other a duty of love and the safeguard of the interest of each other. The duty of love necessarily calls for protection most especially under such circumstances where the liberty of one of the parties is at stake. The law makers are not blind to this reality.

It is within the same context that a person guilty of theft, misappropriation, false pretences [475], special theft and misappropriation[476], credit by fraud and fraudulent retention[477] are immune when such acts described are against a spouse, against a legitimate or adopted or adoptive ascendant or , descendant, or against a natural ascendant or descendant up to the second degree either living with the victim or after recognition, or to a surviving spouse in respect of necessaries belonging to the deceased spouse[478]. Family immunity should not be confused with the situation of prior complaint which is a legal obstacle to prosecutorial discretion.

II. LEGAL OBSTACLES TO PROSECUTORIAL DISCRETION

If it is true that criminal proceedings shall be instituted and prosecuted by the Legal Department[479], it is equally true that the same reserves part of these prerogatives to particular administrations and to victims under specified conditions.

A. Prior Complaint of Victims: A condition to the institution of proceedings

The offences for which prior complaint are required are offences which can put to peril the honour, the integrity of the dignity of the family and couples. The protection of the entity, family, is at the origin of the enactment of this principle that seeks to safeguard the interest of the family, which happens to be the base

[475]Section 318(1) (a) (b) (c) of the penal code.
[476]Section 319(1-4) of the penal code.
[477]Section 322(1) (2) of the penal code.
[478]Section 323 of the penal code.
[479] Section 60 CPC.

of every society. Protection here is equally grounded on the fact that the offences involved are of a private nature, thus acting otherwise can infringe private life. Offences that fall within this category include, abuses [480], defamation [481], adultery [482], desertion[483] and incest[484]. The institution of criminal proceedings in such cases therefore is subject to a prior complaint by the victim of the offence. The Legal Department cannot of its own motion engage proceedings for these offences without a prior complaint of the victim. The importance of the preservation of family or private interest is further demonstrated by the fact that even where prosecution was commenced after a prior complaint of the victim, the Legal Department will not proceed if the civil party proceeded with the withdrawal of his complaint[485]. In certain cases, prosecution can only be engaged if the administration concerned files a complaint.

B. The Complaint of the Administration

While emphasising that criminal proceeding shall be instituted and prosecuted by the Legal Department, Section 60 of the CPC notes that they may also be instituted by any government Department. The CPC, apart from indicating that other government departments can as well institute criminal proceedings does not go further to give a list of such government departments. It should however be noted that special criminal provisions attributing the power to prosecute to certain government departments vary according to the nature and importance of the administration in question. Some can act of their own motion, some institute criminal proceedings concurrently with the Legal Department, while others subject prosecution by the Legal Department to the introduction of a

[480] Section 307, penal code.
[481] Section 307, penal code.
[482] Section 361, penal code.
[483] Section 358, penal code.
[484] Section 360, penal code.
[485] Section 62(1), (g) CPC. Criminal proceedings will be discontinued in the following cases; the withdrawal of a complaint where the lodging of such complaint is a precondition for the commencement of prosecution.

complaint by the concerned administration[486]. He cites the following laws as examples:

- Law n° 2002/003 of the 19 February 2002 on the general tax code;
- Law n° 94/01 of the 20 of January 1994 on the regime of forestry, fauna and fishery, completed by ordinance n° 99/001 of the 31 August 1999;
- Law n° 96/12 of the 5 August 1996 on the management of the environment.

1. Taxation Administration

For all offences with pecuniary sanctions only, the taxation department solely has the right to set in motion criminal proceedings. On the contrary where such offences are punished with both pecuniary as well as imprisonment term or better still where the infringement against the tax code is coupled with a common law offence the right to set in motion criminal proceedings shall be that of the Legal Department. The taxation administration can however come in to lay claim for damages.

2. Customs Administration

The institution and prosecution of custom offences geared towards the sanctioning of defaulters is the prerogative of the Legal Department. On the other hand, the customs administration has jurisdiction for the application of fiscal sanctions.

3. As regards Fauna

The administrations of fishery and forestry concurrently with the Legal Department reserves the right to institute and prosecute criminal offences in the afore-cited domains, irrespective of the nature of the sanction, (fine or imprisonment term).[487]

C. Extinction of criminal liability

The term "extinction" translated "discontinuance" in the English version of the CPC was misconstrued.

---

[486] Ndjere (E.), op.cit , p. 254

[487] Ndjere (E.), *op.cit.*p. 254.

Discontinuance under the common law has been defined as a formal notice filed with the Court and served on the defendant, ending active litigation[488]. Simply put, it means to abandon a claim that is in progress. Under this system, only a plaintiff can file discontinuance and he or she can do so over the objection of the defendant. In fact, in **Young v. Valcourt (1982) 1WWR 575 (BCSC),** the Court held that ***"the plaintiff is the master of this litigation and may proceed or not as he chooses. He is therefore entitled to the order he seeks. If the defendant has some claim against him, her remedy is not in this action, which is now at an end."*** In the British Columbia, rules related to discontinuance are set out in the British Columbia Rules of

Court at section 36 and are remarkably similar to the Civil Procedure Rules in Great Britain. It provides that "At any time before an action is set down for trial, a plaintiff may discontinue it in whole or in part against a defendant by filling and delivering a notice of discontinuance… to each party of record. After an action has been set down for trial a plaintiff may discontinue it in whole or in part against a defendant with the consent of all the parties of record or by leave of Court. … a person wholly discontinuing an action…. Shall pay cost of that party to the date of delivery of the notice of discontinuance….".

From the common law terminology used, notably, Plaintiff[489], we can easily infer that discontinuance within the context of the common law applies to civil and not criminal law. Discontinuance within the framework of the Criminal Procedure Code was not properly used by the law maker. A better way of putting it would have been "extinction" to suit the context "criminal procedure". In common law we talk of extinction of criminal liability.

Section 62 of the CPC lay down the circumstances of extinction of criminal proceedings. According to this provision death of the suspect, defendant or accused, prescription,

---

488 www.duhaime.org.

489 « Plaintiff » is the term used in civil cases in most English speaking jurisdictions, the notable exception being England and Wales, where a plaintiff has since the introduction of the Civil Procedure Rules in 1999, been known as a 'claimant'. In criminal cases the prosecutor brings a case against the defendant, but the key complaining party is often called the 'complainant'."

Amnesty, repeal of the law a successful plea of convict or acquit, by agreement between the parties and withdrawal.

1. Extinction by death

The CPC lays down the principle according to which the death of the offender at any stage of the proceedings, automatically leads to the extinction of criminal proceedings. It is for this reason that it lays emphasis on the death of the suspect (in the course of police investigation), the defendant (in the course of preliminary inquiry) and the accused in the course of the trial before a Court of law. As regards corporate bodies the French Courts have attributed the death of a company as pertains to criminal responsibility with merger-absorption, "fusion-absorption" of the company, which automatically leads to its dissolution with transfer of assets to the absorbing company thus the loss of its legal existence[490]. Extinction of criminal proceedings by death can be justified by the fact that criminal responsibility is personal[491]. Extinction is not however extended to co-offenders and accessories who remain criminally liable. The extinction of criminal responsibility by death does not affect the civil liability which remains intact and can be engaged against the next of kin.

Its civil liability effect is similar to that of amnesty.

2. Amnesty

On an inclusive node amnesty in criminal law can be defined as sovereign acts of oblivion of forgetfulness (from Greek amnesia) for past acts, granted by government to persons who have been guilty of crimes. It is often conditional upon their return to obedience and duty within a prescribed period. Amnesty is usually granted for political crimes against the State, such as treason, sedition, or rebellion. It is addressed generally to classes or communities and takes the form of a legislative act or other

---

[490] Crim. 20 juin 2000; Bull.n° 237, D. p. 865 note H. Matsopoulou; Crim. 14 Oct. 2003, Bull. n° 189 (cite dans Bouloc 2010, p. 165);

[491] Section 74(1) of the penal code « no penalty may be imposed except upon a person criminally responsible.

(2) Criminally responsibility shall lie on him who intentionally commits each of the ingredient acts or omissions of an offence with the intention of causing the results which completes it.

constitutional, statutory act of the supreme power of the State[492]. The pardon granted can either be absolute[493] or conditional[494]. Some local legislation makes a distinction between pardon and amnesty.

Within our context the law on amnesty, which is conditional, usually lay much emphasis on the condition. It can for example exempt fines, limited to a given category of offenses, or for offences with a given range of imprisonment term. Amnesty does not have any effect on the civil liability.

3. Repeal of criminal law (l'abrogation de la loi pénale)

Repeal is the removal or reversal of a law. There are two basic types of repeal, a repeal with a re-enactment (or replacement) of the repealed law or a repeal without any replacement. Under the common law of England and Wales the effect of repealing a statute was "to obliterate it completely from the records of parliament as though it has never been passed"[495].

Repeal removes the felonious aspect of an offense while obliterating its legal character, when it is done before the seizure of the court with jurisdiction[496].

It would seem then that the repeal of a statute completely destroys the possibility of continuing any prosecution which were pending at the time the statute upon which the prosecution is founded is repealed, unless there is a saving clause within the repealing statute or another statute which controls generally the effects of repealing statutes upon pending prosecution. This was the principle laid down by **Lord Campbell C.J**, in the leading English case of ***Regina v. Denton***[497] wherein he declared that; ***"The general rule is that a statute from the time that it is repealed cannot be acted upon"***; in the same line **Earl, J.**, in his

[492] www. Britannica.com.

[493] The total extinction of criminal liability, of the individual to whom it is granted, without any condition. It restores the individual his civil and political rights and remits the particular offense of which he was convicted.

[494] The exemption of an individual within certain limits or conditions from punishment which the law inflicts for the offense he had committed resulting in the partial extinction of his criminal liability.

[495]www.wikipedia.org

[496] Keubou (Ph.), op. cit. p. 88.

[497]Q.B.D761 ;188 Reprint 287 (1887).

concurring opinion said; ***"To say that proceedings can nevertheless be followed up contravenes the sense of the word repeal... The repeal takes away the ground and makes the indictment bad in substance as well as in form"***[498]. This is the position of Phillipe Keubou who goes a step further, by précising that if the matter was pending before the Examining magistrate, he must enter a no case ruling to the benefit of the defendant, and if before the Court, the accused must be found not guilty and acquitted. But just like in the case of amnesty, civil liabilities subsist.

4. Resjudicata (La chose jugée)

A successful plea of convict or acquit as per the provisions of Section 62 of the CPC is one of the causes of discontinuance of criminal proceedings, summarised in the legal maxim *"non bis in idem"*. Res judicata also known as preclusion claim, is the Latin term for "a matter already judged", and refers to either of two concepts: in both civil and common law legal systems a case in which there has been a final judgement and is no longer subject to appeal; and the legal doctrine meant to bar (or preclude) continued litigation of a case on same issue between the same parties. In case of res judicata, the matter cannot be raised again either in the same court or a different Court, a court will use res judicata to deny reconsideration of the matter[499].

The doctrine of res judicata is a method of preventing injustice to the parties of a case supposedly finished but perhaps also or mostly a way of avoiding unnecessary waste of resources in the Court system. Res judicata does not only avert judgements from contradicting earlier ones, but also prevents litigants from multiplying judgements and confusion.

The elements of res judicata are as follows:

- The former judgement or order must be final;
- The judgement or order must be on the merit;

---

[498] Albert Levitt, « Repeal of penal statutes and effects on pending prosecutions», in *American Bar Association Journal*, vol.9, no. 11 (November 1923), p. 715-721.

[499] Larson Aaron," Issue preclusion and claim preclusion; How prior litigation can block your claim", 3 November 2017, ExpertLaw.com. Retrieved 12 December 2017, cited at www. Wikipedia. com

- It must have been rendered by a Court having jurisdiction over the subject matter and the parties
- There must be between the first and second action identity of parties, of subject matter and cause of action[500].

As per the provisions of section 62 a previous acquittal or conviction under the above conditions constitutes a cause of extinction of criminal proceedings, which is different from an agreement between the parties.

5. Agreement between parties

Agreement between parties has been provided for by the law makers as a cause of the extinction of criminal proceedings. Agreement between the parties is possible only where the law so provides. Such can be the cases of offences for which just pecuniary sanction has been provided for notably fines. In this case a valid agreement must be reached prior to the setting in motion of criminal action, at this stage, the extinction is absolute. Any subsequent agreement after the verdict has been handed may only affect damages to be awarded.

6. Withdrawal of a complaint

A withdrawal of complaints has been contemplated in the provisions of section 62 as one of the causes of the extinction of criminal action. The CPC does not give a definition of the term withdrawal nor the reasons for its existence. Withdrawal of something can be defined as the act or process of removing or ending it. It is an indication that a complainant no longer wishes to proceed with their own complaint in accordance with any explicit policy for the managing of a complaint. The rationale behind withdrawal was finely stated before the Kenyan High Court Seating at Nairobi through the mouth of **Lady Justice Lesiit** thus "***under section 176 of the Criminal Procedure Code, the Court is enjoined to promote reconciliation to parties in a misdemeanour, even on its own motion. Assault, contrary to section 251 of the penal code, is a misdemeanour and is one of***

[500] https://www.lawPhil.net

the best cases where section 176 of the Criminal Procedure Code could be invoked by the Court on its own motion in a bid to reconclle the parties and end the matter in Court"[501].

Withdrawal of complaints under the Cameroonian Criminal Procedure Code initially is only possible where the lodging of such a complaint is a precondition for the commencement of prosecution[502]. Such is the case with offences such as adultery[503], defamation[504], insult[505] etc. Within the Kenyan context, the court can of its own motion proceed with withdrawals for the reasons mentioned above and even for offences whose lodging is not a precondition for prosecution. Such is the case with assault, contrary to section 251 of the Kenyan Penal Code.

---

[501] ShenZhanghua V. Republic [2006], cited at www. Kenyalaw.org. A brief summary of the facts of this case are as follows. ShenZhanghua had been charged with occasioning bodily harm, contrary to section 251 of the Penal Code. The charge arose pursuant to a complaint filed with the Muthaiga Police Station, following which Shen was arrested and charged before the Chief Magistrates Court at Makadara. He was arraigned in Court on May 19 and pleaded not guilty to the charge.

On July 10,2006, when the case came up for hearing before one of the judicial officers at the station, as the Court record was not clear who was presiding, the complainant applied under section 204 of the Criminal Procedure Code, to withdraw the case. He stated under oath that he had decided to forgive Shen. The Court reserved the case for ruling. Three days later, on July 13, 2006, the magistrate declined to allow the withdrawal and directed that the matter should proceed to hearing.

Section 204 provides that, if a complainant, any time before a final order is passed in a case under this part (procedures of trial under subordinate Courts) satisfies the Court that there are sufficient grounds for permitting him to withdraw his complaint, the Court may permit him to do so and shall, thereupon, acquit the accused.

The matter came before Lady Justice Lesiit, challenging the refusal by the magistrate to allow the complainant withdraw the matter, in Makadara Criminal case No. 2850 of 2006, under section 204 of the Criminal Procedure Code.

Lady Justice Lesiit, upon perusal of the file remitted it back to the trial Court with the direction that the considered ruling be given as to why the application for withdrawal was denied.

The ruling made by the Court according to Lady Justice Lesiit, gave the reason for declining to grant the withdrawal on the fact that the trial Court was not satisfied that the grounds put forth by the complainant were sufficient.

The trial Court also questioned the sudden change of heart by the complainant. Lady Justice Lesiit said the trial magistrate was ignorant of two factors. On, that under section 176 of the Criminal Procedure Code, the Court is enjoined to promote reconciliation to parties in misdemeanours, even of its own motion.

Assault, contrary to section251 of the Penal Code, is a misdemeanor. It is one of the best cases where section 176 of the Criminal Procedure Code could be invoked by the Court on its own volition in a bid to reconcile parties and end the matter in Court.

[502] Section 62(1) (g) CPC .

[503] Section 361(3) (4), Penal Code.

[504] Section 305(3),Penal Code.

[505] Section 307(2), Penal Code.

It is however different from withdrawal in Section 62(1) (h) of the CPC[506]. This paragraph while excluding lodging of a complaint as a precondition for the commencement of prosecution, includes withdrawal of civil claim as well as specifying the nature of the offences for which it is applicable (simple offences and misdemeanour). Withdrawal as per this provision is only possible and can only be granted by the Court under the following conditions:

- Where the withdrawal is voluntary;
- The matter has not been heard on the merits;
- The offence committed does not disturb public order or good morals[507];
- In case of many civil claimants, all of them must withdraw their complaint or civil claim,
- The withdrawal is not as a result of violence, fraud or deceit[508].

Unlike under the Kenyan context, withdrawal as per the provisions of 62(1) (h) of the CPC can only be granted by any Court of law if the conditions are fulfilled.

7. Nolle prosequi

As already analysed above, the Procureur General of a Court of Appeal may by express authority of the Ministry in charge of Justice, enter a nolle prosequi at any stage before judgement on the merits is delivered[509]. Serious perils to social interest or public order are reasons that are likely to justify the entering of a nolle prosequi.

8. Prescription

Prescription has been defined as the means of extinguishing rights through the inaction of the legal owner. It has equally been

---

[506] « the withdrawal of the complaint or the civil claim by the civil party who lodged the complaint in respect of a simple offence or a misdemeanor».

[507] The term "public order" widely used by the Cameroonian lawmakers within the context of the 1990 liberty laws and the maintenance of order, has never been given a concise definition by the legislative organ. The resulting consequence has been that its interpretation has always been a source of controversy to both professionals such as administrative officers and academicians of law, everybody attributing to it a definition that suits his motive and interest.

[508] Section 62(2) (3), CPC.

[509] Section 64(1) CPC

defined by **Madam Justice Shannon Gremillion of the Court of Appeal of Louisiana** as ***"a mode of barring of action as a result of inaction for a period of time.... In other words prescription sets a time limit within which one is allowed to seek enforcement of a right"***[510]. In other words, "prescription" is "the extinction of a title or right by failure to claim or exercise it over a long period. It is the effect of the lapse of time in creating and destroying rights"[511]. According to S. Tabe Tabe prescription and time-bar are distinct and not synonymous, defining time-bar as per the aforementioned dictionary[512]as "a bar to a legal claim arising from the lapse of a defined length of time, especially one contained in a statute of limitation".

In common law it is known as *statute of limitation*, which has been defined as the legislation that sets a timeframe (limitation period) within which affected parties must initiate proceedings to enforce their rights or to seek redress after a damage or injury. This period varies according to the nature of the case. Its objective is to encourage diligent prosecution of certain offences while evidence is available and fresh, and thus ensure finality and predictability in litigation. In other words, it is enacted to protect persons against claims made after disputes have become stale, evidence has been lost, memories have faded, or witnesses have disappeared.

The CPC in the same line summarily defines prescription as the barring of prosecution following the failure to commence action within the prescribed limitation period[513], prescription of prosecution within this context is a matter of public policy[514].

---

[510] See the case of Yen v. Avoyelles Parish Police Jury, 5 So. 3d 1002 (2009), cited at www.duhaime. org

[511] Bryan A. Garner, «Black's Law Dictionary» 7th Ed., West Group, St Paul Minn, 1999, P. 1202 as cited by Tabe Tabe (S.), « Prescription period for making a private complaint in cases of misdemeanours-whether offence was time barred? Isaiah Mbunkur V. The People of Cameroon. Appeal n° BCA/MS/32C/2008» in *Les grandes décisions de la jurisprudence pénale Camerounaise*, URDA, (Dir. Anoukaha (F.)), Juillet 2018, p. 253-268

[512] Ibid., p. 1492

[513]Section 65(1), CPC.

[514]Section 69(1), CPC

Prescription of offences should not therefore be mistaken for prescription of penalty[515].

In cases of felony, criminal proceedings are barred after 10 years have elapsed from the day following the commission of the offence i.e. if within the interval no step was taken[516]. As regards misdemeanours the period has been fixed at 3 years [517] .This was the position of the Court in **suit No. BCA/MS/32C/2008: Isaiah Mbunkur V. The People of Cameroon & 1 OR** [518] as analysed by S. Tabe Tabe, wherein the North West Court of Appeal held that

---

[515] Section 67(1) , penal code « Where a principal penalty has remained unenforced for the following periods after judgment has become final, neither it nor any accessory penalty or preventive measure accompanying it ,may any longer be enforced:

a) For felony 20 (twenty years);
b) For misdemeanor and simple offences tried with misdemeanor, 5 (five years);
c) For any other simple offence,2 (two) years

2) Prescription shall be suspended while enforcement of the sentence is prevented by any consideration of law or of fact apart from the offender's will.

Time shall begin to run again on the intervention of an enforcement measure taken before the completion of the period.

[516]Section 65 (2), CPC.

[517]Section 65 (4), CPC.

[518] This case was a criminal appeal against the judgment of his worship Mr. Agbor James Eyong (as he then was) delivered on the 5th day of February 2008. The brief facts of the case are that the 2nd respondent, one Tamjong Bako Umaru was the complainant at the trial and he was a herdsman serving the appellant for more than 18 years. He had to go to Nigeria for a death ceremony, so he left work as herdsman. Before leaving and with the consent of the appellant, he kept his bull in the appellant's herd of 85 cows. On his return two months later, he could not find his bull among the appellant's herd of cows. On questioning the appellant, he was informed that the appellant had sold his bull because he did not have a male cow to sell. All this happened when the complainant was still working for the appellant. He quit his job as appellant's herdsman in 2001. But before quitting the complainant for more than 11 to 12 years kept demanding for his bull to be returned to him. After about 12 years, he realized that the appellant did not intend to refund his bull so he lodged a complaint of misappropriation against the appellant at the Public Security Nkambe and case file C.R.No 040/2006 was established. The appellant was tried in court on a one count charge under section 318(1) (b) P.C and the trial magistrate found him guilty and sentenced him to one month imprisonment term; to pay cost to the State of Cameroon of the sum of 169.288 FRS and awarded the complainant the sum of 150.000 FRS for the bull. He ordered that failure to pay the sum of 150.000 FRS he will serve four and a half month imprisonment in default of payment. The trial magistrate relying on section 565 CPC, suspended the term of imprisonment in default of cost and civil damage award; but ordered that the cost and civil damage award shall be recovered from him by decision after the supposed term of imprisonment in default of payment has expired, should he fail to pay voluntarily. Dissatisfied with the decision the appellant appealed on the following grounds;

1. That the learned trial magistrate erred when he convicted, sentenced and remanded into prison custody the accused/appellant to a term of imprisonment of one month when the later was 70 years old.
2. That the judgment is altogether unreasonable and unwarranted having regard to the weight of the evidence adduced at the trial.

"We associate ourselves with the submissions of the learned counsel for the appellant under this ground of appeal. The offence in this matter is a misdemeanour. Therefore, as per Section 65(4) C.P.C, the prescription period is 3years. In perusing through the evidence in record we noticed that no act or step was taken by the 1st respondent to initiate investigation within the prescription period of three years. The step of persistently asking the appellant to refund his cow for 12 years does not qualify an act under section 66 C.P.C; therefore, it cannot cause the time to run afresh. We hold that the action was time barred under section 65(4) C.P.C. Therefore, the trial court erred in entertaining and adjudicating on it».

It should, however, be noted that there are special provisions as regards the prescription of misdemeanours. In some cases, the Penal code has provided for a more limited prescription period. Such is the case with misdemeanours such as abuse (Section 307(3)), defamation (Section 305(5)), and contempt (Section 152(3)). The Penal code fixes the prescription period of this offences at 4months. Such is equally the case with press offences[519], whose prescription period is fixed at 3 years.

Simple offences according to the provisions of Section 65(5) are time barred by the elapse of one year after the commission of the offence. In case of prosecution for several related offences, the prescription period to be considered is that of the offence with the most severe punishment[520].

a. Suspension and Interruption of prescription

The prescription period can be affected either by suspension or by interruption. Prescription is said to be suspended when proceedings are momentarily suspended such that in the computation of the dateline, the time already used even before the suspension is calculated. On the contrary, prescription is said to have been interrupted when the dateline starts running afresh after the accomplishment of certain acts. The following acts that can set the time to start running afresh have been identified; the

[519] Article 87 of Law N° 90/52 of 19 December 1990 on the freedom of social communication.
[520] Section 65 (6), CPC.

lodging of a complaint, writ or orders issued by the Legal Department instituting measures of investigation, processes served by the bailiff, reports of police investigation, Court processes, hearing of the parties and the witnesses during preliminary inquiry or in Court, interlocutory rulings and declarations of appeal.[521] Its effect extends even to those who are not implicated or named in the said acts[522], i.e. offenders, co-offenders and accessories. They must not necessarily be cited personally in any of the acts. A complaint for example against a suspect automatically implicates his co-offenders and accessories if there are any.

According to an author jurisprudence has transposed to criminal law, a principle of civil law according to which prescription cannot reasonably be expected to run against someone who cannot validly act. Such is the justification of suspension of prescription summarised in the maxim *"contra non valentine"*[523]. The causes of the suspension of prescription are both de facto and de jure.

b. De jure causes of suspension of prescription

Section 68(2) of the CPC sets out the following as de jure bars; an interlocutory plea against the judgement being given, parliamentary immunity, a fiat to prosecute, an appeal to the Supreme Court has been lodged and where there is conflict of jurisdiction.

c. De factor causes of suspension of prescription

The same provision in its paragraph 3 list the following as de facto bars; the invasion of the territory by enemy forces, insanity of the suspect, the defendant or the accused after the commission of the offence, the escape of the suspect, the defendant or the accused, the enlisting of the case for hearing, adjournment of the case entered in the record book and the fact that a Court by failing to perform an act within its jurisdiction, prevented a party

[521] Section 66, CPC.
[522] Section 67, CPC.
[523] Keubou (Ph.) ,op.cit.,p. 86

from exercising his legal rights to take action or to defend himself.

In the absence of any impediment the Legal Department proceeds with the prosecution of offences brought to his knowledge. The role of the Legal Department varies depending on the various phases of the procedure.

PART IV

THE PROSECUTORIAL ROLE OF THE LEGAL DEPARTMENT

The Legal Department as regards criminal proceedings can be qualified as the alpha and omega. It is present at the inception of proceedings; it is present and takes active part in the investigating offences, collecting evidence, identifying offenders and accomplices; it is present even at the phase of preliminary inquiry, and takes an active part in the hearing phase where it is the principal party. It is charged with the execution of all decisions, and the final outcome of proceedings.

CHAPTER XI
THE LEGAL DEPARTMENT AND POLICE REPORT

Every investigation ends up with the drawing up of a police report irrespective of the nature of the offence. The reports drawn up have as destination the Legal Department or the Commissioner of Government depending on the nature of the offences committed. The jurisdiction of the military Tribunal, which is a Court with special attributes, is laid down in the code of military justice[524]. This text formally excludes minors from the jurisdiction of the Military Tribunal[525].

Case files with offences that fall under the jurisdiction of the Military Tribunal are directed to the Public Prosecutor Department of the said Tribunal, on the other hand case files with common law offences are directed to the Public Prosecutor Departments of Common law Courts (Court of First Instance or High Court), depending on the gravity of the offences. The treatments of case file in the various Departments are not similar.

---

[524] Law N° 2017/012 of 12th July 2017 to lay down the code of military Justice, section 8: The military Tribunal shall have exclusive jurisdiction to hear and to determine:

a) Military offences and war crimes;
b) Crimes against humanity and crimes of genocide;
c) Offences related to acts of terrorism and State security;
d) Offences of piracy and unlawful against the safety of maritime navigation and platforms;
e) Offences committed by servicemen or civilian personnel serving in the defense forces, with or without civilian co-offenders or accomplices, in a military establishment or in the exercise of their duties;
f) Offences against the law governing 1st, 2nd ,3rd and 4th category weapons as specified in the law to lay down general weapons and ammunition regulations in Cameroon;
g) Offences committed using the weapons falling under the categories referred to in section 8 (f) above;
h) Armed robbery;
i) Offences involving servicemen or persons considered as such, committed in wartime or in an area subjected to the state of emergency
j) Offences committed by civilians in a military establishment affecting military equipment or installations, prejudicial to the to the physical integrity of a serviceman or disrupting normal service;
k) Offences related to the purchase, importation, sale, production, distribution, wearing or keeping of military effects or insignia as defined by the regulation in force;
l) All other offences related to those referred to above.

[525] Section 9: Minors aged 18 (eighteen) years who are offenders, co-offenders or accomplices in the cases referred to in section 8 above shall fall within the jurisdiction of courts dealing with juvenile delinquency. In such cases, the State Prosecutor shall refer the case file to the competent Legal Department after separation of the proceedings, as appropriate.

I. GENERAL CONSIDERATIONS IN THE TREATMENT OF CASE FILE AT THE LEGAL DEPARTMENT

A state counsel or deputy irrespective of the Court, who receives a file from an investigating unit, must take into consideration the following preliminary items when perusing:

- The place of commission of the offence, to ensure that it is within his jurisdiction[526];
- The nature of the offence (felony, misdemeanour or simple offence), the nature of offence here equally includes verifying if the offence is a common law offence or an offence that fall within the jurisdiction of a court with special jurisdiction. He equally verifies if the offence is one for which a fiat for prosecution is required;
- The person implicated is equally an element to be considered. Such is the case with offences by the President of the Republic, parliamentarians, and diplomats, covered by immunity. Such is equally the case with Magistrates, Administrative officers (governors, senior divisional officers, divisional officers, high profile government officials) and judicial police officers, for whom the law has provided a special procedure of prosecution[527], as well as minors[528] etc. Many suspects fall under this category and in most cases the obligation of reporting comes to play;
- The prosecutor ensures that the offences contained in the case file has not been extinguished by the factors of section 62 of the CPC such as death of the suspect, prescription, amnesty, repeal of law, res judicata, agreement of the parties or withdrawal of the complaint;
- The Public Prosecutor must equally ensure that all the operations of investigations (arrest, search and seizures)

---

[526] Section 140 (1) CPC, « The competent State Counsel shall be either;

a) That of the place of commission of the offence; or

b) That of the place of residence of the suspect; or

c) That of the place of arrest of the suspect.

2) When more than one State Counsel are seized of the same matter, priority shall be given to the State Counsel in whose jurisdiction the offence was committed.

[527] Section 629-634 CPC

[528] Section 700 CPC

were regularly conducted and are not subject to nullity[529], that the recording of statements were done in compliance with the law (informing the suspects of their rights and making mention in the police report)[530], compliance to rules pertaining to remand in police custody[531]. They must as well ensure that the police reports are signed by the various parties concerned.

II. PROBABLE SOLUTIONS AFTER TREATMENT

After considering the aforementioned elements, the reaction of the State Counsel depends on the content of the case file. He may:

A. Return case file to the investigating unit

Returning a case file to an investigating unit is an option that has as objective, correcting lapses observed during treatment. Apart from returning for the purpose of requesting for further investigation as per the provisions of section 144 (b) of the CPC, the State Counsel may equally request the JPO to rectify certain irregularities observed such as; the non-respect of the provisions as regards the recording of statements (information of rights of suspects and making mention in the police report), failure of the parties to sign the various reports, non-compliance with rules as regards arrest, remand etc. When faced with certain factors he may as well close the case file in chambers.

B. Closure in Chambers

The State Counsel may as well decide to close the matter in chambers and inform the complainant of his decision. This decision is proper under the following circumstances; where there is prescription, amnesty, death of the suspect, and non-identification of the suspect, agreement of the parties or withdrawals. The law provides that the decision closing the file must be forwarded to the Procureur General at the Court of

---

[529] Section 92-100 CPC

[530] Section 116, CPC

[531] Section 118-126 CPC

Appeal within a month[532]. Can the decision of closure of the State Counsel be appealed against? This decision does not meet the requirements of a judgement as per sections 387-389 of the CPC, thus cannot be appealed against. By virtue of the principle of hierarchical obligation, he may be constraint to report to the PG.

C. Report to the PG

The State Prosecutor may as well report to the Procureur General. Section 141 of the CPC has not however made provision for this. Reporting is one of the consequences of the principle of hierarchical subordination. It obliges the State Prosecutors to systematically report matters of certain importance notably; matters relating to the security of the State and repression of subversive activities, all matters involving parliamentarians, ex-parliamentarians, mayors and traditional chiefs, administrative officers (senior divisional officers, District officers and high ranking civil servants as a whole), law officers and those with the status of law officers. Such is equally the case with matters which though falling under common law jurisdiction, present an exceptional character or gravity (i.e. mutiny among different ethnic groups). However, where the investigation was regularly conducted and there is no obstacle, the State Counsel institutes criminal action.

D. Instituting Criminal Proceedings

The last option opened to the State Prosecutor is instituting criminal proceedings against the suspect[533]. The institution of proceedings varies depending on whether it is before the Court of First Instance or High Court.

When the State Counsel is settled on prosecuting a suspect one other issue that remains unsettled is the liberty of the suspect, will he be remanded or granted bail?

---

[532] Section 141(c), CPC.

[533] Section 141(e), CPC

III. THE LEGAL DEPARTMENT AND BAIL

The right to be presumed innocent as a guarantee to the right to a fair hearing is intrinsically linked to the right to bail. According to international instruments duly ratified by Cameroon "Anyone arrested or detained on a criminal charge shall be brought promptly before a judge or other judicial officers authorised by law to exercise judicial power and shall be entitled to trial within a reasonable time or to a release. It shall not be a general rule that the persons awaiting trial shall be detained in custody, but release may be subjected to guarantees to appear for trial, at any stage of the judicial proceedings, and should occasions arise, for the execution of the judgement[534].

Such is the recommendation contained in the United Nations Minimum Rules for Non-Custodial Measure otherwise known as the Tokyo Rules. These rules have as fundamental aim, encouraging the widest possible use of non-custodial measures and to ensure that non-custodial measures are imposed and implemented in a fair and just manner, while insisting that enthusiasm for no-custodial measures should not lead to the infringement of human rights.

In compliance to this international legal instrument the Cameroonian constitution provides that "no person shall be prosecuted, arrested or detained except in the cases and according to the manner determined by law"[535]. The law to this regards provides that "remand in custody shall be an exceptional measure which shall not be ordered except in the case of a misdemeanour or a felony, further that it shall be necessary for the preservation of evidence, the maintenance of public order, protection of life and property, or to ensure the appearance of an accused before the EM or the Court"[536]. It is thus clear from the above provision that the Cameroonian lawmakers have conceived remand in custody as an exceptional measure, making bail the principle and remand in custody an exception.

[534] Article 9(3) of the International Covenant on civil and political rights.

[535] Law N° 2008/001 of 14 April 2008 to amend and supplement some provisions of Law N° 96/6 of 18 January 1996 to amend the constitution of 2 June 1972.

[536] Section 218, CPC.

A. The empowerment of the State Counsel to grant bail

Bail has been defined as set of pre-trial restrictions that are imposed on a suspect to ensure that they comply with the judicial process. It can equally be considered as the conditional release of a suspect, a defendant, or an accused with the promise to appear in court when required[537]

Application for bail may be made to the judicial police officer, to the State Counsel, to the Examining Magistrate or to the court seized of the matter[538]. The law has made provisions for bail at each phase of the procedure (at the level of investigation, at the level of the Legal Department and during the hearing or trial) with each of the actors at each phase empowered to grant bail.

In principle any person lawfully remanded may be granted bail on condition that he fulfils one of the conditions referred to in section 246(g), in particular to ensure his appearance either before judicial police or any judicial authority[539]. Curiously, any person on bail is considered being lawfully in custody. Persons charged with felonies punishable with imprisonment for life or deaths are explicitly excluded from the benefit of bail[540].In spite of the fact that bail is the principle and remand in custody an exception, its attribution is not a haphazard operation, it is highly regulated and subjected to the fulfilment of prescribed conditions thus the use of the term conditional bail.

B. Conditions for bail at the Legal Department

The conditions to which the attribution of bail is subjected are laid down by the provisions of section 246(g) as read with Section 224 of the CPC. According to this provision bail may be granted to a suspect subject to the deposit of sums of money or after the provision of one or more sureties.

---

[537] www.wikipedia.org

[538] Section 225, CPC .

[539] Section 224(1), CPC

[540] Section 224(2), CPC.

1. **Caution or Security as a guarantee of appearance**

The Legal Department is just a channel for all criminal matters destined for the Courts of law. Even though the Legal Department has been attributed the power to grant bail, in the exercise of this discretion it must ensure that the suspect appears before the court. One of the measures put in place to ensure future appearance is the deposit of sum of money (caution or security) into the State treasury. In fixing the caution the law provides that the resource of the suspect should be taken into consideration. In most Legal Departments State Counsels equally take into consideration the gravity of the offence committed. A suspect is likely to be charged a high caution for offences of a serious gravity.

Far from ensuring the appearance of the suspect before the court, caution or security deposited is equally destined to the reimbursement of cost incurred by the civil party, the compensation of damages caused by the offence and the payment of fines and cost[541]. The security deposited in the event of an acquittal is reimbursed. However, such reimbursement must be specifically ordered in the judgment or ruling[542]. Where a person jumps bail, the security deposited at the public treasury shall, without prejudice to the rights of the civil party be forfeited[543].The State Counsel may, however, prefer one or more sureties as condition for bail

2. **Conditional bail by a surety or sureties**

The State Counsel in the course of granting bail may require the suspect to provide one or more sureties who must enter a recognizance[544] to guarantee his appearance before any judiciary authority. Where the applicant presents several sureties for bail the recognizance entered into by them may be taken separately[545]. The surety shall be responsible for the appearance of the person

[541] Section 232(1),CPC.

[542] Section 232(2),(3), CPC

[543] Section 234, CPC

[544] An obligation of record entered into before a court or magistrate requiring the performance of an act (such as appearance in court) usually penalty of a money forfeiture.

[545] Section 226, CPC

released on bail[546]. The consequences of entering a recognizance are however drastic to the suspect and on the surety.

In case of non-appearance of the person released on bail, the competent authority orders the arrest of the accused or defendant and summons the surety to produce him[547]. Failing such production, the surety forfeits the sum mentioned in the recognizance, subject to being imprisoned in default of payment. The surety is however discharged of his obligation if he proves that the non-appearance of the defendant was due to a force majeure[548].

Considering the enormous risk taken by the surety, the law has given him the possibility of withdrawing his recognizance. Every surety wishing to withdraw bail is required to produce the person on bail before the competent authority who takes note of the withdrawal, while informing the person that he may remain on bail if he provides another surety or securities[549]. A surety who suspects that the person on bail is trying to evade his obligations to appear before the court, may as well inform the authority who granted bail. The said authority may order his arrest and remand him or cause him to provide another surety[550]. The State Counsel may equally with the use of his discretional power grant self bail.

3. Self bail

In practice most State Counsel in the process of granting bail do not necessarily subject it to the deposit of a security in the state treasury or the production of one or more sureties. They equally take into consideration the status of the suspect. A suspect with a stable employment, married and with a known place of abode may likely benefit from self bail.

In practice however most of the courts of French expression make use of securities or caution as a guarantee of appearance of person granted bail. Most litigants decry the exorbitant sums often demanded as securities, which at times are

546 Section 228(1) ,CPC
547 Section 228(2), CPC
548 Section 228(3), CPC
549 Section229, CPC
550 Section 230, CPC

hardly ever less than 50.000francs. In a country where the interprofessional guaranteed minimum wage abbreviated in French as (SMIG)[551] is less than 40.000 francs most counsels for the defence see the securities as exaggerated. Sometimes between 2012 and 2014 the Legal Department of the Court of First Instance Edea and the High Court Sanaga Maritime Division, situated on the very busy Douala-Yaoundé highway in a bit to curb the exceedingly high rate of unintentional killing and harm through the high rate of accidents, fixed the sum of caution at a million francs, without which most of the suspects were remanded in custody awaiting trial. For offences such as simple theft, misappropriation, false pretences, destruction, disturbances of quiet enjoyment equally legion in this area, the security or caution ranged between 100,000-250,000 francs.

On the contrary, in the courts of Anglo-Saxon extraction, most magistrates make use of Surety as a mechanism of guarantying the appearance of suspects or defendants. However, sureties usually enter a recognizance or a property bond[552]. Courts in the North West and South West Regions equally make use of both surety who enter both a recognizance and a property bond backed up by a land title.

C. Remand in Custody pending Hearing

Although bail is the principle and remand the exception, the discretion of the State Counsel can as well lead him to remand a suspect in custody while pending the hearing and determination of his matter. Apart from the cases expressly provided for by law wherein bail is prohibited, there are so many considerations that can lead a State Counsel to remand even where bail is authorised.

Most State Counsels take into consideration the gravity of the offence as a determinant factor. Aggravated offences committed flagrante delicto wherein suspects are opened to mob justice will hardly ever be subject to bail. Offences such as

---

[551] Salaire minimum interprofessionnel garanti

[552] A property bond uses a person's personal possession as a way to ensure bail payment. Usually this involves larger items such as house or landed property. Practically the suspect deposits copies of the property as guarantee. If the suspect jumps bail the court can possess the items and force the accused to forfeit ownership in order to cover the cost of bail. Using one's property as a way to pay bail should be very carefully considered and used only as last resort.

unintentional killing or harm through accident most especially accidents that cause the loss of many lives, the reflex of a smart State Counsel will be to remand the suspect for his security and protection.

Most State Counsels are reticent to grant bail to criminals who are ex-convicts for fear of exposing the society to identified dangerous elements. Remand in custody is always considered for habitual criminals with the hope of re-socialisation.

Women with children are always given special consideration when it comes to taking decisions on bail or remand. Generally however, where the suspects can neither produce a surety to guarantee their appearance or pay a caution or security into the State treasury where such guarantee is required, the State Counsel is left with no other option but remand.

When the Legal Department is settled on the liberty of the suspect, the institution of proceedings is the next step. Proceedings are however instituted depending on the nature of the offence which by itself determines the court to be seized and the procedure to be engaged. While felonies automatically command that preliminary inquiries be opened [553], misdemeanours and simple offences obviously calls for charging before Courts of First Instance. The State Counsel with the use of his discretionary power direct that preliminary inquiries be opened even in misdemeanours and simple offences[554]

IV. INSTITUTION OF PROCEEDINGS BEFORE THE COURT OF FIRST INSTANCE

Criminal proceedings before the Court of First Instance are commenced either by way of a committal order of an Examining Magistrate, an order of the Inquiry Control Chambers, by "direct summons" or by application of the procedure relating to offences committed flagrante delicto [555]. Apart from direct summons instituted by individuals, all the other methods of seizure contain charges.

---

[553] Section 142(1), CPC

[554] Section 142(2),CPC

[555] Section 290, CPC

A. Charging before the Court of First Instance

It is a fundamental principle of law that the accused should know the exact nature of the allegation brought against him. It is therefore imperative that before a person is convicted of any offence he should be formally charged, i.e. informed of the offence allegedly committed by him and be given the opportunity to defend himself against such charge. He is entitled to be informed with the greatest precision what acts he is said to have committed and under what section of the penal law theses act falls.

Unlike the Criminal Procedure Ordinance used in the then Anglophone provinces, the CPC does not define a charge, specify its elements, or sanction a charge poorly drafted. This deficiency has led some legal practitioners to question whether the charge still has a place in our criminal procedure, with some arguing that the use of charges is contrary to public policy. Responding to this overly sensitive issue the **Court of Appeal of the North West Region**[556] stated:

"Learned counsel further argued that it (the charge) was contrary to public policy. Public policy is said to be a very unruly horse. It is a term that does not admit of any precise definition. However, broadly speaking, it constitutes principles and standards regarded by the legislature or by the courts as being of fundamental concern to the State and the whole society. An infringement is therefore said to be contrary to public policy, where it outrages a sense of justice and decency, where it offends our conception of human liberty and freedom of action and above all, where it is prejudicial to the interest of the State. From the foregoing can we say, can it be said that by instituting criminal proceedings in the Court of First Instance on a filed charge, in lieu of a direct summons, when an accused has been properly summoned to appear in court and stand trial on the said charge, is prejudicial to the rights of defence, or contrary to public policy? The answer is patently in the negative. We hold that while it is desirable to institute criminal proceedings in the Court of First Instance by direct summons,

[556] Fuh Gideon Bakeh & 4 ORS Vs The People of Cameroon & 3 ORS, Suit N0.CANWR/MS/39C/2014: SLR 4 (2016), p. 30-31

pursuant to section 290 of the CPC, commencing the same on the charge which is an excerpt of the summon served on the accused in strict compliance with the provisions of section 40 et seq of the code in essence serves the same purpose. After all the bottom line is that the accused was summoned to court directly and arraigned on the charge. Instituting criminal proceedings as such was neither prejudicial to the right of defence nor was it contrary to public policy. In other words, there was no miscarriage of justice. To hold otherwise would be an unnecessary display of pedantry"

In the same line and responding to a similar question the **Court of Appeal of the North West Region**[557] in another suit came to the same conclusion though with much precision when it held inter-alia that:

"The learned advocate General Magnaguemabe Pascal, representing the 1st respondent argued that the instrument of accusation filed by his department at the trial court was a nullity because it was a charge sheet. He maintained that the charge is an old practice under the CPO which has been repealed by section 746(K) of the CPC and that this charge is against the rights of the defence and public policy. With all due respect, we wish to differ with some aspects of this seemingly charming argument. There is no doubt that section 746(K) of the ordinance has been repealed; But this does not mean that all the words or legal terms that were in the ordinance are anathema to the CPC. The said CPC itself in many of its sections used the word "CHARGE". It is our considered opinion that a close study of the CPC can lend credence to the conclusion that the charge is still a proper instrument of bringing persons before the court of law in the present dispensation of the CPC. The question then is this; if the charge was no longer a legal instrument of accusation in the CPC, what then is the instrument that is being referred to in the above sections of the CPC and many other sections that we have cited here? Since the code, that is the CPC has not given a definition of a charge anywhere in its provisions, we think that

---

[557] Bangha Grace & 1OR Vs The People of Cameroon and 1OR. Suit N0.CANWR/MS/30C/2015, SLR 6(2017),p.44-45

a charge as drafted in the trial court is still a legal instrument of accusation in the CPC".

The bone of contention here is the facts that direct summons, as a mode of commencement of proceedings is not exhaustively presented. It does not make mention of a charge, or precise its definition and constitutive elements. This lack of precision as to the content of direct summons was identified by the then president of the North West Court of Appeal as an obstacle to prosecution. However, he proposed that a formal procedure should be laid out and included in the CPC, since the notion was called from the "*Code d'Instruction Criminelle*"[558].

The Chief Justice as regards charges and indictments, proposed that the code should provide in book I section (a) for interpretation of words and phrases, wherein various legal terms will be defined, proposing further that the format and content of charge and indictment should be included in the code and specified just like in the order of commencement of inquiry[559]as well as defects of charges such as duplicity.

While wholly adopting the solution of the Learned Chief Justice, which is specific to indictment, we will like to add that if such changes will be made in the nearest future by the law makers, the following requirements regarding a charge properly speaking should be emphasized:

- It should be in writing;
- It should be in the language of the Court;
- It should state the offence with which the person is charged;

---

[558] Paper presented by Chief Justice Morfaw Henry Njinjun President of the Court of Appeal North West Provence on "Shortcomings and problems relating to the application of the CPC and proposed solutions in the Jurisdiction of the North West Court of Appeal" on the 6th October 2007.

[559] Section 164(1) « the order for commencement of inquiry may be made against a known or unknown person ;

It shall specify;

a) The full names and the functions of the magistrate who made it;
b) The statement of the offence committed;
c) The full name and identity of the defendant if he is known, or the sign if he is unknown;
d) A precise statement of the provisions of the law which has been violated;
e) The place and date of the commission of the offence;

- It should give particulars as to the time and place of the alleged offence and the person against whom or the thing in respect of which the offence was committed;
- It should state the law and section of the law against which the offence is said to have been committed;

Any such changes in the CPC should equally inculcate the notions of defective charges and charges bad for duplicity.

B. Defective charges

As regards the notion of a defective charge, the principle of law governing a charge sheet is that an accused should be charged with an offence known in law. The offence charged should be disclosed and stated in a clear and unambiguous manner so that the accused may be able to plead to a specific charge that he can understand. The Kenyan decisions of the Courts of Appeal[560] and the High Court[561] holds that a charge sheet is fatally defective if it does not allege an essential ingredient of the offence. The Court of Appeal of the North West Region in the afore-cited case use the notion of a defective charge, relating to a charge that was addressed to a non-existing Court, in the excerpt of the judgement the court held inter-alia that the

"Learned counsel for the 2nd respondent maintained that the legal issues raised by the Appellant and 1st Respondent that the charge addressed to a none existing court is bad at law[562] is not a ground of appeal. Consequently, it shall be a violation of section 449(3) of the CPC, If this Court takes into consideration the above arguments…. He argued that throughout the trial at the Court, the defence never raised the issue of a defective charge and that it was too late for them to do so at the level of the Court of Appeal….We very much appreciate and

[560]Case of Yosefa v. Uganda [1969]E.A. 236.

[561]Sigilani v. Republic [2004] 2 KLR 480.

[562] Learned Counsel for the Appellant in a further submission had drew the attention of the Court to the fact that the instrument of accusation (charge) upon which the Appellants were convicted in the trial Court was addressed to the Court of First Instance Boyo Judicial Division in place of the Court of First Instance Fundong, which according to the Appellants acted in vain when it received a charge that was not destined to it. The charge was addressed to the Court of First Instance Boyo (which in essence is none existent) was entertained by the Court of First Instance Fundong, which is existing but to whom the charge was not destined or addressed.

sympathise with these arguments of the 2nd Respondent raised by her learned counsel. We are also embarrassed by this attitude of the Legal Department, that should have sought to correct its own errors committed at the trial court, instead of relying on the errors to urge that the proceedings and judgements of the trial Court should be annulled. However, we wish to note here that the unambiguous provisions of section 3(2) of the CPC are that "nullity as referred to in subsection (1) of this section shall not be overlooked. It may be raised at any stage of the criminal proceedings by the trial court of its own motion". In the light of the above, even if the appellant and the 1st respondent did not raise that procedural virus in the charge; this court trying this matter; ought to raise it of its own motion".

The Court of Appeal consequently declared the entire proceedings a nullity in consonance with the provisions of section 3 of the CPC, setting aside the Judgement since it was tainted with an irreparable illegality which could not be reviewed as per the provisions of section 463 of the CPC.

C. Charges bad for duplicity

The rules against duplicity prohibit the prosecution alleging two or more offences in a single charge sheet or indictment. The rules against duplicity are based on the following considerations:

- The accused must know the case alleged so that he or she can prepare and present a defence;
- The Court must know the charges alleged so that it can determine the admissibility of evidence, determine the appropriate punishment in case of conviction;
- The Court must know the précised charges in order to focus on the relevant fact finding task and consider the possibility of defences operating at different times;
- The accused must be able to use a Court record to support a defence of a previous conviction or previous acquittal.

Duplicity may take two forms:

1. **Patent duplicity**
   Patent duplicity exists when a single charge in the charge sheet or indictment alleges the commission of two or more offences;
2. **Latent Duplicity**
   Latent duplicity arises when the evidence in respect of a single charge reveals the commission of two or more possible offences.

It will just be proper that in any future amendments of the CPC, the law makers should specify these notions of charges or indictments which were merely shallowly and passively treated. It is worth noting that these precisions participate in fostering the right to a fair trial by its nature and essence.
As it stands for the time being the drafting of charges and indictment as indicated by the chief justice is not regulated. While the Courts in the two English speaking regions have adopted the drafting style of the former CPO, Courts across the Moungo maintained the drafting rules inspired from the "*Code d'Instruction Criminelle*", respecting in passing forms that were designed to this effect by the Minster in charge of Justice.

D. Samples of Charges within the Courts of the North West and South West Regions

1. For theft under Section 318(1) of the penal code

That you Man Nolap on or about the 7th day of February 2019 at Kumba in the Meme Judicial Division, caused loss to one God Power by theft, that is by removing his property to wit; a bag of rice, a radio set, four shirts and two pair of shoes and thereby committed an offence contrary to and punishable under Section 318(1) of the Penal Code.

2. Where several offences were committed by the same person at the same time and place (disturbance of quiet enjoyment, destruction and conditional threat under Sections 239, 316 and 302(2) of the Penal code)

Count One:
That you Ngong Joshua on or about the 7th day of March 2019 at Awing in the Mezam Judicial Division in a manner liable to

disturb the public peace entered upon land quietly enjoyed by one Che Divine and thereby committed an offence contrary to and punishable under Section 239 of the penal code.

Count Two:
That you Ngong Joshua at the same time and place destroyed crops and trees belonging to the said Che Divine to wit; four ridges of maize, two young mango trees aged approximately 1year, four pear tress of the same age, 3 guava trees of approximately 3years and thereby committed an offence contrary to and punishable under Section 316(1) of the penal code.

Count Three:
That you Ngong Joshua at the same time and place threatened same Che with dead if he dared set foot on the said piece of land and thereby committed and offence contrary to and punishable under Section 302(2)(a) of the penal code[563].

The drawing up or drafting of indictment though containing almost similar elements are different in form or structure with regards to charges.

E. Samples of Indictments within the Courts of the North West and South West Regions

1. Aggravated theft

Statement of offence

Aggravated theft contrary to and punishable under Section 320(1)(b) of the penal code;

Particulars of offence

That you Mbah Sampson on or about the 11th day of February at Nsongwa in the Mezam Judicial Division, caused loss to one Ndutu Paul by breaking into his residence and collecting therefrom; a 32 inch TV set, a gas bottle, a laptop, three iPods and the sum of 500.000 (five hundred thousand) FCFA .

[563] Where an offence was committed at the same time and place and by one or several persons, it will be redundant in for example a four count charge to for each count mention the date and place. In such cases the format «…at the same time and place…», is used to avoid monotony. In such cases the charges are numbered in counts with each offence constituting a count.

2. **Aggravated Misappropriation**

Statement of offence

Aggravated misappropriation contrary to and punishable under Section 321 of the penal code

Particulars of offence

That you Ndola Jude on or about the 25th of November at Babungo in the Ngoketunjia Judicial Division being the manager of ambiance bar, by misappropriation, caused loss to your employer one Dogo George of the sum of 300.000 (three hundred thousand) FCFA, being proceeds of sales of drinks, entrusted to you for accounting and thereby committed an offence.

3. **Capital murder**

Statement of offence

Capital murder contrary to and punishable under section 276 of the Penal Code

Particulars of offence

That you Galim Clinton on or about the 14th of February 2019 at Bali in the Mezam Judicial Division caused the death of one Doh Lawson after premeditation.

F. Charging and Indictment before Courts of French Speaking Courts

The drafting of a charge or an indictment in jurisdictions of French expression is unique in that it makes precision on the time factor (en tout cas dans le temps légal des poursuites) as well as the intentional factor, *mensrea* (i.e. Section 74 of the Penal code)[564]. Section 74 is not always cited for unintentional offences such as unintentional harm or killing[565], simple harm[566], or slight harm [567], when the harm caused in both circumstances are unintentional. These elements though primordial are not highlighted with as much emphasis within the Anglo-Saxon context. Whereas the use of this factors in the drafting of charges

[564] The precision of the time and intentional factors observed in charges before courts of French expression is an important factor to be considered in any future amendments of the CPC, as regards the drafting of charges most especially.

[565] Section 289, Penal Code

[566] Section 280, penal code

[567] Section 281, penal code

across the Moungo are mandatory, its absence is liable to rendering the charge defective. No Court will readily entertain a matter wherein the elements are absent in the document seizing the Court.

G. Charge Samples before Courts of French expression (One Count Charge)

1. Simple theft (vol simple)

ABATSON Cyrille a été traduit devant le Tribunal de Première Instance statuant en matière correctionnelle pour y répondre de la prévention d'avoir à Aviation Edéa, ressort judiciaire du Tribunal de Première Instance d'Edéa, le 23/07/2015 en tout cas dans le temps légal de poursuite ; porté atteinte à la fortune de sieur SIGOUE Louis par vol c'est-à-dire en soustrayant a son préjudice une scie sauteuse, cinq fraises, un tournevis, une paire de sécurité, un manteau, une paire de gang, une paire de ciseau ,un rallonge de 50m, qu'il a enfoui dans un sac, fait prévus et réprimés par les articles 74 et 318 (1) a du code penal.

2. Unintentional killing and harm (homicide involontaire)

BTCHOKA Paul a été traduit devant le Tribunal de Première Instance d'Edéa, statuant en matière correctionnelle pour y répondre de la prévention d'avoir à Pouma, ressort judiciaire d'Edéa, le 18/11/2012 en tout cas dans le temps légal des poursuites, par maladresse, négligence, imprudence ou inobservation des règlements causé la mort de nommé Billong Bienvenue et des blessures aux nommés MPECKMPECK,OUM Robert, EYIKE Paul, YEMBA Herve, NGUETANG Marie Laure, MAKON Fils, HAMGA Jeanne Clarisse et NKOUGABINAM Paul , faits prévus et réprimés par les articles 289 du code pénal ;

Two or more count charges

3. Missapropriation and non possession of National identity card (Abus de confiance et défaut de CNI)

HAMAN BOUBA a été traduit devant le Tribunal de Première Instance statuant en matière correctionnelle pour y répondre de la prévention d'avoir à Yassa Douala, mais appréhendé à Edéa ressort judiciaire du Tribunal de Première Instance d'Edéa, le 23/09/2015 en tout cas dans le temps légal des poursuites ; porté atteinte à la fortune de Sieur SOULEYMANOU OUMAROU par abus de confiance c'est-à-dire en détournant une motocyclette de marque BAJAJ qu'il a reçu à charge de la conserver, de la rendre, ou d'en faire un usage déterminer, notamment les fait pour lui de ne pas pourvoir le représenter à son propriétaire ; dans les mêmes circonstances de temps et lieux que ci-dessus , été trouvé dépourvu de la carte nationale d'identité dont le port est obligatoire ,fait prévus et réprimés par les articles 74 et 318 (1) b du code pénal, 1 et 5 de la loi N° 90/042 du 19 Décembre 1990 ;

4. **Practice of witchcraft and destruction (Pratiques de sorcellerie et destruction)**

NTILME Roger a été traduits devant le Tribunal de Premier Instance d'Edéa statuant en matière correctionnelle pour y répondre de la prévention d'avoir à Edéa-Ekité ressort judiciaire du Tribunal de Première Instance d'Edéa, le 23/08/2013 en tout cas dans le temps légal des poursuites;

1) livré à des pratiques de sorcellerie, magie ou divination susceptible de troubler l'ordre ou la tranquillité publique ou de porter atteinte aux personnes, aux bien ou à la fortune de MAHI Job même sous forme de rétribution[568] ;

2) Détruit des cacaoyers, des arbres fruitiers notamment 15 orangers, 10 kolatiers, 08 safoutiers et autres, faits prévus et réprimés par les articles 74,316 et 251 du Code Pénal[569] ;

H. Indictments before Courts of French expression

Indictments before jurisdictions of French expression are slightly different from those of the English regions of the North and South west Regions of Cameroon. The format used is faintly

---

[568] It is common practice in the courts of the North and South West Regions of Cameroun that the commencement of prosecution for the offence of witchcraft is subject to the deliverance of a fiat to prosecute by the competent PG. Such is not the case with courts east of the Moungo.

[569] We note that charges of more than one count are either drafted in a block or numbered without any clear-cut separation. The Anglo-Saxon counts system is not applied. If duplicity was to be considered in any future amendments the counts system should equally be put in place, without which such charges which are not separate in essence will be bad for duplicity. Harmonisation is required in this domain.

different, but the content is almost similar. Below are samples of indictments before courts of French extraction. (one count)

1. **Indecency to child under sixteen (Outrage à la pudeur en présence d'une personne mineure de seize ans)**

Suivant l'ordonnance du 13 Février 2004, OMA Julius a été renvoyé devant le Tribunal de Grande Instance de la Sanaga maritime statuant en matière criminelle pour y être jugé sur la prévention d'avoir à Songmbengue, ressort judiciaire du Tribunal susvisé, le 01er Avril 2013 en tout cas dans le temps légal des poursuites, commis un outrage à la pudeur en présence de NGO NTOGO Marie, mineure âgée de 11 ans comme née le 13 Mars 2003 avec cette circonstance qu'à l'aide de violences physiques ou morales, il l'a contrainte à avoir avec lui des relations sexuelles ; faits prévus et punis par les articles 74, 346 (1) et (4) ;

Below is a three count indictment.

2. **Aggravated theft, receiving and accessory (vol aggrave, recel et complicité)**

Suivant l'ordonnance du 30 Mars 2015 les nommés NGUIAMBA Bidias et MILLARD Linus ont été renvoyés devant le Tribunal de Grande Instance de la Sanaga Maritime, statuant en matière criminelle pour y être jugés sur la prévention d'avoir à Edéa ressort du Tribunal de Grande Instance de la Sanaga Maritime, le 01 février 2015, en tout cas dans le temps légal de poursuites,

1) porté atteinte à la fortune de la société HALGED SARL prise en la personne de son chef d'agence par vol aggravé, c'est-à-dire en soustrayant à son préjudice, des spiritueux évalués a la somme de 1.737.922 FCFA avec cette circonstance que ledit vol a été commis à l'aide d'une fausse clé ;
2) Qu'il a également été reproché au nommé BITJOKA Romaric d'avoir détenu ou disposé des choses obtenus à l'aide de vol, soit en connaissance de cause soit en en ayant des raisons d'en soupçonner l'origine délictuelle avec cette circonstance que ce vol a été commis à l'aide d'une fausse clé et

3) enfin au nommé MAYO Alfred de s'être rendu complice des faits de vol et recel reprochés respectivement à NGUIAMBA et MILLARD, notamment en s'abstenant de les dénoncer alors même qu'il était au courant de tous leurs mouvements délictueux ; Que ces faits sont prévus et réprimés par les articles 74, 97,318(1) a, 320 (1) et 324 d du code Pénal.

Whatever the case, a charge be it in courts of English or French expression is a component of either a direct summons or procedures engaged by way of Flagrante delicto procedure.

V. THE DEPARTMENT OF PUBLIC PROSECUTIONS AND THE INSTITUTION OF PROCEEDINGS

As far as the Legal Department and the institution of proceedings is concerned, the law has provided for a dual mode of seizure of the Court to wit; by way of direct summons (A) or by the use of the flagrante delicto procedure (B).

A. The Legal Department and seizure of the Court by way of direct summons

One of the innovations of the CPC is the introduction of the seizure of the Court of First Instance by way of Direct Summons. If it is true that this mode of seizure was widely used in jurisdictions that applied the CIC, it is equally true that it was not known to jurisdictions of Anglo-Saxon extraction. While its application posed little or no problem in Courts of French extraction, it has not been an easy birth with the Courts of the North and South West Regions. This is so because the Court of First Instance prior to the introduction of other modes of seizures in section 290 was basically seized by way of a charge sheet, with new matters introduced to Court as «overnights». Old habit they say die hard. It has not been easy adapting to this new mode of seizure introduced by the CPC. As such most of the jurisdictions have maintained the use of the charge sheet as a mode of seizure not without objections from counsels.

1. Definition of Direct Summons

The CPC has not given us the definition of the direct summons and the exact form it should take, it is a concept drawn from the repealed "*Code d'instruction Criminelle*". The French translation is "citation directe". In "*Lexique de termes juridiques*", by Daloz 6th edition 82, "citation directe" is defined as;

> "Acte de procédure par lequel le ministère public ou la victime peuvent saisir directement la juridiction de jugement en informant le prévenu des cordonnées de l'audience".

In other words, it is a procedure whereby the Legal Department or the Victim of an offence may cause the accused to be brought directly to the competent court without going through the red tape of preliminary inquiries"[570]

In an earlier decision the Court of Appeal[571]responding to the issue as to what amounts to direct summons, stated:

"The CPC does not specifically define "direct summons". However, Section 40(1) of the code affords a simplistic definition of summons thus, "summons shall be an order requesting a person to appear before a Court". By extrapolation therefore, direct summons, as a mode of commencement of criminal proceedings, would mean direct committal or summon bringing the accused directly before the court without passing through the rigmarole of the conduct of preliminary inquiries. It equally embraces private prosecution… The CPC has neither defined direct summons nor has it furnished us with the form and content. We are therefore constraint to draw inspiration from the provisions of section 40 and 41 of the Code, which deals with summons simpliciter. The provisions of the above-cited sections 40 and 41 of the CPC define the form and content of the summons. It is issued at the request of the Legal Department, the aggrieved party or any other interested party. It is issued by the bailiff who equally affects service. It states the affiliation and other

---

[570] Loh Emmanuel & 2ORS Vs The people of Cameroon & 1or, Suit N0.CANWR/MS/70C/2014; SLR 6, {2017}, p. 54

[571] Fuh Gideon Bakeh & 4ORS Vs The people of Cameroon & 3ORS, Suit N0.CANWR/MS/39C/2014; SLR, 4 {2016}, p. 30-32

material particulars and the address of the complainant or addressee as the case may be. It further states the Court seized of the matter, the place, date and hour of hearing. The summons shall equally state the facts of the case and the provisions of the law under which the accused is charged".

From the above definition of direct summons by the Court of Appeal, one notes that there is no great difference between direct summons and private prosecution which is equally engaged by way of direct summons. The elements contained in both, that is direct summons from the Legal Department and direct summons from aggrieved parties (private prosecution) are similar. What differentiate them is that an aggrieved party who engages criminal action by way of private prosecution is obliged to pay a deposit, (consignation) and stamp duty, without which his action will be declared inadmissible. The Legal Department is not constrained by any such obligations.

From the opening statements of a direct summons one can easily dictate its origin. When it originates from the Legal Department it takes this form; "*Attendu qu'à la requête du Procureur de la République près les Tribunaux d'Edéa et de la Sanaga Maritime et suivant exploit en date 11/04/2015 de Me NJINE Guy Magloire, huissier de justice, près la Cour d'Appel du Littoral et le Tribunaux d'Edéa…*".

On the contrary, when it emanates from an aggrieved party (private prosecution) it is presented thus; "*Attendu qu'à la requête de EDJENGUELE Stepane et par exploit du 02 Septembre 2014 de Me Adalbert NLENDMAPOUT Huissier de justice prés la Cour d'Appel du Littoral et le Tribunaux d'Edéa enregistré le 27 Septembre 2014 au volume 17 Folio 452 au droit de 20697 FCFA….*" Direct summons introduced by an aggrieved party specifies the registration number and the cost of stamp duty.

2. Procedure of Seizure of the Court

The procedure of instituting criminal proceedings through direct summons by the Legal Department was succinctly laid down by the Court of Appeal of the North West Region thus:

"When the Legal Department decides to commence criminal proceedings by direct summons, it is incumbent on them to forward what is termed "An order to summon" to the bailiff. This is a request addressed to the bailiff to issue and serve the direct summons on the accused. The order to summon states the affiliation, the material particulars of identification of the accused, the facts of the case and the provisions of the law under which the accused is charged. The bailiff then uses the information on the "order to summon" (mandement de citation) to draw up the direct summons which is an extra-judicial act. In effect, its content should mutatis mutandis be similar to those of the summons as ordained under section 41 of the code. After drawing it up, it behoves the bailiff to immediately forward an original copy to the State Counsel and serve the accused with a copy thereof in conjunction with a copy of the original order to summon. Thereafter the document captioned "direct summons" which is addressed to the trial court is filed in the Registry of that Court. On the date indicated thereon for hearing, the matter is called and after complying with the provisions of section 338 of the CPC, the accused is arraigned. As such criminal proceedings have been instituted and set in motion. And this is the procedure that should now obtain with the coming into force of the CPC".

In spite if this clarification from the Appeal Court, Courts with original jurisdiction within the North and South West Regions are still very reluctant to adapt to this innovation, haunted by the old demon of the CPO.

Apart from direct summons, instituting proceedings by the way of the flagrante delicto procedure has equally been problematic in Courts of the North West and South West Regions.

B. The Legal Department and the Institution of Proceedings by way of the Flagrante delicto procedure.

One of the modes of commencement of proceedings by the Legal Department introduced by the CPC is by "... application of the procedure relating to offences committed flagrante delicto"[572]. It is a more expedient, special, and simple mode of institution of proceedings instituted by virtue of section 114 of the CPC. The code expressly explains the notion of felonies and misdemeanours committed flagrante delicto[573], while précising that suspects arrested under the said circumstances shall be brought by the JPO before the State Counsel who shall proceed to check his identity, interrogate him summarily[574] and if he decides to prosecute shall place him under temporary detention or release him on bail or with sureties.

The peculiarity of this procedure is instant prosecution in the "nearest session of Court". To my mind this procedure is intended to breach the inertia that characterized the institution of criminal proceedings prior to the putting in place of the CPC. Inertia, that had as consequence, the disappearance of evidence which could have been exploited properly and efficiently while it was still fresh.

The code has however failed to precise the form and content of this mode of commencement of proceedings. This lapse has been compensated by the provision of forms to this effect by the Ministry in charge of Justice. In Courts of French expression proceedings commenced by way of offenses committed flagrante delicto opens thus: *"Attendu que suivant procès-verbal d'interrogatoire au parquet en cas de flagrant délit du 08 Juin 2015..."*.

While lauding the efforts made to this regard, we suggest that the form and content of the procedure in the future should be defined in the CPC. Unlike direct summons, most Legal Departments of the North and South West Regions are fast adapting to this mode of seizure.

---

[572]Section 290, CPC

[573]Section 103, CPC

[574] Interrogation here should not be confused with questioning for the purpose of obtaining evidence. The State Counsel in this case is not out to complete investigations already conducted by JPOs. Interrogation here is geared towards a proper identification of the suspect, notification of the facts for which he will be standing trial, the provisions of law violated and obtaining his response(to the question if he acknowledges the offences for which he is reproached or not). The interrogation equally lays emphasis on the fate of the freedom of the suspect, i.e. he is supposed to be informed if he has been granted bail or not as well as the conditions thereto.

Whatever the case, it should be noted that the role of the Legal Department is not limited to the reception, treatment of police reports as well as institution of proceedings in the Court of First Instance. The treatment sometimes extends this role to the chambers of the Examining Magistrate which is a gateway to the High Court for felonies.

CHAPTER XII
THE LEGAL DEPARTMENT AND THE SETTING IN MOTION OF PRELIMINARY INQUIRY

One of the ground-breaking innovations of the CPC is the fact that preliminary inquiry, hitherto confined to the Legal Department by virtue of the 1972 ordinance relating to judicial organisation, has been handed over to an independent organ i.e. the Examining Magistrate. The Legal Department was criticized severally for playing the role of inquiry and prosecution in the same matter. The CPC instituted the office of the Examining Magistrate, who is a member of the bench and thus independent not only with regards to the jurisdiction in which he carries out his activities[575], with regards to the President of Court[576], with regards to the Inquiry control Chambers[577], with regards to the State Counsel[578] as well as the litigants.

With the introduction of the Examining Magistrate as the new master of preliminary inquiry, many scholars thought and wrongly so, that the Legal Department had completely been scrapped out in the conduct of preliminary inquiry. The Legal Department still plays a primordial role in the conduct of

---

[575] The Court after noticing some irregularities in the reports or rulings of the Examining Magistrate can neither order him to correct or complete same. On the contrary, the Court may Order a JPO or a magistrate of the bench of the same Court to do same to the exclusion to the Magistrate who was initially assigned the file.

[576] As per the provisions of section 146(2),(2) of the CPC, the President of Court cannot single handedly withdraw a matter from the Examining Magistrate. He can only do so on the initiative or request of one of the parties or the legal Department.

[577] The CPC in its logic of the protection of the independence of the Examining Magistrate against the inquiry chambers implicitly prohibits the Inquiry Control Chambers from ordering the EM to carry out certain measures, such is the case with appeals against rulings relating to remand in custody, judicial supervision, or restitution of objects seized. In such cases the Inquiry control Chambers proceeds as it deems fit (section 277 CPC). He can only return the file to same Examining Magistrate in case of appeal against a ruling relating to any other matter other than remand, after quashing the order, with the view of continuing the preliminary inquiry (section 278 CPC).

However where the inquiry Control Chambers annuls a Committal, It may in the interest of the law and for the proper administration of justice appoint another Examining Magistrate or in default another Magistrate of the same Court to continue with preliminary Inquiry (Section 286 CPC).

[578] The State Counsel cannot withdraw an Examining Magistrate assigned a particular matter. In the same line, the Examining Magistrate is not bound by the statement of offence in the complaint or that stated by the State Counsel in his submission (Section 163 CPC).

preliminary inquiry and we can dare say that it is the principal party. He is at the initiation of preliminary inquiry, even when the proceedings are commenced by a complaint with a civil claim, he assist throughout the hearing, his final submission is essential to the closure of preliminary inquiry, and finally he has the right to appeal.

I. THE LEGAL DEPARTMENT AND THE SEIZURE OF THE EXAMINING MAGISTRATE

The Legal Department holds the key that opens the door of preliminary inquiry. Preliminary inquiry can hardly ever commence if the State Counsel does not give his blessings to the Examining Magistrate to proceed.

A. The holding charge

The judicial act by which the State Counsel seizes the Examining Magistrate is called a holding charge[579]. The absolute nature of this act can be justified by the fact that even where an aggrieved party opts for a complaint with a civil claim, the use of this act is never ruled out. It may not be called exactly a holding charge; it may take the form of a submission[580] but what is of essence is that it is at the origin of all preliminary inquiries.

Considering the importance of the act of the State Counsel, the law makers have succinctly spelt out its content. Section 144 of the CPC provides that the holding charge preferred by the State Counsel shall be in writing and made against known or an unknown person. It further provides that it shall contain the statement of the offence committed[581], and

---

579 Section 143, CPC

580 Section 160 (1) « As soon as the civil party has deposited the sum of money provided for in section 158, the Examining Magistrate shall forward the complaint to the State Counsel for his submission;

(2) the submission of the State Counsel may;

a) declare the complaint inadmissible;

b) order the commencement of an inquiry against a known or unknown person;

(3) The State Counsel may also in the case of complaint without sufficient grounds or inadequate justification having regard to supporting documents, request that the person mentioned in the complaint be heard as a witness by the Examining Magistrate.

581 Statement of offence within the Anglo Saxon context of an indictment simply refers to the offence committed as well as the provision of the law violated. Section 144 (2), fails to mention that the particulars of offence as well are supposed to be contained in the holding charge of the State Counsel. This lapse has however been rectified on the forms from the

mention that prosecution has not been discontinued by virtue of the circumstances referred to in Section 62 of the CPC. An author has questioned the pertinence of the inclusion of this provision on the holding charge[582], arguing and reasonably so, that it is impossible for any right-thinking magistrate to commence any proceedings where one of those factors stand as an obstacle. Lastly it must be signed by the State Counsel.

After complying with the provisions, the holding charge is forwarded to the Examining Magistrate through the President of the Court. Forwarding of the case file does not however stops the State Counsel from requesting the Examining Magistrate to perform any act which he deems necessary for the discovery of the truth and in particular to prefer a new charge. This he does by way of an additional holding charge[583].

Yohanes Mbunja[584] identifies the following as the effects of the holding Charge:

- the holding charge have as principal effect putting in motion preliminary inquiry within the limits of the statement of offence cited. Its nullity incidentally leads to the nullity of the entire procedure, as the Examining Magistrate will not be deemed as having been regularly seized;
- as soon as the holding charge is transmitted to the President of the Court, the State Counsel is functus officio and cannot carry out any prosecutorial acts in the matter, until the response of the Examining Magistrate;
- Finally, the holding charge is an act that interrupts prescription in spite of its omission in the enumeration of such acts in the provisions of section 66 of the CPC.

---

ministry of justice, which in its structure, provides space for the particulars of the offence. The form alone is not enough to remedy this shortcoming; we recommend that it should be taken care of in the event of amendments in the CPC.

[582]Mbunja (Y.), op.cit., pp.63.

[583]Section 145 (1) and (2) CPC.

[584] Ibid.

B. The Legal Department and Complaints with Civil Claims

Any person who alleges that he has suffered injury resulting from a felony, or a misdemeanour may when lodging a complaint with the competent Examining Magistrate, file a civil claim. The complaint in which a victim claims damages shall set the criminal action in motion. These provisions are not applicable to simple offences or to offences, the prosecution of which is exclusively reserved for the Legal Department[585].

As we noted above the role of the State Counsel in preliminary inquiry proceedings set in motion is as capital as by holding charge. After the payment of the deposit fixed by the Examining Magistrate to whom the case file is assigned, the file is forwarded to the State counsel who by his submissions can either make or mar the proceedings. The submissions of the state counsel initially open two options, with a negative and positive connotation.

1. Inadmissibility of Complaint with civil claim

It may declare the civil claim inadmissible. A submission of inadmissibility automatically brings the procedure to an end. One of the causes of inadmissibility is failure to deposit at the registry of the Court of First Instance an amount considered sufficient for defraying the cost of the proceedings[586]. It is a rather complex situation since by virtue of the provision; the forwarding of the file for submission is conditioned by the defrayment of the said sum. It is however comprehensive considering the fact that the law is silent on the fate of a complaint with a civil claim wherein the civil complainant defaults defrayment of deposit. It is just logical that the Examining Magistrate forwards such a file for the steps to be taken (submission on inadmissibility for non-defrayment of deposit). Among other causes of inadmissibility, an author [587] has identified offences for which the Legal Department has the sole right of setting in motion prosecution, which are offences for which a civil party cannot apply for

---

[585] Section 157 (1), (2) and (3) CPC

[586]Section 158(1), CPC.

[587] Mpinda (F.),op.cit., pp. 41

damages (non-possession of identity card, traffic of drugs and contraband goods etc).

2. Order of commencement

It may as well order the commencement of an inquiry against a known or unknown person. An order of commencement gives the Examining Magistrate green light to commence inquiry within the frame of the statement of offence retained by the State Counsel. We insist on the statement of offence retained by the State Counsel because the State Counsel when making his submissions is not bound by the statement of offence as given by the complainant[588], even though the Examining Magistrate is as well not bound by the statement of offence stated by the State Counsel in his submissions[589].

The law makers have provided for a third option. This option gives the State Counsel the possibility of ordering for the commencement of inquiry in the face of a complaint without sufficient grounds, inadequate justification having regards to the supporting documents, on condition of requesting the complainant to be heard as witness by the Examining Magistrate. [590] The law lays emphasis on request leaving compliance at the discretion of the Examining Magistrate.

Apart from this hypothesis Ferry Armand [591] equally brings to light other hypothesis not foreseen by the law makers. Such is the case with lack of jurisdiction both material and personal, immunity, and privilege of jurisdiction or prescription. That notwithstanding, it is worth noting that his role is not limited to setting in motion preliminary inquiry.

II. THE LEGAL DEPARTMENT AND THE PRELIMINARY INQUIRY

Apart from the role of setting in motion inquiry proceedings, the Legal Department plays active part in the course of inquiry. The

---

[588] Section 163(1) CPC.
[589] Section 163(2) CPC.
[590] Section 160 (3) CPC.
[591] Mpinda (F.),op.cit., p. 42

CPC makes him a party in the proceedings and some authors are even tempted to call him a principal party by virtue of his role.

A. Prior Information: A Condition of the Participation of the State Counsel in Preliminary Inquiry

The law provides that the State Counsel may be present at the interrogation and the confrontation of the defendant, as well as the hearing of the civil party and witnesses. It further provides that he shall inform the Examining Magistrate of his intention to do so[592]. The CPC makes the presence of the State Counsel optional in all the phases of the inquiry, while subjecting the said presence to prior information of the Examining Magistrate [593] "He shall inform the Examining Magistrate..." However, the mandatory nature of the information is not subject to any sanction in case of non-compliance. The spirit of this compulsory provision to our mind is thus one of courtesy which in our opinion needs not be mandatory.

B. Examination, Cross-Examination and Confrontation: An Ambiguous Mode of Intervention of the State Counsel in PI

The essence of the presence of the State Counsel during preliminary inquiry is stipulated in Section 176 of the CPC, which refers us to Section 175 of same. This provision gives the State Counsel right to directly examine, cross-examine the witnesses, the defendants, and to carry out a confrontation of the parties. This applies to the counsels of the defendant and the civil party as well. Unlike in preliminary investigation where the role of counsel of the suspect is limited to assisting his client without any further precision, his role just like that of the State Counsel has been expressly stated as regards preliminary inquiry.

If we go by the premise that investigations and inquiry are just preparatory phases of trials and have as objective the search

[592] Section 175(1) CPC.

[593] Each time the lawmakers make use of the word « shall » in a provision of law, it gives an obligatory nature to the required action. The actor charged with its execution must scrupulously comply with the said provision, he has no option. This applies even when the non-compliance is not sanctioned. On the contrary where the law desires to give an option to the actors, it expressly provides for that possibility by the use of the word «may»

for ingredients favourable or unfavourable to the defendant, then the role of counsel and the State Counsel at the preliminary inquiry phase poses a problem in our opinion. The role of examination, cross-examination and confrontation attributed to the State Counsel and counsels in the course of preliminary inquiry has assimilated the proceedings to a pre-trial and not the inquiry that it was designed to be.

More so, considering the fact that the law gives the Examining Magistrate the latitude to stop the witness, or any other party from answering any question which he deems irrelevant, injurious or against public policy only at the phase of confrontation. An Examining Magistrate who is not smart may find himself conducting a trial, whereas the lawmakers did not intend to make preliminary inquiry as such, or better still "*audience en form réduit*" in the words of the former President of the Appeal Court of the Center Region Mbenoun Christopher [594]

Examination, cross-examination and confrontation has rendered preliminary inquiry not only unnecessarily long and delaying the dispensation of justice but has equally transformed this investigating phase into a full trial. This confusion has further created uncertainty on the role of the Examining Magistrate; is it adjudicating or investigating? The Inquiry Control Chambers of the Court of Appeal of the North West Region in ***Nyamsekwen Christopher Kunbuma Vs the People of Cameroon & 2ors*** [595], clarified the role of the Examining magistrate in the following words:

"***The Examining Magistrate states that; " these are the facts to be adjudicated upon"...It is only a Court that adjudicates on facts because per the oxford Advanced Learner's Dictionary of the Current English and even Black's Law Dictionary, to adjudicate means the judging of a matter by a judge and giving a judgment or a decision on the liability or the guilt or the innocence of the accused or on the issues raised in the cause of action. To adjudicate means to evaluate the evidence adduce and take a decision as in what is right and what is wrong and what the true situation is. This is certainly***

[594]In the preface of the book of Yohanes Mbunja, cited by Ferry Armand Mpinda, supra, p. 45
[595]Suit NO.CANWR/ICC/2C/2014,SLR 6 {2017}, pp.124

the duty of the Court and not that of the Examining Magistrate who is just a superior investigator...We have held in many cases and still hold with emphasis here that the role of the Examining Magistrate is limited to the tracing of the slightest indication or suspicion, even from only one witness, that the defendant is implicated or involved in the commission of an offence and he is bound to commit him to stand trial before the competent Court. The Examining Magistrate's duty is to be satisfied that a prima facie case has been made out from the evidence of even one witness against the defendant to justify that he is being properly charged before the trial court. The search for concrete proof of the commission of an offence, and the proof of veracity of the evidence of the witnesses, as well as the decision whether the defendant is guilty or innocent of the offence, are the reserved duty and business of the trial court and not the concern of the Examining Magistrate who is conducting only an inquiry"

It is for this reason that most Examining Magistrates limit the participation of the State Counsel and Counsel of other parties to a one or two questions and observations, contending that they have the full autonomy to defend their case before the law court or file an appeal.

C. The State Counsel and Visit to the Locus Inquo during PI

This assimilation of preliminary inquiry into a trial, with the intervention of the State Counsel and Counsels of the parties as provided for in the CPC, leads us to wonder if the said parties can as well take part in other acts of preliminary inquiry such as search and seizures or even to the *locus inquo*. This question is more pertinent as regards visits to the *locus inquo*, considering the fact that at times they are organised not only to make necessary observations but to proceed to the interrogation of some parties or witnesses as well as to confrontation. Unfortunately, the law is silent on this issue. That notwithstanding, some authors[596] are of the opinion that for the

[596] Mpinda (F.),op.cit.,p. 44, citing Mbunja (Y.), supra, p. 129

sake of transparency of preliminary inquiry towards the parties not subjected to secrecy[597], the Examining Magistrate is supposed to take an order fixing the visit to the *locus inquo*, which he must serve on the State Counsel and the counsel of other parties.

D. Submissions: An Indirect means of Participation in PI

The participation of the State Counsel in inquiry proceedings far from being direct can as well be indirect. This participation can be manifested by the exercise of his generalised power of submissions, by virtue of which he can request the Examining Magistrate to carry out acts which he deems necessary. Such is the case with an additional holding charge for the purpose of charging, expertise, visit to the *locus inquo*, remand in custody, when he feels that the defendant does not merit bail.[598] It is however regrettable that the law in most cases has not fixed a time limit within which the Examining Magistrate must respond to the additional holding charges of the State Counsel. The silence of the Examining Magistrate cannot be assimilated to an implicit refusal or rejection neither. He is obliged to wait and most often the time spent renders the act requested to be of no essence.

E. Preliminary Inquiry and the Submissions of the State Counsel

The forwarding of the case file to the State Counsel equally materialise the non-negligible role he plays in the conduct of inquiry proceedings. While observing that the other parties to the proceedings are not beneficiaries of this obligation, the law has gone as far as making the forwarding of proceedings obligatory in some cases and optional in others.

The forwarding of the case file to the State counsel for his submissions is obligatory in the following cases:

[597] Section 154(2), CPC, « Anyone participating in the proceedings shall be bound by professional secrecy subject to the penalties provided for in section 310 of the penal code; provided that the secrecy shall neither apply to the Legal Department nor to the defence.

[598] Mbunja (Y.), op.cit., p. 108.

1. **Setting in motion of PI by way of complaint with civil claim**

Where criminal action is set in motion by an aggrieved party by way of a complaint with a civil claim, the law makes the transmission of the case file to the State Counsel mandatory after the payment of deposit[599];

2. **Application for bail**

Such is equally the case with the granting of bail. The law provides that where bail is not granted as of right, or by the Examining Magistrate of his own motion, it may be granted on application of the defendant or his counsel and after the submissions of the State Counsel. This was the position of the **Inquiry Control Chambers of the Court of Appeal South West Region**[600] responding to the issue as to whether it is mandatory for the Examining Magistrate to forward the application for bail to the Legal Department for submission. The Court ruled thus:

It is crystal clear to us that section 222 envisages two situations under which bail can be granted by the Legal Department: (a) under subsection (1), the Examining Magistrate grants the bail on his own motion and (b) under subsection (2), he may grant the bail, if he does not do so of his own motion, on the application of the defendant or defendants counsel. We hold that it is under situation (a) that is, where the Examining Magistrate acts of his own motion that is that the submission of the Legal Department/State Counsel are not required by law but under situation (b), that is, where the Examining Magistrate is acting pursuant to the application of the defendant or defendants counsel, the law requires that the Examining Magistrate should obtain the submissions of the Legal Department/State Counsel before ruling on whether to grant the bail or not. We hold that it is mandatory, in that situation (b), for the submissions of the Legal

[599]Section 157 as reard with section 160 CPC.

[600] The People of Cameroon Vs Gabriel Lyonga, Suit N0. CASWR/04ICC/2015, SLR 6 (2017),p.170

Department/State Counsel to be obtained and accordingly agree with the Appellants that the learned trial Magistrate erred in law by granting the bail on the application of the defendant/respondent's counsel without getting the submissions of the State Counsel, thereby acting in violation of section 222of the CPC.

3. Entering of recognizance

Whenever the defendant enters a recognizance to appear before the Examining Magistrate wherever convened and undertake to inform the later of his movements[601]

4. Restitution of Exhibits

The CPC, while giving the latitude to anyone to lay claim to articles and documents seized, subject the ruling to such an application to a prior submission of the State Counsel[602];

5. At the close of PI (for final submission)

Lastly the law provides that where the Examining Magistrate deems that the inquiry is ended, he shall forward the file to the State Counsel for his «final submission». Considering the importance of this provision, the law has fixed the dateline for the final submissions to be returned to five (5) days[603]. The law has not provided for guidelines on the nature of the submissions of the Legal Department. This lapse has however been filled up by forms from the Ministry of Justice fashioned to this regard. However, in some jurisdictions, far from just filling the blank spaces with the required information, State Counsels actually make reasoned submissions, setting forth the law and the fact on which it is based.

The other cases of forwarding of files not provided for by law are optional and at times at the request of the Legal Department perform any acts which he deems necessary for the discovery of the truth.

---

[601] Section 222(2), CPC.
[602] Section 179(5), CPC.
[603] Section 256(1), (2), CPC.

The law has made provisions for the transmission of files from the chambers of the Examining magistrate to the State Counsel. In fact, it provides that whenever the Examining Magistrate forwards the file of inquiry to the State Counsel, he must by a ruling make an order known as forwarding order which shall be included in the case file[604]. The forwarding of the case file at the request of the State Counsel is not automatic; the Examining Magistrate can as well go contrary to the request of the State Counsel. In this case his refusal must as well be motivated by a reasoned order, known as an order of refusal of further inquiry, notified to the State Counsel within twenty-four (24) hours.

Practically the transmission of the file is materialised by the transmission of the complete case file to the State Counsel, directly, without transiting through the President of Court. The transmission of the complete case file is not an absolute rule; the law in some cases requires that only the duplicate be transmitted to the State Counsel. Such is the case with section 25(3), (d) of Law N° 2006/015 of 29 December 2006 on judicial Organisation[605]. According to this author the transmission of the case file does not hamper the continuation of hearing or interrogation or better still the carrying out of any act which is not linked to the initial motive of the transmission such as search, seizures etc.

F. The Legal Department and Appeal in the Course of PI.

The decisions of the Examining Magistrate just like every other legal decision may be subject to appeal before the Inquiry Control Chambers[606] within the conditions laid down by law. Unlike other legal decisions, the law has fixed the time-limit for appeal to forty-eight hours following the date of service of the ruling[607]. Practically and summarily they are made by way of an unstamped application in four (4) copies and addressed to the

[604] Section 145(3) CPC.
[605] Mbunja (Y.), op.cit., p. 109
[606] Section 267, CPC.
[607] Section 271, CPC.

president of the Inquiry Control Chambers, with a copy of the ruling attached thereto[608]. Generally, the law while listing persons with the *locus standi* to appeal against the rulings of the Examining Magistrate limit their scope of appeal. It provides that, the defendant[609], the civil party[610] and the Legal Department are endowed with the power of appeal.

The principle of appeal against the orders of the Examining Magistrate by the Legal Department is laid down by the provisions of section 268 of the CPC, which provides inter-alia that "The legal Department may except otherwise provided by law [611], appeal against the rulings of the Examining Magistrate [612] in accordance with the provisions of sections 252(3), 254(1) and (3), and 271 of the CPC. According to these provisions, the Legal Department can file appeals against all the rulings of the Examining Magistrate but for the cases listed hereunder. This act gives the State Counsel a very extensive power of surveillance on the acts of the Examining Magistrate.

The Courts have held that the Legal Department can appeal against the no-case or partial no-case ruling of the Examining Magistrate[613].

But according to an author [614], paradoxically even a committal order of the Examining Magistrate is subject to appeal by the State Counsel. His contention is grounded on the principle that the said committal order may have been taken contrary to his stand in his submissions wherein he submitted for inadmissibility or a no case ruling, or according to him, there exist elements or circumstances in the case file that exonerate the defendant. According to him "the representative must not be a blind,

---

[608] Section274, CPC.

[609] Section 269, CPC « the defendant may only appeal against rulings in respect of remand in custody, judicial supervision, request for an expert or counter-expert opinion and of restitution of articles seized».

[610] Section 270, CPC « the civil party may appeal against the rulings in respect of the refusal to commence an inquiry, the inadmissibility of an application to be a civil party in a criminal case, the rejection of an application for expert or counter expert opinion, the restriction of articles seized and no case ruling ».

[611] Such is the case with the provisions of section 146(4) and section 179(5) of the CPC.

[612] It should be noted here that the acts concerned here are purely jurisdictional acts and not acts of administration; such is the case with forwarding orders, which are purely administrative acts.

[613] Chambre de contrôle de l'instruction de la Cour d'appel du centre: Aff. . MP et CNPS contre ELOUNDOU Pierre Jean Marie et autres. Inédit, cited by Kenmoe (E.), op. cit., p. 292

[614] Mpinda (F.), op.cit., supra, p.60

diabolic and mechiavelic prosecutor, thirsty of the blood of vengeance"[615]. He must show proof of probity, honesty and neutrality, submitting for a no-case ruling where necessary and appealing where he feels that the committal order of the Examining Magistrate is vitiated by an error of appreciation, disrespect of formal rules or by outright violation of the law.

Section 252(3) of the CPC gives the State Counsel the right of appeal against acts of the Examining Magistrate that he considers a nullity. Prior to this action, the law has provided for preliminary steps to be taken. One of such steps is informing the Examining magistrate in writing and directs that the duplicate of the case file of inquiry be forwarded to the President of the Inquiry Control Chambers of the Court of Appeal for the annulment of the act violated. It is only when the parties and notably the State Counsel is notified with a refusal order through a reasoned ruling of the Examining Magistrate, that he can proceed with an appeal against the ruling.

The law has provided for a time- limit of forty-eight hours within which the State Counsel must appeal, from the day of notification. This time limit poses a practical problem with regards to Courts which are far off from the Court of Appeal. It will be very difficult for an appeal from Nkambe to reach Bamenda the seat of the North West Regional Court of Appeal within forty-eight hours. Ferry Armand [616] while equally acknowledging the difficulties in the application of this provision for such Courts; propose the use of a cyber-justice system as a solution. This can be done by a cybernetic or internet connection between Courts of Appeal and Courts in the periphery for a more rapid and low-cost transmission of appeal proceedings.

The Registrar in Chief is charge with the immediate forwarding of the duplicate of the inquiry file together with the State Counsel's submission to the President of the Inquiry Control Chambers[617].

---

[615]Citing Ndjere (E.), op.cit, p. 320

[616] Ibid., pp. 62

[617]Section 253(3), CPC.

G. Impacts of Appeals Against the Rulings of the Examining Magistrate

An appeal against the decisions of the Examining Magistrate by the Legal Department has diverse impacts. Such is the case with hearings on appeals against the rulings of the Examining Magistrate relating to remand in custody, judicial supervision, or the restitution of the objects seized. The Inquiry Control Chambers may quash such rulings, cancel a remand or arrest warrant, or a judicial supervision measure, or issue an arrest or a remand warrant against the defendant set free in execution of a ruling in issue, or order the restitution or not of the objects seized.[618] The far reaching effects of the appeal of the Legal Department in case of restitution of seized objects, is that even the Procureur General is expected to immediately ensure the execution of the said decision given not withstanding any eventual appeal by the party concerned[619].

Another consequence of such appeals is that it risks depossessing an Examining Magistrate of an inquiry file. In fact the law provides that where the Inquiry Control Chambers are seized of an appeal filed against the ruling of the Examining Magistrate relating to any matter other than remand in custody, quashes the order, it may either return the inquiry file to the Examining Magistrate initially seized of the matter or to another Examining Magistrate of the same court with a view of continuing the preliminary inquiry[620]. In this regards he may interrogate the defendant, hear witnesses and proceed where necessary with searches and seizures, give rogatory commissions and issue warrants. The law however prohibits him from neither deciding on applications for bail nor making orders closing inquiry. He simply returns the case file to the Inquiry control Chambers at the end of his mission.[621]

As regards rulings, where the Inquiry Control Chambers quashed the ruling relating to the closure of the preliminary inquiry, it may of its own motion hear and determine the enquiry

---

[618]Section 277(1), CPC.
[619]Section 277(2), CPC.
[620]Section 278, CPC.
[621]Section 280, CPC.

de novo.[622] Apart from the right to appeal, the Legal Department is the principal party in all criminal proceedings before the Court.

[622] Section 279, CPC

CHAPTER XIII
THE ROLE OF THE LEGAL DEPARTMENT IN THE COURSE OF HEARING BEFORE THE COURT

After questioning the role of the Legal Department in criminal proceedings notably as regards remand of suspects in custody in the light of the MEDVEDEV jurisprudence[623] of the European Human Rights Court, an author[624] came to the conclusion that in the actual state of the Cameroonian criminal law and with regards to international evolution, ***"il est urgent de repositioner le Ministère Public en dehors de la justice, comme le sont la partie civile et la defense, en ce qui garatirait la preservation de l'equilibre théorique entre les trios parties de chaque, procés penal,équlibre qui n'existe pas encore véritablement aujourd'hui***". This conclusion is predicated on the question "how can we comprehend the fact that even before the setting in motion of criminal proceedings, one of the parties has an ascendency on the other through the possibility of remand in police custody or remand in prison custody?"

One would have expected the law makers to take this in consideration in the CPC, because the right to a fair trial is at the centre of the code. Unfortunately, nothing much has changed as regards the ascendency of the Legal Department over the other parties in the criminal proceeding.

I. THE PLACE OF THE DEPARTMENT OF PUBLIC PROSECUTION BEFORE A TRIAL COURT

As aforementioned, the CPC has maintained the Legal Department as a party in all criminal proceedings before the Court. Far from just being a party like all others (the civil party

---

[623] The European Court of Human rights in this case responding to the question as regards remand in custody by the Legal Department stated that « magistrates must present the required guarantee of independence towards the executive as well as the parties, which excludes them from acting subsequently against a defendant under the capacity of Legal Department, and must be endowed with the prerogative of ordering for his release, after having recorded statements from the said person and controlled the legality of the arrest and remand in custody" According to the European Court, the Legal department at the same time plays the role of referee and party, thus in his capacity of referee the equation is unbalance, and discredited apriori by virtue of the absence of independence.

[624] ETEME ETEME, "Le parquet et la privation des libertés : mauvais ménage ? reflection sur le devenir d'une relation antinomique", *in Miroir de droit*, N° 02, avril-mai-juin 2011, pp.14-21.

and the defence) the Legal Department has been given a place of honour.[625] One would understand that the statute of "principal party" given to the Legal Department both at the level of Courts with original jurisdiction and at the level of appellate Courts[626] stems from the fact that the Legal Department is at the origin of more than half of the cases enrolled for trial in every Court, coupled with its role of the safeguard of general interest.

The importance of the place of the Legal Department in the course of the trial is materialised by the fact that his absence during hearing renders the whole proceeding null and void. This is not the case with the civil party or the defence whose presence though important as well can be overlooked without such a drastic legal consequence. The accused can be constrained to appear before the Court as well as the civil party[627] but in cases where such constraint fail to produce the required results the court can proceed in their absence and at their detriment.

A. The Exorbitant Powers of the Legal Department

The power of the Legal Department as compared to that of the other parties before the same Court and with regards to the same trial is exorbitant. The Legal Department enjoys certain privileges not accorded to the other parties. Apart from his mandatory presence in the course of all trials, the law provides that he can intervene at any stage of the trial, though subject to the power of the Presiding Magistrate to maintain order.[628]

The law has equally made the intervention (address) of the Legal Department at the close of hearing in every case mandatory.[629] This is not the case with the other parties, whose

---

[625] Section 128, CPC "the Legal Department shall be the principal party in a criminal trial before the Court and shall always be represented at such trials under pain of rendering the entire proceeding and the decision null and void»

[626] Section 132(1) "The Procureur General at the Supreme Court shall be a party to appeals lodged by the parties and may of his own motion raise grounds for the annulment of the decision appealed against"

(2) "He shall be a principal party in all appeals brought before the court"

[627] This can be done by way of a bench warrant issued against accused or defaulting witnesses. A witness regularly summoned but who fails to appear may be prosecuted under section 173 of the Penal Code.

[628] Section 128(2), CPC

[629] Section128(3), CPC « The legal Department shall at the close of the hearing in every case, address the Court or tender written submissions without been denied the right of hearing or stopped when addressing the court »

submissions can be dispensed with. This intervention is not limited to the purely criminal aspect of the trial which is the centre of his intervention. The Legal Department must be heard even when its submissions are based only on civil claim.[630]

Whatever the case, the accused persons are given the place of pride as the last person to address the court. This was the stand of the **Judicial Bench of the Supreme Court**, in ***Arret N° 72/P du 16 Juillet 2015, affaire Kingue Paul Eric c/ commune de Njombe-Penja***[631]. The facts of the case are as follows; sometimes in the month of June 2009 the Examining Magistrate of the High Court of Moungo was seized with a holding Charge issued by the State Counsel of the said jurisdiction, curiously enough this was done while the defendant was already serving an imprisonment term for a similar offence by virtue of a judgment handed down on the 19th of January 2009, wherein he was sentenced to a six years imprisonment term. After having been seized the Examining Magistrate made an order of commencement of inquiry duly signed and stamped (it is worth noting that in the initial case wherein Paul Eric Kingue was sentenced these elements were absent), subsequently he established a report of first appearance (process-verbal de premiere comparution) and finally a remand warrant which was due to expire on the 30th December 2009. On the 30th of September 2009, he was committed before the High Court, charged with the fraudulent retention of sums belonging to the Njombe-Penja council, notably the sum of ten million two hundred and ninety six thousand eight hundred and fifty one (10.296.851) francs, being sums recovered partly from the exploitation of heavy weight engines and a second part made up of sums donated to the council by the plantation enterprise and a third part made up of a fictive supply of fuel. At this level, the counsel for the defence raised an objection *in limine litis*, which was rejected by an interlocutory ruling of the 17 of August 2011. By a final judgment of the 29 of February 2012 the accused was found guilty as charged and sentenced to life imprisonment and

---

[630]Section 129, CPC.

[631]Commented by Bedel (L.J.), in *Les grandes décision de la jurisprudence pénale Camerounaise*, URDA, juillet 2018, p. 317 à 341.

equally subjected to the forfeitures under section 30 of the Penal code, ordering the publication of the judgment in “Cameroon Tribune” and “Nouvelle Expression”.

As regards compensation he was ordered to pay damages to the civil party, fixed at ten million two hundred and ninety-six thousand eight hundred and fifty-one (10.296.851) francs. His lawyer filed an appeal at the Littoral Court of Appeal. The court by ***Arret N° 68/Crim du 14 November 2012*** rejected the nullity of the entire proceedings solicited, while at the same time nullifying other aspects of the judgment. After ordering and opening hearing afresh, the Court found Paul Eric Kingue not guilty of the misappropriation of the sum of one million three hundred and twenty-one thousand, three hundred (1.321.300) francs, corresponding to the provision of fuel. The Court found the appellant guilty of the charge of misappropriation of the sum of one million four hundred thousand (1.400.000) francs, a part of the donation, four million nine hundred and sixty thousand, five hundred and fifty one francs, received from the Plantation company of Mbanga and two million sixty thousand francs (2.060.000) francs, sums originating from the exploitation of heavy duty machines. While according to the appellant mitigating circumstances, the Littoral Court of Appeal sentenced him to ten years imprisonment, ordering the confiscation of his property by virtue of section 35 of the penal Code and a forfeiture under section 30 of same code. The Njombe-Penja Council was awarded damages amounting to the sum of three million four hundred and sixty thousand (3.460.000) francs as well as cost. Disappointed once more his counsel filed an appeal at the Supreme Court. By this appeal the Supreme Court was called upon to respond to the following preoccupations; whether the report of the last interrogation of the defendant by the Examining Magistrate was optional, whether witnesses could be dispensed of the obligation of oath taking, if the Presiding Magistrate could overlook the prescription according to which after the submissions of counsel, the accused is supposed to address the court and present the final word of his defence, whether the ruling stating the grounds of remand in prison custody was optional and whether an imprisonment warrant is necessary when an accused is on bail. Responding to these preoccupations, the Supreme Court among other grounds (absence of signature of the report of final interrogation, the recording of statements from witnesses without the formality of oath taking, absence of a ruling grounding the remand in prison custody and omission to issue an imprisonment warrant) nullified the judgment of the Littoral Court of Appeal on grounds that the record of proceedings didn't mention that the accused addressed the Court last.

One of the fundamental traits of the exorbitance of the prerogatives of the Legal Departments is its irresponsibility faced with malicious prosecution.

B. The Department of Public Prosecution and Malicious Prosecution

The Legal Department in spite of its excessive prerogative is not responsible for malicious prosecution. The law provides that where there is a ruling of no case or where there is an acquittal, the Legal Department shall not be made to bear the cost of the proceedings or to pay damages to the prosecuted party [632]. Ironically, where a complaint involving a civil claim results in a no case ruling, the defendant may bring a civil action for damages against the complainant for malicious prosecution [633]. One would have reasonably expected the Legal Department to take responsibility considering the fact that it is the principal party who has the power of stopping frivolous or abusive lawsuits by way of its prosecutorial discretion, which permits it to close such files in chambers.

The Canadian Supreme Court [634] has defined malicious prosecution as "***an intentional tort designed to provide redress for losses flowing from unjustified prosecution...***", providing three elements of the test of malicious prosecution.

---

[632]Section 131, CPC.
[633]Section 161, CPC.
[634]Maizga v. Kvello Estate, 2009 SCC 51, cited on duhaime. Org.

1. Elements of Malicious Prosecution

Under the first element, the plaintiff must prove that the prosecution in issue was initiated by the defendant. This element identifies the proper target of the suit, as it is only those who were actively instrumental in the setting the law in motion that may be held accountable for damages that result.

The second element of the tort demands evidence that the prosecution terminated in the plaintiff's favour. This requirement precludes a collateral attack on a conviction properly rendered by a criminal court, and thus avoids conflicts between criminal and civil justice. The favourable termination requirement may be satisfied no matter the route by which the proceedings conclude in the plaintiff's favour, be it an acquittal, a discharge at the preliminary hearing, or a withdrawal.

The third element which must be proven by a plaintiff- absence of reasonable or probable cause to commence or continue the prosecution further delineates the scope of the potential plaintiffs.

Finally, the institution of criminal proceedings in the absence of reasonable and probable grounds does not itself suffice to ground a plaintiff's case for malicious prosecution regardless of whether the defendant is a private or public. Malicious prosecution, as the label implies, is an intentional tort that requires proof that the defendants conduct in setting the criminal process in motion was fuelled by malice.

2. The Public Prosecutor and the dilemma of malicious prosecution

From the definition above, it may be interesting to know who actually has the power of prosecution in Cameroon. Can a plaintiff influence the powers of the Legal Department to set in motion prosecution or not? According to Anyangwe, in common everyday cases the State Prosecutor decides whether to prosecute or not. No law requires him to prosecute all charges for which there is sufficient evidence to justify a conviction. In theory therefore, he may decline to prosecute even in a case of provable criminal liability and no one else may make good his refusal to do so. He however emphasizes that the State Prosecutor generally prosecutes where he is convinced that there is sufficient evidence to sustain a prosecution[635]. How then can the Legal Department with such all-embracing powers of prosecution not be responsible on the consequence of a situation over which he alone is solely responsible? The civil party is a parasite to a criminal proceeding instituted by the Legal Department and his sole interest is compensation for the damages suffered[636]. The civil party is simply a witness of the prosecution who cannot single handedly decide to end the proceedings except under certain conditions and in case of particular isolated offences (defamation, insults, adultery etc). One would have expected the Legal Department to take responsibility not only on the cost incurred, but the compensation of the victim of malicious prosecution under the conditions laid down by the Canadian Supreme Court in the afore-cited case.

3. The consequence of prosecutorial irresponsibility of the Public Prosecutor

The prosecutorial irresponsibility of the Legal Department has led to the indiscriminate prosecution of all matters originating from the investigating unit, in most Legal Department such that it is common to find a lawsuit before a law court wherein the accused has never been identified, talk less of the succession of suits that are thrown out of Court daily for want of diligent prosecution, insufficient or lack of evidence etc. Most often the price of the irresponsibility and may be the negligence of the Legal Department is paid by the civil parties who are sued before the same court, prosecuted by the same Legal Department, for a proceeding over which the said Legal Department had exclusive right, for false report[637]. Most courts have systematically resorted

---

[635] Anyangwe (C.), op.cit., p. 89.

[636] This is perhaps why in every criminal proceedings the suit name is always « The People of Cameroon V. …… or across the Moungo, Ministére public c/

[637] Section 304(1), Penal Code, "whoever makes to any person in authority, whether public or private, a false report liable to lead to prosecution or to any disciplinary measures shall be punished with imprisonment for from 6 (SIX), months to 5 (five) years and with the fine of from FRS 10 000 (ten thousand) to FRS 1 000 000 FRS (one million) unless he shows that he had good reasons to believe the report to be true.

(2) Imprisonment shall bc from 2 (two) months to 5 (five) years where the false report is anonymous.

to finding civil parties against whom lawsuits were instituted after an acquittal, guilty for false report. The question as regards the responsibility for malicious prosecution in cases where there is no civil party is yet to be answered by the code. More so, in proceedings whose investigation is initiated by the Legal Department, who proceeds to prosecution where there is no civil party witness?

C. The Qualities of a Public Prosecutor before a Trial Court

A good Public Prosecutor far from having a comfortable mastery of the law must be very smart, with an exceedingly high degree of self-confidence, prompt with much vivacity and spontaneity. He must as well be master of the arts of public speaking. He must at all times command a good mastery of his case files and apt in presenting his facts and logical in such presentation[638]. Moral rectitude is one of the virtues of a good prosecutor which must not be sacrificed at any moment irrespective of the reason. He must not resort to any physical or mental constraints, threats, pressure, deceit, insidious manoeuvres, or false proposal to secure a conviction. He must be honest enough to admit or submit that there is no evidence that warrants that the accused be put to his defence, where there is no evidence. In spite of the fact that the Legal Department investigates offences, institute and prosecute criminal offences, its prime objective is not conviction at all cost. The enforcement of the law being one of its fundamental missions, the Legal Department must be honest enough to submit for an acquittal where the elements before the court warrants an acquittal, submit for nullity when the elements at his disposal reveal a violation of a substantial formality. In other words, he must be as impartial as the judge.

---

(3) Where in consequence of the report a criminal prosecution is commenced in the trial court in the respect of the fact reported, any prosecution for false report shall be stayed until final judgment.

[638] Just like lawyers, most State Prosecutors in Courts of the North West and South West Regions used to hold briefings with the prosecution witnesses in a sort of pre-trial in their Chambers days before the trial proper. This enabled them not only to get a proper mastery of the facts of the matter, the importance of every witness to his case, the eradication of immaterial facts to the case but more importantly it helped the prosecutor to avoid contradiction among his witnesses, as well as avoiding any surprises in the course of the trial.

An ideal State Prosecutor is very attentive during a trial such that he has a good grasp of the legal issues raised which he confronts with the facts. By so doing he understands what was said, what was left out, such that he may be able to illuminate any doubts, fill all loopholes, shed light on any contradictions.

These qualities are exhibited both in the course of criminal as well as civil proceedings wherein the Legal Department is called upon to present written or oral submissions.

D. Submissions of the Legal Department in Civil Matters

As regards the intervention of the Legal Department in civil matters, it is worth noting that its institution and practice in the Cameroonian legal system is inspired from the French civil Code. The civil code applied in Courts of French expression in its article 36 gives an exhaustive list of matters for which the submission of the Legal Department is primordial. The forwarding of civil proceedings to the Legal Department has been justified by the need to preserve public policy, state interest and the protection of vulnerable persons. Such matters for which the investigation and written submissions of the Legal Department is solicited include the rectification or reconstitution of civil status acts, oath taking ceremonies during which the Legal Department is expected to make oral submissions, defence against provisional execution etc.

If the internal application of the provisions of section 36 cited above as it stands poses little or no problem, its transposition at the community level with the OHADA law has been a subject of controversy. The Common Court of Justice and arbitration has consistently been very hostile towards internal provisions which make the transmission or forwarding of matters to the Legal Department that falls within the OHADA framework mandatory[639]. The court holds that such provisions are contrary to the letters and the spirit of the OHADA law. It should be noted that the Court is not hostile to the idea of forwarding or transmitting matters to the Legal Department, its hostility is

---

[639] Arrêt N°003/2002 du 10 Janvier 2002 (affaire Siem C/ Société Atou et Bicici) et N° 016/2004 du 29 avril 2004 (affaire scierie d'Agnibilekrou Wahab Nouhab dite SDA, Wahab Nouhab Rachid C/ Hassan Hahly, cited by Mpinda (F.), op.cit., p. 112.

towards the obligatory and systematic nature of such transmission, which favours delay in the dispensation of justice in a domain where the respect of datelines is fundamental to the final outcome of almost every proceeding.

CHAPTER XIV
THE DEPARTMENT OF PUBLIC PROSECUTION AND THE EXECUTION OF COURT JUDGMENTS

Out of the three phases of the judiciary activities, i.e. prosecution, judgment, and execution, the most important is the last phase. Every litigant is interested not only in the outcome of a proceeding which is the judgment but more importantly in its execution. Summarily put, the credibility of justice is largely subject to the level of execution of the judgments handed down[640].

A judgment has been defined as the decision of a court regarding the rights and liabilities of parties in a legal action or proceeding. [641] Judgments generally provide the Courts explanation of why it has chosen to make a particular order.[642]

I. TYPES OF JUDGMENTS

Types of judgments subject to execution are as varied as the nature of the matter at stake, the level of proceedings, the attitude of litigants and the issues raised in the course of the proceedings. Such is the case with interlocutory rulings, default judgments, summary judgments, declaratory judgments, and consent judgment.

A. Default Judgment

A default judgment has been defined[643] as a judgment rendered in favour of one party based on the failure of the other party to take action. Default judgments are commonly used when the accused fails to appear before the Court and submit a defence after being summoned. That notwithstanding, a judgment is always said to have been delivered after full hearing in respect of the Legal Department.[644]

---

[640]Mangin Gilbert, "L'exécution des décisions judiciaire selon les conventions franco-africain", *Penant* 1974 N° 743, pp. 87, cited in an expose presented by Daniel Mekobe Sone on the occasion of the Heads of Courts of Appeal meeting held on the 17,18 and 19 October 2007 on the theme "l'exécution des décisions de justice en matière pénale, pp. 2.

[641] Black's Law Dictionary, 10th ed. 2014, pp. 970.

[642] Black's Law Dictionary, 10th ed. 2014, pp. 970.

[643]Black's Law Dictionary, 10th ed. 2014, pp. 507.

[644]Section 387(2), CPC

B. Interlocutory Judgment or Ruling

An interlocutory ruling[645] is an intermediate or interim judgment providing a temporal decision on an issue that requires timely action. Interlocutory orders are not final and may not be subjected to appeal or may follow an appeal procedure different from that of other kinds of judgments.

C. Summary Judgment

It is an accelerated judgment that does not require a trial and in which the court's interpretation of the pleadings forms the basis of the judgment. The court consider the content of the pleadings, the motion and additional evidence adduced by the parties to determine whether there is a genuine issue of material fact rather than one of law.[646]

D. Declaratory Judgment

It is a judgment that determines the rights and liabilities of the parties without enforcing a judgment or otherwise requiring the parties to do anything.[647] It may be useful where the parties have differing views about their rights and duties or are wishing to clarify them without seeking any other remedy. Though it is not binding, it is expected that the parties will act in accordance with what the Court determines in its judgments.

E. Consent Judgment

Also referred to as an "agreed judgment", a consent judgment is a settlement agreed upon by the parties and authorised by the judge.[648] Though the Legal Department plays a primordial role in the execution of judgments, it does not enjoy a monopoly in this domain.

---

[645] Black's Law Dictionary, 10th ed. 2014, pp. 971

[646] Black's Law Dictionary, 10th ed. 2014, pp. 1664.

[647] Black's Law Dictionary, 10th ed. 2014, pp. 971.

[648] Black's Law Dictionary, 10th ed. 2014, pp. 970.

II. THE ROLE OF THE LEGAL DEPARTMENT IN THE EXECUTION OF JUDGMENTS

The execution of judgment is a chain action wherein many other actors play a non-negligible role. The role of the Legal Department in the execution of court judgment is regulated by law and provides that "The Legal Department shall ensure the enforcement of laws, regulations and judgments and may in the interest of the law make any request it considers necessary before any Court".[649] This role is further elucidated in the CPC in the following words "The prosecution and the parties shall each in their own sphere, follow up the execution of judgments that have become final".[650]

However, the role of the Legal Department in the execution of judgments varies depending on whether the sanctions are pecuniary or imprisonment terms.

A. The Legal Department and the Execution of Principal Penalties

The following penalties as per the provisions of Section 18 of the Penal Code are classified as principal penalties for natural persons, death penalty, imprisonment and fine.

1. The execution of death penalty by the Legal Department

Capital punishment, often referred to as the death penalty is a practice of crime deterrence, whereby a person is killed by the State as a punishment for a crime committed. Crimes that are punishable by death are known as capital crimes or capital offences and most often include such offences as murder, treason, terrorism, espionage, piracy, trafficking, war, crimes against humanity, genocide etc.

As tribal societies developed into social classes and humankind created its own self-governed republics, capital punishment became a common response to a variety of crimes. One of the earliest written documents that supported death penalty was the Code of Hammurabi which was written on stone

---

[649] Section 29 Law N° 2006-15 of 29 December 2006 on judicial organisation.

[650] Section 545(3), CPC.

tablets around 1760 BC. It contained 282 laws that were collected by the Babylonian King Hammurabi, including the theory of an "eye for an eye". Several other ancient documents supported capital punishment including the Jewish Torah, the Christian Old Testament etc.

Early forms of capital punishment were designed to be slow, painful, and torturous such as boiling in oil, strangling, burying alive, thrown to wild animals, stoning, and crucifixion, burned at the stake. Considered subsequently as cruel and inhumane, the 18th and 19th Century saw the coming up of legal bodies advocating for a less painful approach to death penalty including hanging and beheading with the guillotine, electric chair, lethal injection etc. Nowadays death penalty has become a very controversial subject. At the end of 2017, 106 countries according to Amnesty international had abolished the death penalty in law for all crimes and 142 had abolished the death penalty in law or practice.[651]

2. Considerations Prior to the Execution of death penalties

Cameroon has been described by the Parliamentarians for Global Action as an abolitionist de facto state, with the last executions taking place in 1997. According to this organisation, although no one was sentenced to death in 2017 and no execution was carried out, 235 individuals remain in the death row. Though Cameroon has ratified the International Convention on Civil and Political Right (ICCPR), in 1984, it has yet to ratify its second optional Protocol aiming at the abolition of death penalty (ICCPR-OP2)[652] On the contrary, Cameroon features among 20 other countries which recorded commutations or pardon of death penalty[653].The absence of execution within the last decades can partially be attributed to the conditions laid down by law[654]. The afore-cited law lays down the following conditions prior to the execution of any death penalty:

---

[651] www.amnesty.org.
[652] www.pgaction.orgs.
[653] Ibid.
[654]Section 22, Penal Code.

- The submission of every death sentence to the President of the Republic for his decision on commutation;
- The execution of any death penalty only after the President of the Republic has taken a decision not to commute;
- No woman with child can be executed until after her delivery;
- No executions may take place on Sunday or a public holiday.

When the following conditions are fulfilled, the decision not to commute taken by the President of the Republic is forwarded to the Procureur General of the jurisdiction wherein the convict is remanded by the Minister in charge of Justice for execution. Shooting or hanging is the official modes of execution of death sentence and must be précised in the judgment. Execution is an act carried out publicly. However, the decision not to commute may decide otherwise.

After execution, the bodies of the persons executed are returned to their families at their request. The granting of such a request is however conditioned by the acceptance of the organization of a quiet funeral. Nothing may be published by the press beyond the official record of the execution and any official communiqué that may be released.

B. The Legal Department and the Execution of Imprisonment Term

Imprisonment has been defined as a means of loss of liberty during which the offender shall be obliged to work, subject to any contrary order of the court for reasons to be recorded in the judgment.[655] The duration of imprisonment is fixed by the Presiding Magistrate based on the law and his conscience. He has the latitude of sentencing even to life imprisonment. Such imprisonment terms as fixed by the Presiding Magistrate are executed by the Legal Department. Execution of imprisonment terms poses no serious difficulties when the convict was sentenced while in prison custody. In such circumstances, he

[655]Section 24, Penal Code.

simply executes the imprisonment warrant issued by the Court with the assistance of law enforcement officers, who accompany him back to prison.

On the contrary when the convict is not present in court, the Presiding Magistrate is obliged to issue an arrest warrant as per the provision of section 18 of the CPC[656] for the apprehension of the convict alongside an imprisonment warrant. The arrest warrant after having been issued is forwarded to the Legal Department charged with its execution. The Legal Department properly speaking does not personally execute an arrest warrant. The Legal Department which supervises the activities of JPO, works in close collaboration with the later for the execution of warrants. As such warrants for the arrest of convicts are forwarded to investigating units which are charged with the search and apprehension of convicts as well as bringing them before the State Counsel. Once arrested and brought before the State Counsel the convict will be forwarded to prison by virtue of an imprisonment warrant.

C. The Legal Department and the Execution of Pecuniary Awards

Generally, fines and cost are paid to the Registrar in Chief of the court that delivered the judgment. This is done after he must have issued to the convict without cost a copy of the judgment containing a breakdown of the pecuniary sentence.[657] The Legal Department properly speaking intervenes in the execution of pecuniary awards in case of default payment of pecuniary awards made to the state by virtue of section 564 of the CPC[658] as well as

---

[656] Section 18(1), CPC, "A warrant of arrest shall be an order given to an officer of the judicial police to arrest a defendant, an accused or a convict and bring him before one of the judicial authorities cited in section 12.

[657] Section 556, CPC

[658] Section 564(1) "in matters of fines and costs, the duration of imprisonment in default shall be fixed as follows;

a) Twenty (20) days for amounts not exceeding 10.000 francs;
b) Forty (40) days for amounts higher than 10.000 francs but not exceeding 20.000 francs;
c) Three (3) months for amounts higher than 20.000 francs but not exceeding 40.000 francs;
d) Six (6) months for amounts higher than 40.000 francs but not exceeding 100.000 francs;
e) Nine (9) months for amounts higher than 100.000 francs but not exceeding 200.000 francs;
f) Twelve (12) months for amounts higher than 200.000 francs but not exceeding 400.000 francs;

when the award is for the civil party[659] and the judgment has become final.

1. Recovery of Cost and fines and imprisonment in default

A convict against whom there is a pecuniary sentence can either pay same spontaneously or be constrained to do so by way of imprisonment in default. Imprisonment in default has been defined as "a procedure which aims at compelling a convict to execute the pecuniary sentence pronounced against him or make restitution ordered by a court in a criminal case[660]. Imprisonment in default is a measure of constraint on defaulting convicts applicable without prior notice at the instance of the Legal Department in the event of the non-execution of pecuniary sentence or non-restitution of property. It consists in the terms of imprisonment as specified in the provisions of section 564 cited above during which the debtor shall be obliged to work.

Where imprisonment in default of payment is ordered against a prisoner, it shall be enforced on the expiry of the previous imprisonment unless he furnishes sufficient sureties to guarantee the payment of the pecuniary sentence within a period of two (2) months from the date of recognizance.[661] Such is the case where for example an accused is sentenced to 3 years imprisonment term with a fine of 100.000 francs and the cost of the proceedings fixed at 100.000 francs. In such a case, it is only after the expiration of the 3 years imprisonment term that the prisoner is expected to serve the additional 9 months corresponding to the sum of 200.000 francs which is a sum of the cost and fines.

---

g) Eighteen (18) months for amounts higher than 400.000 francs but not exceeding 1.000.000 francs;
h) Two (2) years for amounts higher than 1.000.000 francs but not exceeding 5.000.000 francs;
i) Five (5) years for amounts exceeding 5.000.000 francs;

[659] It should be noted that civil actions are mostly intended to provide compensation for the damages resulting from an offence.

[660] Section 557, CPC.

[661] Section 558(2), CPC.

2. Recovery of civil awards

One of the main innovations of the CPC is that it has exceptionally provided the possibility to a civil party to recover civil awards by the use of the mechanism of imprisonment in default. This is so because generally, civil awards are recoverable by way of a civil action. To this regards section 558 of the CPC provides that "where the award is for the civil party and the judgment has become final, an imprisonment warrant shall be issued at the instance of the civil party who has not been satisfied". Section 564 of the CPC further precise that "in matters of damages to the civil party, the periods provided for… shall be reduced by half". According to the preceding provisions, recovery for civil awards is initiated at the instance of the judgment creditor. This measure can only be envisaged when the judgment has become final. A judgment is said to be final or enforceable when it can no longer be set aside or appealed against, except otherwise provided for by law. [662] The enforcement of a civil award by a judgment creditor is only possible within the prescription period of the penalty.[663]

3. Limits to recovery by imprisonment in default

The CPC has excluded three categories of persons from the measure of imprisonment in default of payment. Such is the case with persons less than 18 years, more than 60 years as well as pregnant women at the time of execution.[664] This exclusion can partly be justified not only by urge of the lawmakers to ensure the respect of the human rights even at the phase of execution of court decisions but by a reinforced protection of vulnerable

---

[662] Section 547, CPC.

[663] Section 67(1), Penal Code, « where a principal penalty has remained unenforced for the following periods after judgment has become final, neither it nor an accessory penalty or preventive measure accompanying it may any longer be enforced;

a) For felony, 20 (twenty) years;

b) For misdemeanour and simple offences tried with simple offences, 5 (five) years;

c) For any other simple offence, 2 (two) years;

2) Prescription shall be suspended while enforcement of the sentence is prevented by any consideration of law or fact, apart from the offenders will.

Time shall begin to run again on the intervention of an enforcement measure taken before the completion of the period.

A person convicted in default may no longer appear to serve his sentence after prescription.

[664] Section 656, CPC.

groups in society among which we have the children, pregnant women and the aged. Within this context, the CPC is more protective of the rights of minors within the framework of prosecution and trial, perhaps why a whole part of the CPC, (part xv) has been reserved for the prosecution and trial of juveniles.[665] The protection of the family as the base of every society is also at the centre of the CPC. The law provides that an order of imprisonment in default shall not be executed simultaneously against husband and wife even for the recovery of sums relating to different sentences.[666]

The execution of court decisions is not a reserve of the Legal Department. Other judicial officers play a non-negligible role in the execution of judgments.

III. THE ROLE OF OTHER ACTORS IN THE EXECUTION OF COURT DECISIONS

The execution of court decisions which is not a monopoly of the Legal Department is a chain procedure that equally calls for the concurrence of other actors such as the JPO, the President of Court, the Registrar in Chief, Bailiffs and personnel of the penitentiary administration.

A. Judicial Police Officers and Agents

Judicial police officers or agents are generally referred to as auxiliaries of the State Counsel. As such they perform their duties under the direct supervision of the State Counsel. Those with the status of judicial police officers for the purpose of reminder include, officers and non-commissioned officers of the gendarmerie, gendarmes in charge even in an acting capacity of a gendarmerie brigade or a gendarmerie post, superintendents of police, deputy superintendents of police, gendarmes and inspectors of police who have passed the judicial police officers examination and taken oath, civil servants even if they are temporarily performing the functions of heads of external

[665] Sections 700-743, CPC.

[666] Section 566, CPC.

services of the national security[667]. Gendarmes who are not JPO, police inspectors and constables have the status of JPA.[668]

Apart from just investigating offences, collecting evidence, identifying offenders and accomplices and bringing them before the Legal Department, one of the fundamental roles of the JPO and JPA is that of executing warrants and court decisions[669]. Practically imprisonment warrants and warrants of arrest are usually transmitted to police and gendarmerie units for execution. It should be noted that such units are not selected arbitrarily; warrants are always transmitted to the place of arrest, place of residence or place of birth. In most Legal Department there is a register of warrants transmitted to these units that enables follow up of the level of execution, considering the supervisory role of the Legal Department.

B. The Role of the President of Court

One of the novelties of the CPC is the fact that the President of Court has been attributed a new role which is that of execution of its decisions. Section 545(1) of the CPC provides that "the Presidents of all courts shall ensure that the orders and judgments of their courts are enforced". The CPC does not however precisely indicate how the President of court can concretely ensure that his decisions are executed. Paragraph 2 of section 545 strangely gives a short list of court decisions which "… shall be immediately executed at the instance of the Legal Department…", emphasizing on the Legal Department and other authorities responsible for execution, under the supervision of the Legal Department, without any clue as to the specific role of the President of Court as regards execution.

The inference one may draw from the use of "ensure" by the lawmakers supposes that the President of court by this provision is not intended to play an active role in execution properly speaking. We are of the opinion that the lawmakers intended that the President of Court provide the Legal

[667] Section 79, CPC.
[668] Section 81, CPC.
[669] Section 82(d), CPC.

Department with the necessary elements for the effective execution of their decisions.

In the same line, Michel Mahouvè and Hermine Kembo see in the emphasis of the nature of court decision i.e. "a bench or warrant of arrest or a decision granting bail or any other court order…." by the lawmaker, a disfunctioning in the system of transmission of documents between judiciary services and the prison. The traditional difficulty of follow up is most often swelled up by the deliberate refusal by the Legal Department to execute court orders, haunted by the ghost of the old law. Most Legal Departments saw in the transmission of Court orders for execution an opportunity of appreciation of execution most especially in rulings granting bail. This is so because under the CIC an appeal of the Legal Department against an order granting bail automatically suspended the execution of the order, such that to outsmart the Legal Department, most EM engaged in the direct transmission of their rulings to the prison authorities [670] .An efficient communication between the Bench and the Legal Department is a primordial condition of the efficacy and effectiveness of this legal prescription. It has been suggested that as solutions to this stalemate, court decisions most especially rulings on bail after having been signed by the Presiding Magistrate be immediately approved and forwarded to the competent authorities for execution. It has equally been suggested to the penitentiary personnel seised by disgruntles parties to approach judiciary authorities for necessary verifications.[671]

But far from the issues raised pertaining to the execution of bail by Michel Mahouvè and Hermine Kembo, prior to the coming into force of the CPC, it was common in most courts of French expressions for the verdict of judgments to be read in open court without any written trace of a judgment , rendering execution impossible. It is perhaps for this reason that the CPC has made the reading of the judgment and not just the verdict in

---

[670]Mahouve (M.) and kembo (H.T.), "Le nouveau juge d'instruction camerounais : un juge a la recherche de son autonomie", RSC, n° 2, avril-juin 2008, p. 319-355

[671]Mahouvè (M.) and Kembo (H.T.),op.,cit.,p.20

court mandatory. [672] A judgment, in its entire ramification, contains the heading[673], the reasoning[674], and the verdict.[675] Even with this, most slothful Presiding Magistrates write and read only the verdict of Judgments, prolonging the writing of the whole judgment to a later date thereby delaying the enforcement of judgments.

The obligation of writing judgments today before delivery equally participates in the guarantee of the right to a judgment, which is a right to fair trial. It provides litigants to dispose of an instrument justifying of backing up a subsequent appeal. The Cameroonian Supreme Court has thus held that the records of proceeding cannot be assimilated to a judgment[676]

C. The Registrar-in-Chief and the Execution of Court Decisions

The office of the Registrar-in-Chief is instituted in all courts and forms part of the organization of the bench at the CFI[677], the HC[678], the Court of Appeal[679], even at the level of the Supreme Court and Courts with special jurisdiction.

---

[672] Section 389(6) CPC

[673] Section389(2) « the parts of the judgment containing the heading shall include ;

a) Date of the verdict,
b) Name of thc court,
c) Full names of the members of the court,
d) Full names and age of the interpreter,
e) Mention of the oath taken by the interpreter,
f) Full names and age of the accused and full names of his counsel if any,
g) Full names of the others and their counsels, if any,
h) Full names of the witnesses,

[674] Section 389(3) « the part of the judgment comprising the reason shall set forth the facts and the law on which the judgment is based. The reason shall relate to the Criminal actions and where applicable to the civil claim.

The court shall in its reasoned judgment deal with each count and reply to the submissions made on it.

[675] The part of the judgment known as the verdict shall indicate the nature of the judgment, the level of the Court and whether the accuse dis guilty or not.

If guilty, it shall state the offence for which he has been found guilty, the relevant sections of the law applied, the sentence pronounced and where necessary the civil award.

If not guilty the provisions of section 395 and 400 of this code shall be applicable.

The verdict shall furthermore tax and make an order as to the payment of costs and also mention the warning provided for in section 399.

[676] Arret n° 27/P du 9 avril 2007, MP, Etondé Ekotto Nathanael et autres c. PAD (Port Autonome de Douala) et al., inédit, cited by Mahouvè (M.) and Kemho (H.T.),op.cit., p. 46

[677] Section 14(1),(a) of law N° 2006/015 of 29 December 2006 on judicial organisation.

[678] Section 17(1),(a) of law N° 2006/015 of 29 December 2006 on judicial organisation.

[679] Section 20(1),(a) of law N° 2006/015 of 29 December 2006 on judicial organisation.

Execution of court decisions is just one of the numerous functions carried out by the Registrar in Chief. As regards the execution of court decisions, the law provides that fines and cost shall be paid to the Registrar in Chief that delivered the judgment.[680] Before any such payment is made, the Registrar-in-Chief issues to the convict without cost a copy of the judgment containing a breakdown of the pecuniary sentence which he has to pay.[681] After payment, the Registrar in Chief must issue to the convict a receipt from a receipt book with counterfoil and when the decision becomes final a copy thereof without cost.[682] A copy of the receipt and an extract of the judgment is forwarded to the Legal Department when it becomes final.

D. The Role of Penitentiary Personnel

The law provides that any person detained by virtue of a judicial warrant shall be confined in a prison.[683] An author has defined prison or penitentiary as a place where persons are confined or restrained from personal liberty or a correctional, detention or penal faculty.[684] In the same line, article 1 of Decree N° 92/052 of the 27 March 1992 on the law organising penitentiary administration in Cameroon, sees a penitentiary as a centre where persons sentenced with loss of liberty as well as those awaiting trial are detained, or an establishment wherein accused persons are kept temporarily and attempts made for the reinsertion of those sentenced with loss of liberty back into the society. Imprisonment has been defined as "a loss of liberty during which the offender shall be obliged to work subject to any contrary order of the Court for reasons to be recorded in the judgment.[685] It should be noted that penitentiary administration in Cameroon which was hitherto attached to the Ministry of territorial administration, by virtue of decree n° 2004/320 of 8 December

[680]Section 556(1), (a), CPC.
[681]Section 556(1), (b), CPC.
[682] Section 556(1), (c), CPC
[683] Section 551,CPC
[684]Ngome (G.), "Prisons' rights ; a case study of Kumba principal prison", an internship report submitted in partial fulfilment of the requirement for the award of a professional Master's Degree in Human rights, international humanitarian law and international criminal law, p.1
[685]Section 24, Penal Code.

2004 on the organisation of government was attached to the Ministry of Justice.

According to article 2 of the law organising prisons in Cameroon, using as a measuring rode, the nature of the various activities in the various prisons classify them in the following categories;

- Orientation selection prison;
- Relegation centres;
- Production prisons;
- Rehabilitation prisons;
- Special prisons.

The execution of an order of transfer in respect of a detainee is executed by police, gendarmerie or by prison authorities. After identification and registration formalities are fulfilled, accused persons on remand must be confined in special quarters separated from those of persons already convicted and as far as possible kept in individual cells. Execution of sentence of loss of liberty equally takes into consideration sex and age of the detainees such that women and children are not detained in the same cell as adult male hardened criminals. It should be noted however that overpopulation of prisons in Cameroon has been a call for concern as many of these lofty ideas cannot be implemented practically due to lack of infrastructures. This situation long decried by experts[686] who proposed alternative sanction has not changed decades after. In 2015 for example, the Bamenda central prison, created on the 20 July 1958, with a capacity of 500 inmates was accommodating over 1000 inmates in its 13 cells.[687]

Whatever the case the penitentiary administration charged with receiving and keeping the various categories of persons must work in close collaboration with the Legal Department for the recovery of cost and fines. That is perhaps why in most jurisdictions the Legal Department carries out a monthly control of prisons.

---

[686] Guimdo (B.R.), "Les alternatives à l'emprisonnement dans des contextes de surpeuplement carcéral : le cas du Cameroun", *juridis périodique* n° 60 du Octobre – Novembre – Decembre 2004, p. 77-85.

[687] Awah (S.),Ibid., pp.27.

E. The Bailiff

One of the main functions of bailiffs as far as criminal matters are concerned and most especially as regards execution is service. Service has been defined[688] as "the delivery of a court process or judgment by the bailiff to the addressee". This provision further provides that «it shall be executed at the instance of the Legal Department or any other interested party». When it comes to execution properly speaking, his role is limited to service for the execution of civil awards resulting from a court decision in criminal matters. Even in that domain, his role has drastically been reduced with the introduction of the mechanism of imprisonment in default of payment, which has significantly reduced his task.

[688] Section 56, CPC.

BIBLIOGRAPHY

A. TEXTBOOKS

1. **Anoukaha (F.),** (Dir.), *Les Grandes Décisions De La Jurisprudence Pénale Camerounaise*, URDA, juillet 2018
2. **Anyangwe (C.)**, *The Magistracy and the Bar in Cameroon*, CEPER 1989
3. Cesare Beccaria, *Traités des Délits et Peine*, trad. Par Mme Khaiat, Paris Cujas, 1966
4. **Charles A. Senewald and John K.Tsukayama**, *The Process of Investigation: Concepts and Strategies For Investigators of the Private Sector*, 2nd Edition, Butterworth-Heinemann,2001
5. **Eba'a** (G.R.), *Les Grands Moments De La Justice au Cameroun* de 1958 à 2010, Presses de l'UCAC, juin 2010
6. **Elizabeth Walter**, *The Cambridge Advanced Learners Dictionary*, 3rd Edition New York, Cambridge University Press, 2008.
7. **Jeuge-Maynart (I.)**, *Dictionnaire Petit Larousse Illustré*, Librairie Larousse, 2011.
8. **Kenmoe (E.)**, *La Pratique De L'information Judiciaire dans le Code De Procédure Pénale du Cameroun*, édition Véritas, 2013,
9. **Keubou (Ph.)**, *Précis de Procédure Pénale Camerounaise*, Presses Universitaires d'Afrique, 2010.
10. **Kitio (E.)**, *Les Délai en Procédure Pénale Camerounaise: Entre célérité et droit à un procès équitable, Edition* Recherche Scientifique universelle (RSC) collections « Droit pour tous », Mars 2016.
11. **Merle (R.) et Vitu (A.)**, *Traité de Droit Criminelle*, Edition Cujas, 1997
12. **Mpinda (F.)**, *Le Procureur de la République au Cameroun*, PUA, 2016,
13. **Mahouvè (M.)** et **Kembo (H.T.)**, *Le Droit De L'homme Au Cœur de la Procédure Pénale Camerounaise: Entre*

Volonté Humaniste Et Tentative Régressive, édition Bruylant, 2016.
14. **Ndjere (E.)**, Le *Ministère Public Ou Parquet*, édit. Apprendre, Tome I, PUCAC, 2009.
15. **Ovono Ondoua (U.),** *Sous le bandeau de thémis, les larmes, panser et repenser la justice camerounaise*, Harmattan 2019.
16. **Pradel (J.)**, *Procédure Pénale,* 6 éditions Paris, Cujas, 1992.
17. **Philip James**, *Introduction to English Law*, E.L.B.S., Butterworths,1989
18. **Yawaga (S.)**, *L'information Judiciaire Dans Le Code Camerounaise De Procédure Pénale*, PUA, 2007
19. **Yawaga (S.)**, *La Garde à Vue, Les Tendances De La Nouvelle Procédure Pénale Camerounaise*, vol.1, PUA

B. ARTICLES

1. **Agbor (A.A.),** "Prosecuting the offences of Misappropriation of public funds: An insight into Cameroons Special Criminal Court" PER/PELJ 2017 (20) pg 12
2. **Albert Levitt**, "Repeal of penal statutes and effects on pending prosecutions", in *American Bar Association Journal*, vol.9, no. 11 (November 1923), pp. 715-721
3. **Anoukaha (F.)**, "Le Procureur de la République « Janus » de la magistrature Camerounaise", *Penant*, 1985, p.115 et suivants
4. **Anoukaha** (F.), "Droit pénal et démocratie en Afrique Noire: l'expérience camerounaise", in *"Juridis Info.* N° 23, p. 79.
5. **Assira (C),** "La loi du 4 Décembre 2014 sur la lutte contre le terrorisme: Le retour de du talion", *Miroir du droit*, N° p.8
6. **Assira (C)**, "Le Tribunal Criminel Special a l'épreuve de la justice", *Miroir de droit,* N° speciale, avril-septembre 2012 p.50

7. **Biboum (L.D.)**, "Le procureur de la république et la privation de la liberté", *Miroir de droit*, N° 02, Avril-Mai-Juin 2011, p. 44-59.
8. **Dashaco (J.)**, "The public prosecutor's power to prosecute in Cameroon: A clash of two legal systems?", *Annales de la Faculté des Sciences Juridique et Politique De L'Université de Dschang*, Tome II 1998, p .103
9. **Djakba (F)**, "Droit pénal général et procédure pénale", *Miroir de Droit*, N° 02, avril-mai-juin 2010, pp.105.
10. **Djila (R)**, "Panorama de la jurisprudence des cours et tribunaux camerounaise en matière de libération immediate", *Miroir de droit*, N° 002, Juillet-Aout-Septembre 2009, p. 10-25.
11. **Djila (R)**, "L'enquête de police à l'épreuve des droits de l'homme", *Annales de la Faculté des Sciences Juridiques et Politiques de l'Université de Dschang*, Tome I, 1997, p. 123-174
12. **Dountsop (Ph.R.)** "La flagrance des crimes et délits dans le code Camerounaise de procédure pénale", *Les Tendances De La Procédure Pénale Camerounaise*, Yaoundé, Presses Universitaires d'Afrique, (novembre 2007), p.50.
13. **Duga (T.E),** "The right to defense under the criminal procedure code of Cameroon: The consecration of international human rights norms under Cameroonian law?" *Juridis périodique,* N° 71, July-August-September 2007, p. 90-96.
14. **Emmanuel Decaux,** "Justice et droit de l'homme", in *Revue des Droits fondamentaux,* N°2, Janvier-Décembre 2003, P .78-79.
15. **Engolo (S.P.)**, "Le droit au procès équitable : Considération générale sur un droit qui donne sens et essence au droit", *Miroir de droit,* juillet, aout et septembre 2010, p.18.
16. **Etémé Etémé**, "Le parquet et la privation de liberté : Mauvais ménage ? Réflexion sur le devenir d'une relation

antinomique", *Miroir de Droit*, N° 02, Avril-Mai-Juin 2011, p. 14-21.

17. **Ewang (S.)**, "Can the state prosecutor discontinue a private prosecution by entering a nolleprosequi?", F. NEKO V. Sam Mofor (1971) Appeal N° WCCA/11/71, unreported _ Judgment per O'Brien Quinn, J.", *Juridis péridique,* N° 31, July-August-September 97, p. 39-44.
18. **Ewang (S.)**, "The organisation of the judiciary in cameroon : An appraisal", *Annales de la Faculté des Sciences Juridiques Et Politique*, Tome 10, 2006, p.24 .
19. **Guimdo (B.R.),** "Les alternatives à l'emprisonnement dans des contextes de surpeuplement carcéral : le cas du Cameroon", *Juridis périodique* n° 60 du Octobre – Novembre – Décembre 2004, p. 77-85.
20. **Keudjeu de Keudjeu (J.R.),** "L'effectivité de la protection des droit fondamentaux en Afrique subsaharienne", *Juridis périodique* N° 109, janvier-février-mars 2017, p. 161-178.
21. **Kitio (E)**, "La garde à vue administrative pour grand banditisme et respect de droit de l'homme au Cameroun (Application de la loi n°90/054 du 19 décembre 1990 sur le maintien de l'ordre)", *Juridis périodique* N° 30, Avril-Mai-Juin 1997, p. 47-56.
22. **Kweku Vanderpuye**, "Traditions in conflict: The internationalisation of confrontation", *Cornell International Law Journal*, vol 43, p. 514
23. **Larson Aaron**, "Issue preclusion and claim preclusion; How prior litigation can block your claim", 3 November 2017, *ExpertLaw. Com.* Retrieved 12 December 2017, cited at www. Wikipedia. Com
24. **Leumega (E)**, "La loi N° 2005/007 du 27 juillet 2005 portant code du procédure pénale et de la protection des droits de l'homme au Cameroun (a propos de garde à vue et de détention provisoire)", *Miroir de droit*, N° spéciale, Avril-Septembre 2012, p. 124-151.
25. **Mahouvè (M.) and kembo (H.T.)**, "Le nouveau juge d'instruction camerounais: un juge a la recherche de son autonomie", RSC, n° 2, avril-juin 2008, pp. 319-355

26. **Mangin Gilbert**, "L'exécution des décisions judiciaire selon les conventions franco-africain", *Penant* 1974 N° 743, pp. 87
27. **Mani Ayong (F.E.)**, "L'égalité des parties au procès pénal: Fiction ou réalité", *Miroir de droit* N° 04, octobre-novembre-décembre 2010, p.43
28. **Merle R.**, "Le problème du contrôle juridictionnel de la garde à vue", in *Détention provisoire, contrôle judiciaire et garde à vue, les problèmes soulevés par leur contrôle juridictionnelle*, XIIe journées franco-Belgo-luxembourgeoises, Poitier, 11 et 12 décembre 1970, PUF, 1971, p. 12-16.
29. **Ngai (C)**, "La loi N° 2005/007 du 27 juillet 2005 portant code de procédure pénale: Excursion autour de la garde à vue", *Juridis périodique* N° 71, Juillet-Août-Septembre 2007 p. 110-116.
30. **Ngono S.,** "L'application des règles internationales du procès équitable par le juge judiciaire", in *Juridis périodique* N° 63, Avril-Mai-Juin 2005, p. 44
31. **Ongolo Foe (J.E)**, "Libre propos sur la privation de la liberté par le procureur de la république", in *Miroir de droit* N° 02, Avril-Mai-Juin 2011, p .22-32.
32. **Ongolo Foe (J.E)**, "La privation de la liberté par les officiers de la judiciaire dans le code de procédure pénale camerounaise" *Miroir de droit*, Octobre-Novembre-Décembre 2009, Janvier-Février-Mars 2010 p. 330
33. **Pougoue (P.G.)**, "Protection des droits fondamentaux et systèmes juridiques (rapport de droit camerounais)", p. 4, in *production des membres du groupe de recherche des droits de l'homme de l'institut Catholique de Yaoundé*
34. **Ronald J.**, "Rethinking the doctrine of nullity" *Louisiana Law Review*, vol.74, number 3, Spring 2014, p. 687-691
35. **Tankoua (E)**, "La libération immédiate, "un jeu de ping-pong dans certaines juridictions"", *Juridis périodique* N° 48, octobre-novembre-décembre, p. 113
36. **Timtchueng (M.) et Assontsa (R)**, "Le nouveau visage de la garde à vue dans la procédure pénale

Camerounaise", *Annales de la Faculté des Sciences Juridiques Et Politique, édition spéciale*, CPP, T.11, p.95.

C. INTERNSHIP REPORTS AND OTHER REPORTS

1. **Awah Fru (S.)**, Access to justice by detainees awaiting trial under the criminal procedure code (CPC): A case sturdy of the Bamenda Central Prison, internship report, University of Dschang, 2011.
2. **Kimbeng (R)**, "Human rights implication in pre-trial detention: The case of the Mezam Judicial Division", DESS report, University of Dschang, 2006.
3. **Morfaw Njinjun (H.)**, "Shortcomings and problems relating to the application of the CPC and proposed solutions in the Jurisdiction of the North West Court of Appeal" on the 6th October 2007
4. **Ngome Ndimbieh (G.)**, Prisoners' Rights: A case study of the Kumba Central prison, internship report, University of Dschang, 2011.
5. Report of the Ministry of Justice on the state of human rights in Cameroon, 2005
6. Report of the Ministry of Justice on the state of human rights in Cameroon, 2005.

D. PRESS

1. The Horizon newspaper of April 20, 2017
2. The Guardian Post Newspaper N° 1977 of Monday, January 28, 2019
3. The Post newspaper N° 01978 of Monday, January 28, 2019
4. The Post weekender, N° 01830 of June 23, 2017.

INDEX

R

W

ANNEX

17

REPUBLIQUE DU CAMEROUN
Paix – Travail – Patrie

REPUBLIC OF CAMEROUN
Peace – Work – Fatherland

PROCES-VERBAL DE PROROGATION DE GARDE A VUE
REPORT ON EXTENSION OF REMAND IN POLICE CUSTODY

L'an deux mil six .... le .... à .... heures ;
In the year two thousand and and the at o'oclock ;

Nous, ...
I,
Officier de Police Judiciaire, auxiliaire du Procureur de la République ;
Judicial Police Officer, auxiliary of the State Counsel ;

Assisté de .... ;
Assisted by
Poursuivant notre enquête,... ;
In pursuance of my investigations
Vu les dispositions des articles 79, 81, 82, 83, 86, 119 et suivants du Code de Procédure Pénale ;
Mindful of sections 79, 81, 82, 83, 86, 119 and following of the Criminal Procedure Code ;
Faisons comparaître devant nous le/la nommé (e) déjà entendu (e) et lui signifions que
Have caused M who has been heard, to appear before me and haven
conformément aux dispositions de l'article 120 du Code de Procédure Pénale, le Procureur de
informed him/her, in accordance with the provisions of section 120 of the Criminal Procedure Code ;
la République près les Tribunaux de ...., a, suite à notre
that the State Counsel of the Court of has, based on my
demande du ...., accordé la prorogation de sa garde à vue pour une
application of , extended his/her remand in police custody for a
durée de .... à compter du .... à ....heures
period of with effect from the at o'clock
Sur quoi il/elle répond : ....
He/she, in reply, states as follows :

Dont procès-verbal de notification que l'intéressé signe avec nous et nos assistants..............
....
In witness whereof, this report of service has been signed by him/her, myself and my assistants.

Le gardé à vue	Les assistants	L'OPJ
The detainee	*Assistants*	*JPO*

REPUBLIQUE DU CAMEROUN
Paix – Travail – Patrie

REPUBLIC OF CAMEROON
Peace – Work – Fatherland

COUR D'APPEL DE ....

COURT OF APPEAL OF ......

PARQUET DU PROCUREUR DE LA REPUBLIQUE DE..........................
....

CHAMBERS OF THE STATE COUNSEL OF....................
....

DOSSIER N°............................

FILE N°.................................

ORDRE DE GARDE A VUE
POLICE CUSTODY ORDER

L'an deux mille .... ;et le.. ;
In the year two thousand and ;and the

Nous,...Procureur de la République ;
I, State Counsel

Vu les articles 118 et suivants, et 137 du C.P.P ;
Mindful of sections 118 and following, and 137 of the CPC

M ....

J'ai l'honneur de vous demander de recevoir, garder à vue
I have the honour to request you to receive, keep in custody

et représenter à mon parquet le ....à ....heures,
and to produce in my chambers on at o'clock

la /les personne (s) ci-après :
the following person (s):

N° D'ORDRE *NUMBER*	NOMS ET PRENOMS *NAME AND SURNAME*	DATE ET LIEU DE NAISSANCE *DATE AND PLACE OF BIRTH*	DOMICILE *RESIDENCE*	MOTIFS *REASONS*	OBSERV-ATIONS

Le Procureur de la République

REPUBLIQUE DU CAMEROUN
Paix – Travail – Patrie

COUR D'APPEL DE ....

PARQUET DU PROCUREUR DE LA REPUBLIQUE DE.................
....

DOSSIER N°...............................

REPUBLIC OF CAMEROON
Peace – Work – Fatherland

COURT OF APPEAL OF ....

CHAMBERS OF THE STATE COUNSEL OF.....................
....

FILE N°.............................

REQUISITION A FORCE DE MAINTIEN DE L'ORDRE
REQUISITION FOR THE FORCES OF LAW AND ORDER

AU NOM DU PEUPLE CAMEROUNAIS
IN THE NAME OF THE PEOPLE OF CAMEROON

L'an deux mille ....,et le...............................;
In the year two thousand and , and the

Nous,..Procureur de la République ;
I, State Counsel

Vu l'article 138 du C.P.P ;
Mindful of section 138 of the C.P.C;

Vu la procédure suivie contre .... ;
Mindful of criminal proceedings instituted against.

Vu les nécessités de services ;
Mindful of the needs of the service

Requérons l'assistance de ....;
Hereby request the assistance of

A l'effet de ;...
For the purpose of
....
....
....

Le Procureur de la République
The State Counsel

REPUBLIQUE DU CAMEROUN Paix – Travail – Patrie	REPUBLIC OF CAMEROON Peace – Work – Fatherland
COUR D'APPEL DE	COURT OF APPEAL OF ....
PARQUET DU PROCUREUR DE LA REPUBLIQUE DE.................	CHAMBERS OF THE STATE COUNSEL OF.................... ....
DOSSIER N°.........................	FILE N°............................

REQUISITOIRE DEFINITIF
FINAL SUBMISSION

L'an deux mil.............................et le .... ;
In the year two thousand and *and the*

Nous, ...Procureur de la République ;
I, *State Counsel*

Vu les articles 145 et 256 du C.P.P ;
Mindful of *Sections 145 and 256 of the C.P.C ;*

Vu le réquisitoire introductif d'instance en date du............................. ;
Mindful of *holding charge of*

Vu l'information judiciaire ouverte contre .... ;
Mindful of *the preliminary inquiry opened against*

Vu le réquisitoire supplétif en date du.. ;
Mindful of *additional holding charge of*

Vu l'ordonnance de soit communiqué en date du................................ ;
Mindful of *forwarding order of*

Attendu qu'il résulte de l'information judiciaire que :
Whereas it results from the preliminary inquiry that:

....
....
....
....
....

Par ces motifs
For these reasons

....
....
....
....
....

Le Procureur de la République
The State Counsel

REPUBLIQUE DU CAMEROUN
Paix – Travail – Patrie

REPUBLIC OF CAMEROON
Peace – Work – Fatherland

COUR D'APPEL DE ....

COURT OF APPEAL OF ......

PARQUET DU PROCUREUR DE LA REPUBLIQUE DE..............
....

CHAMBERS OF THE STATE COUNSEL OF...................
....

DOSSIER N°.............................

FILE N°.............................

REQUISITOIRE SUPPLETIF
ADDITIONAL HOLDING CHARGE

L'an deux mille ....,et le...............................;
In the year two thousand and , and the

Nous,..Procureur de la République ;
I, State Counsel;
De...;
Of

Vu le articles 143, 144 et 145 du C.P.P ;
Mindful of Sections 143, 144 and 145 of the C.P.C;

Vu l'information judiciaire ouverte contre .... ;
Mindful of the preliminary inquiry opened against
.... ;

Vu notre réquisitoire introductif d'instance du..;
Mindful of our holding charge of

Vu l'ordonnance de soit communiqué en date du................................. ;
Mindful of forwarding order of

Attendu qu'au cours de l'information judiciaire ouverte contre le (s) susnommé (s), des faits nouveaux constituant une ou des infractions d'une toute autre nature que celle (s) relevée (s) au réquisitoire introductif d'instance susvisé, ont été portés à notre connaissance ;
Whereas in the course of the preliminary inquiry opened against the above named person (s), new facts constituting one or more offences, other than those contained in our holding charge mentioned here above were brought to my knowledge;

EN CONSEQUENCE,
CONSEQUENTLY

Requérons le Juge d'instruction du Tribunal de..
Request the Examining Magistrate of
Aux fins de..
To...
....
..../.

Attendu que dans le cas d'espèce, l'action Publique n'est pas éteinte par l'un des évènements visés à l'article 62 du C.P.P. ;
Whereas , in the present action, prosecution has not been discontinued by virtue of any of the circumstances referred to in section 62 of the C.P.C;

/.

EN CONSEQUENCE,
CONSEQUENTLY

Requerrons le juge d'instruction de..
Request the Examining Magistrate of

Aux fins d'ouvrir une information judiciaire contre le/la/les susnommé(e)(s).
To open preliminary inquiries against the above named person(s)

Le Procureur de la République
The State Counsel

REPUBLIQUE DU CAMEROUN
Paix – Travail – Patrie

REPUBLIC OF CAMERON
Peace – Work – Fatherland

COUR D'APPEL DE ......

COURT OF APPEAL OF ....

PARQUET DU PROCUREUR DE LA REPUBLIQUE DE ....
....

CHAMBERS OF THE STATE OF COUNSEL OF..............
....

DOSSIER N°..............................

FILE N°.............................

REQUISITOIRE INTRODUCTIF D'INSTANCE
HOLDING CHARGE

L'an deux mille .... et le .... ;
In the year two thousand and *and the*

Vu les articles 143,144,145 et 160 du C.P.P;;
Mindful of *sections 143,144, 145 and 160 of the C.P.C ;*

Nous, ...Procureur de la République
/ *State Counsel*
De ....;;
Of

Vu la procédure suivie contre le/la (s) nommé (e)(s) ....;
Mindful of *criminal proceedings n°* *instituted against*
.... ;

Attendu qu'il résulte des procès–verbaux d'enquête n°..............du.......................
Whereas it results from the preliminary investigations report n° *of*

Diligentée par ....
Carried out by..
Indices suffisants contre :..
Enough evidence against :
....
....
....
D'avoir à...le..
For having at *on*

ressort judiciaire du...
in the Judicial Division of
....
....
.... ;
Crime (s)/ délit(s) / délit(s) connexes prévu(s) et réprimé (s) par les articles ....
Offence(s) contrary to and punishable under sections
....

La (les) personne(s) dont les noms suivent :
The following person(s) :

N°	Noms & Prénoms *Name & Surname*	Date & lieu de naissance *Date & place of birth*	Fils/fille de et de *son/daughter of and of*	Domicile *Residence*	Profession *Occupation*	Adresse *Address*

Pour être entendue (s) sur l'inculpation/accusation (1) / d'avoir/de s'être à.................
In order to be heard on the charge of having at

Ressort judiciaire du ....
In the judicial Division of

Le.. en tout cas dans le temps légal des poursuites
On *within the time limit for prosecution*
....
....
....

Faits prévus et réprimés par les articles ....
Contrary to and punishable under sections
....

Fait à .... le ....
Done at *on*

Le Procureur de la République
The State Counsel

REPUBLIQUE DU CAMEROUN
Paix – Travail – Patrie

REPUBLIC OF CAMEROON
Peace – Work – Fatherland

COUR D'APPEL DE ....

COURT OF APPEAL OF ....

PARQUET DU PROCUREUR DE LA REPUBLIQUE DE..................

CHAMBERS OF THE STATE COUNSEL OF....................

DOSSIER N°.............................

FILE N°............................

MANDEMENT DE CITATION
ORDER TO SUMMON
A/TO
INCULPE – PREVENU – ACCUSE (1)
DEFENDANT – ACCUSED

Nous, ...Procureur de la République ;
I, *State Counsel* ;

vu l'article 40 du C.P.P;
Vu la procédure suivie contre *Mindful of* *section 40 of the C.P.C*

....
Mindful of criminal proceedings instituted against
....
....
....
.... ;

Requérons Maître ....Huissier de justice près la
Hereby request *Sheriff/Bailiff*

Cour d'Appel et les Tribunaux de .... ;
Of the Court of Appeal and Courts of

Aux fins de citer à comparaître par devant le Cabinet d'instruction/Tribunal de ......
To summon to appear before the:Examining Magistrate/Court of First Instance/ High Court of
(1)..;

Le ....à .... *heures précises*
On at o'clock precisely

(1) Rayer la mention inutile
Delete where necessary

REPUBLIQUE DU CAMEROUN Paix – Travail – Patrie	REPUBLIC OF CAMEROON Peace – Work – Fatherland
COUR D'APPEL DE	COURT OF APPEAL OF ....
PARQUET DU PROCUREUR DE LA REPUBLIQUE DE..........................	CHAMBERS OF THE STATE COUNSEL OF............... ....
DOSSIER N°............................	FILE N°...../........................

REQUISITION AUX FINS D'EXPERTISE MEDICALE (D'AUTOPSIE)

ORDER FOR EXPERT OPINION (POST-MORTEM EXAMINATION)

L'an deux mille ....,et le.. ;
In the year two thousand and , and the

Nous, ...Procureur de la République;
I, State Counsel
Vu les articles 92 et 137 du C.P.P ;
Mindful of sections 92 and 137 of the C.P.C;

Ayant été informé de la mort suspecte de .... ;
Whereas I am reliably informed that one has died in circumstances which require the conduct of a post-mortem examination;

Requérons le Docteur ....,Médecin ....;
Hereby request Doctor ,Medical officer

En service à ....;
In service at

De procéder à l'autopsie du corps de l'intéressé (e) ,
To conduct a post-mortem examination of the body of the said person;

qui sera mis à sa disposition par les soins de .... ;
which shall be put at his/her disposal by

Disons que le médecin requis prêtera, le cas échéant et avant toute opération, le serment prévu par l'article 204 du C.P.P ;
The said doctor shall, where necessary, and before carrying out any act of the exercice, take the oath provided for in section 204 of the C.P.C;

Disons que son rapport d'expertise nous sera remis au plus tard le .... /-
His findings shall be forwarded to me in the form of a report latest on

Le Procureur de la République
The state Counsel

PAR CES MOTIFS
FOR THIS REASON

Ordonnons un transport sur les lieux aux fins ci-dessus spécifiées ;
Hereby order a visit to the locus in quo for the above purpose

Fixons le montant des frais y afférents à la somme de .... francs CFA ;
Assess the costs related thereto in the sum of
à la charge de.. ;
to be paid by

Disons qu'il y sera procédé par nos soins le...................à..................heures précises.
The visit shall be effected by me on *at* *o'clock precisely*

Le Juge d'Instruction
The Examining Magistrate

REPUBLIQUE DU CAMEROUN Paix – Travail – Patrie	REPUBLIC OF CAMEROON Peace – Work – Fatherland
COUR D'APPEL DE	COURT OF APPEAL OF ....
CABINET D'INFORMATION JUDICIAIRE	CHAMBERS OF THE EXAMINING MAGISTRATE
DE	OF ....
DOSSIER N°....................................	FILE N°...............................

ORDONNANCE DE TRANSPORT SUR LES LIEUX
ORDER FOR A VISIT TO THE LOCUS IN QUO

AU NOM DU PEUPLE CAMEROUNAIS
IN THE NAME OF THE PEOPLE OF CAMEROON

L'an deux mille............... ....et le .... ;
In the year two thousand and *and the*

Nous,......................... ....Juge d'Instruction ;
I, *Examining Magistrate*

Assisté de Me...Greffier.;
Assisted by *Registrar*

Vu l'article 177 du C.P.P ;
Mindful of *section 177 of the C.P.C;*

Vu l'information judiciaire ouverte contre... ;
Mindful of *the preliminary inquiry opened against*

Inculpé(e) de... ;
Charged with

Libre/détenu(e) suivant mandat de détention provisoire du....................................... ;
Free/detained pursuant to remand warrant of

Assisté de...;
Assisted by

Attendu que pour une bonne administration de la justice et dans le souci de la manifestation de la vérité, un transport sur les lieux est nécessaire ;
Mindful that the requirement for a proper administration of justice, and the need to take measures to ensure the discovery of the truth, render a visit to the locus in quo necessary;

Qu'il échet en conséquence d'ordonner cette mesure à l'effet de :
And thus the necessity to order such a visit. for the purpose of

....
....
.... ;

REPUBLIQUE DU CAMEROUN Paix – Travail – Patrie	REPUBLIC OF CAMEROON Peace – Work – Fatherland
COUR D'APPEL DE	COURT OF APPEAL OF......
PARQUET DU PROCUREUR DE LA REPUBLIQUE DE.................	CHAMBERS OF THE STATE COUNSEL OF.............. ....
DOSSIER N°.............................	FILE N°............................

MANDAT D'EXTRACTION
PRODUCTION WARRANT

AU NOM DU PEUPLE CAMEROUNAIS
IN THE NAME OF THE PEOPLE OF CAMEROON

L'an deux mille ....,et le....................................... ;
In the year two thousand and , and the

Nous, ... Procureur de la République ;
I, State Counsel ;

Vu les articles 11, 12, 17 et 26 du C.P.P ;
Mindful of sections 11, 12, 17 and 26 of the C.P.C ;

Vu la procédure suivie contre ....
Mindful of criminal proceedings instituted against
....

Détenu (e) à la prison ....
Detained at the prison

Ordonne au Régisseur de ladite prison de conduire sous bonne escorte le/la
Hereby orders the superintendent of the said prison to produce him/her before
susnommé (e) à l'audience du ....à................. heures précises
the Court on at o'clock precisely

Le Procureur de la République
The State Counsel

Département de................................Domicilié (é) à ....
Division of *Resident at*

Marié (é)/Célibataire.........................nombre d'enfants ....
Married/Unmarried *number of Children*

De nationalité...
Nationality

Exerçant la profession de...
Of the profession of

Déjà/jamais condamné (é) ....
Had been / never been sentenced

Procédons à l'inculpation :
The charge is read to the accused as follows :

Vous êtes prévenu(e) d'avoir /de vous être à ....le........................
That you have been charged for having at *on*

Ressort judiciaire de.....................en tout cas dans le temps légal des poursuites
Judicial division of *within the time limit for prosecution*

....
....
....
....
....

Faits prévus et réprimés par les articles ....
Contrary to and punishable under sections

....

Réponse du prévenu...

Nous avisons le/la prévenu(e) qu'en raison des indices relevés contre lui/elle, nous le/la plaçons en détention provisoire/laissons en liberté et qu'il/elle sera traduit (e), devant le Tribunal de Première Instance statuant à l'audience de flagrant délit
The accused person has been notified that because of the gravity of the evidence against him/her, he/she is being remanded in prison custody/released on bail, and that he/she will appear before the Court of First Instance sitting in matters of offences committed flagrante delicto

du ....à..............heures ....minutes précises
of *at* *o'clock* *minute precisely*

Lecture et traduction faites, le/la prévenu(e) persiste et signe avec nous, ainsi que l'interprète.
After translation and reading over, the accused certifies as being correct and signs this report with me and the interpreter.

Le Procureur de la République, **L'interprète,** **Le prévenu**

REPUBLIQUE DU CAMEROUN Paix – Travail – Patrie	REPUBLIC OF CAMEROON Peace – Work – Fatherland
COUR D'APPEL DE	COURT OF APPEAL OF ....
PARQUET DU PROCUREUR DE LA REPUBLIQUE DE.................	CHAMBERS OF THE STATE COUNSEL OF.............. ....
DOSSIER N°............................	FILE N°...........................

PROCES-VERBAL D'INTERROGATOIRE AU PARQUET EN CAS DE FLAGRANT DELIT

REPORT OF INTERROGATION AT THE LEGAL DEPARTMENT IN OFFENCES COMMITTED FLAGRANTE DELICTO

L'an deux mille..et le..;
In the year two thousand and *and the*

Nous,..Procureur de la République ;
I, *The State Counsel*

Assisté de......................................interprète, âgé de...........ans, ayant prêté serment;
Assisted by *interpreter, aged* *years, having taken oath*
Prescript par l'article 183 du C.P.P ;
Prescribed by section 183 of the C.P.C;

Vu .l'article 114 du C.P.P ;
Mindful of *Section 114 of the C.P.C;*

Vu la procédure suivie contre..;
Mindful of *criminal proceedings instituted against*

Avons entendu le/la nommé (e)...
Upon hearing M.

Arrêté(e) en flagrant délit de........................ ....,
Arrested committing flagrante delicto the offence of

Attendu que l'interressé nous a declaré:
Whereas the person concerned states as follows:

Je me nomme...
I am called

Fils/fille de ....et de..
Son /daughter of *and of*

Agé (e) de.......................................ans, comme né (e) le/vers....................
Aged *born on*

A..Arrondissement de...............................
At *Sub-Division of*

Le Procureur de la République L'interprète Le prévenu

2

Informons le mis en cause qu'il peut demeurer en liberté s'il présente un autre garant

The accused is informed that he/she will be released on bail if he/she presents another surety

Ou s'il verse un cautionnement d'un montant de(1) ....francs CFA
Or if he/she makes a deposit in the sum of (en chiffres et en lettres/*in figures and words*)(1)

Le Procureur de la République
The State Counsel

(1): Rayer les mentions inutiles
Delecte where necessary

REPUBLIQUE DU CAMEROUN
Paix – Travail – Patrie

REPUBLIC OF CAMEROON
Peace – Work – Fatherland

COUR D'APPEL DE ....

COURT OF APPEAL OF ......

PARQUET DU PROCUREUR DE LA REPUBLIQUE DE......................
....

CHAMBERS OF THE STATE COUNSEL OF...........
....

DOSSIER N°............................

FILE N°..........................

RETRAIT DE CAUTION
WITHDRAWAL OF SURETY'S RECOGNIZANCE

L'an deux mille..et le...;
In the year two thousand and and the

Nous, ...Procureur de la République
I, State Counsel

Vu les articles 229 et 245 du C.P.P ;
Mindful of sections 229 and 245 of the C.P.C;

Vu la procédure suivie contre .... ;
Mindful of criminal proceedings instituted against

Vu l'engagement en date du ....enregistré sous le n°..........
Mindful of surety's recognizance of registered under N°

Attendu que le/la nommé(e)..garant du mis en cause
Whereas M. surety of the accused

Nous a présenté ce dernier et a sollicité retirer sa caution ;
Has presented the latter and applies to withdraw his/her recognizance;
Qu'il échet de lui en donner acte ;
And given the necessity to grant his/her application;

EN CONSEQUENCE
CONSEQUENTLY

Donnons acte à ....
Hereby authorize the said

Du retrait de sa garantie à l'égard de ....
To withdraw his recognizance in respect of

Né(e) le ....à...
Born on at
Fils/fille de ....et de ....
Son/daughter of and of

Exerçant la profession de .... de nationalité...............................;
Of the profession of nationality

Domicilié(e) à ....B.P................Tél.................... ;
Resident at P.o box

REPUBLIQUE DU CAMEROUN Paix – Travail – Patrie	REPUBLIC OF CAMEROON Peace – Work – Fatherland
COUR D'APPEL DE	COURT OF APPEAL OF ....
PARQUET GENERAL DE...	CHAMBERS OF THE PROCUREUR GENERAL OF............................
DOSSIER N°............................	FILE N°..

ARRET DES POURSUITES
NOLLE PROSEQUI

AU NOM DU PEUPLE CAMEROUNAIS
IN THE NAME OF THE PEOPLE OF CAMEROON

L'an deux mille ....,et le...;
In the year two thousand and , and the
Nous, ...Procureur Général près la Cour d'Appel de .... ;
I Procureur General of the Court of Appeal of
Vu l'article 64 du C.P.P ;
Mindful of section 64 of the C.P.C;
Vu l'autorisation écrite en date du...;
Mindful of the written authorization of
de Monsieur le Ministre chargé de la Justice ;
of the Minister in charged of Justice;
Vu la procédure suivie contre........ ....;
Mindful of criminal proceedings instituted against
Né(e) le..à ....,
Born on at
De ....et de ....
Of and of
Exerçant la profession de ....de nationalité.................................;
Of the profession of nationality
Domicilié(e) à.......................................Bp..............Tel.........................;
Resident at P.o.box
Prévenu(e)/accusé(e)/ inculpé(e) de.. ;
Charged with
Devant .... ;
Before
Attendu que les poursuites engagées contre le/la susnommé (e) sont de nature à compromettre l'intérêt social ou la paix publique ;
Given that the proceedings commenced against the above named person are likely to imperil social interest or public order,

En consequence,
Consequently,

REQUERONS, l'arrêt desdites poursuites en ce qui concerne l'action publique.
Submit that the said proceedings be discontinued in respect of the criminal action.

Le Procureur Général
The Procureur General

REPUBLIQUE DU CAMEROUN Paix – Travail – Patrie	REPUBLIC OF CAMEROON Peace – Work – Fatherland
COUR D'APPEL DE	COURT OF APPEAL OF ......
PARQUET DU PROCUREUR DE LA REPUBLIQUE DE................	CHAMBERS OF THE STATE COUNSEL OF......................
DOSSIER N°.................................	FILE N°............................

AUTORISATION D'INTERCEPTER, D'ENREGISTRER, DE TRANSCRIRE ET DE PROCEDER A DES PRISES DE VUE
AUTHORIZATION TO INTERCEPT, RECORD, TRANSCRIBE AND TAKE PHOTOGRAPHS

AU NOM DU PEUPLE CAMEROUNAIS
IN THE NAME OF THE PEOPLE OF CAMEROON

L'an deux mille....................................... ;.et le..;
In the year two thousand and ;and the

Nous,..Procureur de la République
I, State Counsel

Vu les articles 92, 137et 245 du C.P.P ;
Mindful of sections 92, 137 and 245 of the C.P.C;

Vu la procédure suivie contre..;
Mindful of criminal proceedings instituted against

Autorisons par la présente, ...;
Hereby authorize

- à intercepter, enregistrer ou transcrire toutes correspondances émises ou reçues par voie de télécommunication, par le/la mis(e) en cause .
to intercept, record or transcribe all correspondences sent or received by means of telecommunication, by the accused person;

- à procéder à des prises de vue dans les lieux privés
and to take photographs at private premises

Pendant la durée de l'enquête.
During the investigations.

Le Procureur de la République
The State Counsel

REPUBLIQUE DU CAMEROUN Paix – Travail – Patrie	REPUBLIC OF CAMEROON Peace – Work – Fatherland
COUR D'APPEL DE	COURT OF APPEAL OF ....
PARQUET DU PROCUREUR DE LA REPUBLIQUE DE.................	CHAMBERS OF THE STATE COUNSEL OF.............. ....
DOSSIER N°............................	FILE N°.............................

REQUISITION DE TRANSFEREMENT
REQUEST FOR TRANSFER

AU NOM DU PEUPLE CAMEROUNAIS
IN THE NAME OF THE PEOPLE OF CAMEROON

L'an deux mille ....,et le...............................;
In the year two thousand and , and the

Nous, ...Procureur de la République ;
I, State Counsel ;

Vu **les articles 14 , 19 et 552 du C.P.P. ;**
Mindful of sections 14 , 19 ad 552 of the C.P.C;

Vu le(s) mandat (s) de détention provisoire/d'arrêt/d'incarcération en date du .... ;
Mindful of remand /arrest/imprisonment warrant of

décerné (s) contre la/le (s) nommé (e)(s)... ;
issued against. M.

....

....

par...
by
Pour (motifs)... ;
For (reasons)

Requérons le Commissaire de police/Commandant de Brigade de Gendarmerie/
Request the Superintendent of police/Gendarmerie Brigade Commander/
Régisseur de la Prison .... ;
Superintendent of prison
De procéder au transfèrement sous bonne escorte du/des susnommé (s) du parquet/de la prison ....
To transfer the above named person from the legal department / prison

Pour être tenu (s) à la disposition de...,
And put him/her/them at the disposal of
Et de nous rendre compte de ce qui est par nous requis.
And to render account to me on the execution of this order

Le Procureur de la République
The State Counsel

Mis en liberté le ....
Released on bail on

Attendu que bien que régulièrement convoqué le mis en cause n'a pas comparu par
Whereas the accused person was regularly summoned and he/she failed to appear

Devant...le ....
Before *on*

Qu'il échet d'inviter son garant à le/la présenter par devant ....
And thus the necessity to request his/her surety to produce him/her before

Le ....à .... heures précises
On *at* *o'clock precisely*

Ou à défaut, à payer la somme sus-indiquée sous peine d'y être contraint par corps.
Failing which he/she shall berequired to pay the above sum of the recognizance, under pain of being imprisoned in default of such payment.

Fait à ....le.....................
Done *at*

Le Procureur de la République
The State Counsel

REPUBLIQUE DU CAMEROUN
Paix – Travail – Patrie

COUR D'APPEL DE ....

PARQUET DU PROCUREUR DE LA REPUBLIQUE DE.................
....

DOSSIER N°.............................

REPUBLIC OF CAMEROON
Peace – Work – Fatherland

COURT OF APPEAL OF

CHAMBERS OF THE STATE COUNSEL OF..................
....

FILE N°............................

MISE EN DEMEURE DU GARANT
WARRANT FOR SURETY TO SHOW CAUSE

Nous,...Procureur de la République;
I, *State Counsel*

Vu les articles les 228, 246 et 563 du C.P.P ;
Mindful of sections 228, 246 et 563 of the C.P.C;

Vu la procédure suivie contre .... ;
Mindful of criminal proceedings instituted against

Attendu que par acte n°............................en date du .... ;

Whereas by undertaking n° of
Le/la nommé(e)...
M.

A pris l'engagement de payer à l'Etat du Cameroun la somme de(1)................
Bound himself/herself to forfeit to the State of Cameroon the sum of
....francs CFA
(en chiffres et en lettres/in figures and words)(1)

En cas de non représentation de la personne mise en cause
In case he/she Fails to produce the accused person
Né(e) le...à .... ;
Born on *at*

De ....et de .... ;
Of *and of*

Exerçant le profession de ....de nationalité.................................;
Of the profession of *nationality*

Domicilié(e) à..Bp................Tel......................... ;
Resident at P.o.box

Inculpé(e) de ....

REPUBLIQUE DU CAMEROUN
Paix – Travail – Patrie

REPUBLIC OF CAMEROON
Peace – Work – Fatherland

COUR D'APPEL DE ....

COURT OF APPEAL OF ......

PARQUET DU PROCUREUR DE LA REPUBLIQUE DE.................

CHAMBERS OF THE STATE COUNSEL OF...................

DOSSIER N°............................

FILE N°...........................

ENGAGEMENT DU GARANT
RECOGNIZANCE OF SURETY

L'an deux mille......................................et le...;
In the year two thousand *and the*
Nous,..Procureur de la République;
I,..State Counsel ;
Vu les articles 224,225, 226, 228, 229, 230 et 246 du C.P.P ;
Mindful of sections 224,225, 226, 228, 229, 230 and 246 of the C.P.C;
Vu la procédure suivie contre ....;
Mindful of criminal proceedings instituted against
Prévenu(e)/accusé(e) de..;
Charged with
Assisté(e) de...;
Assisted by
Par la présente, le/la nommé (e) ....;
By this recognizance, M.
Né (e) le..à ....;
Born on *at*
De .... et de ....;
Of *and of*
Exerçant la profession de............................B.P .... Tel.....................;
Of the profession of *P.o.box*
De nationalité...;
Nationality
Domicilié(e) à..quartier.....................rue............;
Resident at *quarter* *street*
CNI/passeport n°...............délivré le ....à ....par ....;
NIC/passeport n° *issued on* *at* *by*
S'engage à assurer la représentation de la personne concernée
Undertakes to ensure the production of the person concerned
Par devant ....
Before
Le ....à..........................heures précises
On *at* *o'clock precisely*
Et à toutes autres réquisitions jusqu'à la fin de la procédure.
And on all subsequent requests until the matter shall be disposed of.
A défaut, il/elle sera astreint à payer au Trésor Public la somme de(1).................
Failing which he/she shall be constrained to pay to the Public Tresury the sum of
....
(en chiffres et en lettres/*in figures and words*)(1)

Fait à ....le..............
Done *at*

REPUBLIQUE DU CAMEROUN
Paix – Travail – Patrie

COUR D'APPEL DE ....

PARQUET DU PROCUREUR DE LA REPUBLIQUE DE.................
....

DOSSIER N°............................

REPUBLIC OF CAMEROON
Peace – Work – Fatherland

COURT OF APPEAL OF ...

CHAMBERS OF THE STATE COUNSEL OF..................
....

FILE N°...........................

ENGAGEMENT DE DEFERER
SELF RECOGNIZANCE

L'an deux mille.................................et le.. ;
In the year two thousand and and the

Vu **les articles 224, 225, 226, 228, 229, 230 et 246 du C.P.P**
Mindful of ***sections 224, 225, 226, 228, 229, 230 and 246 of the C.P.C***

Vu la procédure suivie contre .... ;
Mindful of criminal proceedings instituted against

Prévenu(e)/accusé(e) de.. ;
Charged with

Par la présente, le/la nommé (e) ....;
By this recognizance, M.

Né (e) le..à .... ;
Born on at

De ....et de .... ;
Of and of

Exerçant la profession de...........................B.P .... Tel....................;
Of the profession of P.o.box

De nationalité..;
Nationalité

Domicilié(e) à.. quartier............rue......................;
Resident at quarter street

CNI/passeport n°...............délivré le ....à ....par ....;
NIC/passeport n° issued on at by

S'engage à se présenter par devant .... ;
Undertakes to appear before

Le ....à.........................heures précises
On at o'clock precisely

Et à toutes autres réquisitions jusqu'à la fin de la procédure.
And on all subsequent requests until the matter shall be disposed of.

A défaut, il/elle sera astreint à payer au Trésor Public la somme de(1)..............
Failing which he/she shall be constrained to pay to the Public Trasury the sum of
....

(en chiffres et en lettres/*in figures and words*)(1)

Fait à ....le.....................
Done at on

REPUBLIQUE DU CAMEROUN
Paix – Travail – Patrie

REPUBLIC OF CAMEROON
Peace – Work – Fatherland

MISE EN LIBERTE
EXECUTION OF RELEASE ORDER

En exécution de l'ordre de mise en liberté
In execution of release order

Signé de ....
Signed by

En date du...
On

Le (la) nommé (e)..
M.

Né(e) le...à ....
Born *at*
De ....et de ....
Of *and of*
Exerçant la profession de ....de nationalité...................................
Exercising the profession of *nationality*

Domicilié(e) à...Bp.........................Tel...........
Resident at *P.O Box*

Inculpé (e)/prévenu (e)/accusé (e)/condamné (e) de/pour ....
Charge with

Détenu (e) en vertu de ....
Detained by virtue of

A été mis (e) en liberté le ....à..heures.
Was released on *at* *o'clock.*

Fait à ....le......................
Done at *on*

L'Officier de Police Judiciaire
The Judicial Police Officer

REPUBLIQUE DU CAMEROUN
Paix – Travail – Patrie

REPUBLIC OF CAMEROON
Peace – Work – Fatherland

COUR D'APPEL DE ....

COURT OF APPEAL OF ....

PARQUET DU PROCUREUR DE LA REPUBLIQUE DE.................
....

CHAMBERS OF THE STATE COUNSEL OF...............
....

DOSSIER N°...........................

FILE N°...........................

ORDRE DE MISE EN LIBERTE
RELEASE ORDER

AU NOM DU PEUPLE CAMEROUNAIS
IN THE NAME OF THE PEOPLE OF CAMEROON

L'an deux mille ....,et le................................;
In the year two thousand and , and the

Nous,...Procureur de la République;
I, State Counsel

Vu les articles 224 et 225 du C.P.P ;
Mindful of sections 224 and 225 of the C.P.C.;

Vu la procédure suivie contre.. ;
Mindful of criminal proceedings instituted against

Né(e) le...à ....;
Born on at

De ....et de .... ;
Of and of

Exerçant la profession de .... de nationalité..................................;
Of the profession of nationality

Domicilié(e) à.. Bp....................Tel..............;
Resident at P.o.box

Gardé(e) à vue en vertu de..;
Detained by virtue of

Ordonnons au .... ;
Hereby order

De le/la mettre immédiatement en liberté s'il/elle n'est détenu (e) pour autre cause
To release him/her forthwith, except he /she is detained for some other offence.

Le Procureur de la République
The State Counsel

que nous présentons à M. .... Pour reconnaissance qui nous déclare ;
and presented to M *for identification and he/she states at follows :*
nous l'avisons de ce que nous saisissons et plaçons sous scellé n° .... (découvert,
and he/she is informed that the object shall be seized and kept as exhibit No .
couvert, ouvert selon le cas) ledit objet,...
(exposed, hidden, overt as the case may be) ;
Nos opérations commencées à .... se sont achevées à ....heures
The search stated at and ended at o'clock
sans incident du tout ;
with no incident ;
Nous dressons le présent procès-verbal ainsi que les fiches des scellés n° .... que
nous signons avec le Maître des lieux, les témoins et nos assistants.
Wherefore this report and exhibit forms No are prepared and signed by the
proprietor, myself, and our assistants.

Le Maître des lieux	**Les témoins**	**Les assistants**	**L'OPJ**
Proprictor	*Witnesses*	*Assistants*	*JPO*

REPUBLIQUE DU CAMEROUN
Paix – Travail – Patrie

REPUBLIC OF CAMEROUN
Peace – Work – Fatherland

PROCES-VERBAL DE REQUISITION EN ENQUETE DE FLAGRANCE
REPORT ON SEARCH DURING THE INVESTIGATION OF OFFENCES COMMITTED FLAGRANTE DELICTO

L'an deux mil six .... le .... à .... heures ;
In the year two thousand and *and the* *at* *o'oclock ;*
on pourra être différente)

Nous,.. Officier de Police Judiciaire ;
I, *Judicial Police Officer ;*
Auxiliaire du Procureur de la République ;
Auxiliary of the State Counsel ;

Assisté de .... ;
Assisted by
Vu ....les dispositions des articles 79, 81, 82, 83, 92 à 100 et suivants du C.P.P ;
Mindful of sections 79, 81, 82, 83, 92 to 100 and following of the C.P.C ;
Nous trouvant à...
Aarrived at
(selon le caractère juridique de l'enquête, la formulation pourra être différente)
Accompagné de M. ....ou (de M. et de M. requis à cet effet, selon le
Accompanied by or (by M. and of M. invited for that purpose,
cadre de l'enquête),
as the case may be)
Somme reçus à.............................. heures par..........................(petite identité)
And we were received at *o'clock by* *(identity)*
A qui nous déclinons notre qualité et après que nous lui ayons notifié les présomptions le concernant (ou concernant un tel) et avisé que nous allons procéder à une perquisition dans le
To whom we identified ourselves, explained the allegations made against him(or against X) and informed him of an impending search to be conducted within
....
Nous l'informons de son droit de nous fouiller avant le début de nos opérations conformément aux dispositions de la loi ;
And informed him/her of his/her right to search me before I conduct the search in accordance with the provisions of the law ;
Sur quoi il déclare : ....
Wherefore he/she states as follows ....
....

En la présence constante de M.. ou (des deux témoins et M selon le cadre juridique)..
Procédons à la perquisition de ....(l'appartement ou de la maison selon cas description des lieux, nombre de pièces, chambres à coucher, cuisine, salon etc…) ;
The search of the (appartment or house depending on the description of the premises, number of rooms, sleeping rooms, kitchen, sitting room etc.) was conducted in the presence of M. or two witness(es) ;

Découvrons à........................(situation) un ....(description de l'objet)......
....
The following object(s) was/were discovered at

De le fouiller aux fins de rechercher et de saisir tous objets ou documents ayant servi à la commission de l'infraction ou qui paraissent en être le produit ;
And search it for the purpose of seizing any articles or documents used in committing an offence, or which appear to be the product of an offence;

Disons que le requis nous fera parvenir dans les meilleurs délais le procès-verbal de ses opérations en même temps que les objets éventuellement saisis.
The executor of this warrant shall, without delay, forward to me the report of his operations, as well as any articles or documents eventually seized.

Le Procureur de la République
The State Counsel

REPUBLIQUE DU CAMEROUN
Paix – Travail – Patrie

COUR D'APPEL DE ....

PARQUET DU PROCUREUR DE LA REPUBLIQUE DE........................

DOSSIER N°............................

REPUBLIC OF CAMEROON
Peace – Work – Fatherland

COURT OF APPEAL OF ......

CHAMBERS OF THE STATE COUNSEL OF....................

FILE N°...........................

MANDAT DE PERQUISITION
SEARCH WARRANT

AU NOM DU PEUPLE CAMEROUNAIS
IN THE NAME OF THE PEOPLE OF CAMEROON

L'an deux mille ....,et le..;
In the year two thousand and , *and the*

Nous, ...Procureur de la République,
I, . *State Counsel*

VU les articles 11, 12, 16, 26, 92, 93, 94 et 99 du C.P.P ;
Mindful of *sections, 11, 12, 16, 26, 92, 93, 94 and 99 of C.P.C;*

VU la procédure suivie contre ....;
Mindful of *criminal proceedings instituted against*

Requérons ....;
Hereby request

De pénétrer dans le domicile/résidence/bureau/magasin/champs ou tous autres lieux publics ou privés connus ou fréquentés ;
To enter the residence/office/business place/farms or any other public or private place familia or known;

Par.......................................né(e) le...........................à.......................................;
To *born on* *at*

Fils/fille de...et de ....;
Son/daughter of *and of*
Domicilié (e) à .... exerçant la profession de ....;
Resident at *of the profession of*

De nationalité...................................... B.P.........................tel...............................;
Nationality *P.o.box*

Prévenu (e) de...;
Charged with

Libre/détenu (e) suivant mandat de détention provisoire du ....;
Free/detained pursuant to remand warrant of

Assisté (e)de...;
Assisted by

RÉPUBLIQUE DU CAMEROUN Paix – Travail – Patrie	REPUBLIC OF CAMEROON Peace – Work – Fatherland
COUR D'APPEL DE	COURT OF APPEAL OF......
PARQUET DU PROCUREUR DE LA REPUBLIQUE DE..................	CHAMBERS OF THE STATE COUNSEL OF...........
DOSSIER N°...........................	FILE N°...........................

MANDAT DE COMPARUTION
SUMMONS

AU NOM DU PEUPLE CAMEROUNAIS
IN THE NAME OF THE PEOPLE OF CAMEROON

L'an deux mille ....,et le.......................................;
In the year two thousand and , and the
Nous,...Procureur de la République;
I, State Counsel
Vu les articles 11, 12 et 13, 26 et suivants du C.P.P;
Mindful of sections 11, 12 and 13, 26 and following of the C.P.C;
Vu la procédure suivie contre le/la (s) nommé (e)(s)..........................;
Mindful of criminal proceedings against
Né(e) le ....à..;
Born on at
Fils/Fille de..et de..;
Son/Daughter of and of
Domicilié(e) à.......................................B.P....................tel..................;
Resident at P.o.box
Exerçant la profession de ....de nationalité.....................................;
Of the profession of nationality
Prévenu(e) de ....;
Charged with
Infraction(s) prévue(s) et réprimée (s) par les articles ....;
Offence (s) contrary toand punishable under sections
Mettons en demeure M/Mme ....;
Hereby requests M
D'avoir à comparaître par devant ....;
To appear before
Le ....à ....heures précises;
on at o'clock precisely
Pour être entendu(e) sur les faits qui lui sont reprochés,
in order to be heard in respect of the matter thereof
Faute de quoi, un mandat d'amener pourra être décerné contre lui ;
Failing which a warrant may be issued for his arrest
Enjoignons à tout officier ou agent de police judiciaire ou toute autre personne habilité, à notifier le présent mandat
Hereby requests all judicial police officers or agents and all other process servers to serve this summons on the person concerned
Observations de l'Exécutant :
Observations of the process-server

Signature/empreintes du concerné *Signature/thumbprints of the concerned*	Le Procureur de la République *The State Counsel*

www.ingramcontent.com/pod-product-compliance
Lightning Source LLC
LaVergne TN
LVHW052251200926
848481LV00002B/340